AMERICAN EDUCATION

Its Men,

Ideas,

and

Institutions

Advisory Editor

Lawrence A. Cremin
Frederick A. P. Barnard Professor of Education
Teachers College, Columbia University

AMERICAN EDUCATION: *Its Men, Ideas, and Institutions* presents selected works of thought and scholarship that have long been out of print or otherwise unavailable. Inevitably, such works will include particular ideas and doctrines that have been outmoded or superseded by more recent research. Nevertheless, all retain their place in the literature, having influenced educational thought and practice in their own time and having provided the basis for subsequent scholarship.

Education and Morals

An Experimentalist Philosophy
of Education

BY

JOHN L. CHILDS

ARNO PRESS & THE NEW YORK TIMES
*New York * 1971*

Reprint Edition 1971 by Arno Press Inc.

Reprinted from a copy in
  The Wesleyan University Library

American Education:
  Its Men, Ideas, and Institutions - Series II
ISBN for complete set: 0-405-03600-0
See last pages of this volume for titles.

Manufactured in the United States of America

Library of Congress Cataloging in Publication Data

Childs, John Lawrence, 1889-
    Education and morals.
    (American education: its men, ideas, and
institutions. Series II)
    1. Education--Philosophy. I. Title.
II. Series.
LB875.C475 1971   370.1   72-165734
ISBN 0-405-03603-5

Education and Morals

Education and Morals

An Experimentalist Philosophy
of Education

BY

JOHN L. CHILDS

Teachers College
Columbia University

New York
APPLETON–CENTURY–CROFTS, INC.

PRINTED IN THE UNITED STATES OF AMERICA

TO

JOHN DEWEY

AND

WILLIAM H. KILPATRICK

Two pioneers in the effort to develop a philosophy of education in harmony with the values of democracy and the methods of experimental inquiry

PREFACE

One of the chief purposes of a preface is to permit an author to put aside the rôle of impersonal expositor and interpreter and to talk in the first person about that which he has written. I should like to indicate why this book in the foundations and philosophy of education has been given the title, *Education and Morals*. I can perhaps do this most simply if I review some of the things which have been of concern to me in recent years as I have talked with parents and teachers about the meaning and the present tasks of education.

I have long been associated with the progressive wing in American education. I share its conception that, viewed from the standpoint of the education of the young, democracy is the most significant pattern in American life. I believe that the democratic conception was given a valid new application by those educators who declared that a child is a person and should be so treated by those responsible for his education. Although the principle of respect for the immature human being does not automatically translate itself into a program of education, it gives necessary moral direction by its recognition that the aim of education should be the growth and the liberation of the child, not his subordination to some external and absolute system.

I am also in full accord with those experimentalist educators who contend that respect for the child as a person includes as its most vital meaning respect for his intellectual potentialities, and that a primary purpose of education in a democracy should be to help each child develop a mind of his own. This necessarily makes *method* in education a moral as well as a psychological and pedagogical affair. We learn as we experience and practice. And the child learns to think by having opportunity to engage in purposeful activities that involve the use of means in the attainment of outcomes. No school meets the democratic criterion unless it provides opportunity for its pupils to participate in activities that nurture their capacity to think and to evaluate.

I also believe that something of enduring worth was contributed by those who conceived education as a process of continuous "reconstruction of experience" that results in the achievement of new meanings and greater powers of control. Viewed from this perspective there is real ground for the assertion that education is its own end: an ongoing process of growth subordinate to nothing save more growth through education.

But this commitment in education to democratic outlooks and experimental procedures is a moral commitment. It is grounded in a definite manifestation of preference for a particular type of group and personal living. Alternative systems of life and thought exist. These alternative systems have their distinctive and rival educational objectives and procedures. The adherents of these alternative systems are now attacking this experimental, functional view of education. I believe that we shall not be able to meet this attack unless we are prepared to defend the moral foundations of our democratic and experimentalist program of education.

And this is only one phase of the problem. Reactionary forces of both the right and the left are also attacking the very fundamentals of our democratic way of life. We may be sure that education for freedom and for the full development of the capacities of individual human beings will not survive under the authoritarian regimentations of any brand of totalitarianism. I am therefore convinced that devotion to democratic and experimentalist values in education involves us in the broader struggle to maintain the conditions essential to a "free" society. Today there is abundant evidence to show that the attitudes, the human dispositions, the loyalties, the understandings, the techniques and the habits which make this coöperative life of freedom possible are not inborn. They are acquired by each new generation through a process of directed experiencing and learning. Educators who believe in democracy must not evade the responsibility of nurturing the young in the morality of this life of organized freedom.

I have written *Education and Morals* because I consider it important for American educators to recognize that devotion to the ideals of democracy in no way bars us from making a deliberate effort to nurture the young in the essential patterns of democratic life and thought. If our schools are to serve as positive agencies for the maintenance of a "free" society, they must be concerned today with "society" as well as with the "child," with "subject-matter" as well as with "method," with "product" as well as with "process," with human "responsibilities" as well as with human "freedoms," and with social and moral "ends" as well as with classroom "procedures" and educational "means."

Our country is now in a period of transition and cultural transformation. The change from human energy to atomic energy, from the self-sufficient family-farm to an interdependent, continental economy, from hand production to mass production, from scarcity to relative abundance, from the police-power state to the positive welfare state, and from the nation to the United Nations and the North Atlantic Pact denotes a change so basic in nature that it calls for the review and the reconstruction of many historic institutions and outlooks. Education has its crucial part to play in this audit of American civilization, and in this effort to reformulate the meanings of democracy and to define the directions in which reconstruction should now move. It may well be that the fate of mankind will depend upon whether the American people can achieve the maturity—economic, political, intellectual, and moral—that is required if we are to use our vast power for the ends of peace and material and cultural progress. I have called this book *Education and Morals* because I have wanted to emphasize the character of the task that now confronts American educators. As I view it, this task is nothing less than the attempt to educate a generation equipped to undertake the formation of the patterns for a new civilization. As I conceive it that task is basically a moral task.

In the development of the foregoing view of education and its present tasks, I am deeply indebted to my colleagues in the Department of Social and Philosophical Foundations of Education at Teachers College, Columbia University. For years we have collaborated in the work of a course that has sought to bring the individual and the social aspects of education into organic unity. Although many problems remain to be solved, we are much encouraged by the response of teachers to this conception and emphasis in education.

With their consent, I have dedicated this book to John Dewey and William H. Kilpatrick, two former teachers of mine. I have gained much from their teachings, and I am confident that both American democracy and American education are in a stronger position because of their pioneer work in education. Responsibility, however, for the views developed in this book rests solely with me; not even pragmatists can be held responsible for the consequences of their teachings in the minds of those who study with them.

I should also like to express my appreciation to the administrative officers of Teachers College who have done so much to make it possible for me to complete this study. In the organization and typing of the manuscript, in the location of sources, and in the preparation of the materials for publication, I owe much to the coöperation of my wife, Grace Fowler Childs, and to Elizabeth V. Rowland, my assistant in philosophy of education.

J. L. C.

CONTENTS

PART TWO

EDUCATION AND THE VALUES OF DEMOCRATIC
CIVILIZATION

PART ONE

The Moral Nature

of

Deliberate Education

CHAPTER I

Characteristics of Deliberate Education

FOR man education is not a mere adornment, it is a life necessity. The human being, at birth, is not nearly so rugged or resourceful as the offspring of many animal forms. The latter are either on their own from the moment they are born or they achieve self-sufficiency after a relatively short period of parental care. The human infant has no such inborn power of efficiency and control. For a period of years he is dependent on others while he matures and learns how to take care of himself. It is by virtue of this adult care and nurture—education—that each new-born human being achieves the competence required for his own existence.

Human societies are equally dependent upon education. Their established modes of life and thought are not biologically transmitted, they are acquired by each successive generation through a process of weighted experiencing and learning. No matter how superior the linguistic, the technological, the scientific, the institutional, the aesthetic, and the ethical attainments of a human group, its young are in no way predisposed by organic constitution to reproduce these cultural patterns in their own original responses. The behavioral equivalents of these cultural affairs emerge in the lives of the immature only as they learn them through participation in the activities of their people. A society continues to exist because of this never ending process of communication and learning.

Education is thus a life necessity in a two-fold sense. It is through nurture that each child becomes a human person. It is

3

also through the education of its immature members that a society provides for the maintenance and the further development of its own ways of living.

§ 1. *Education and the School*

Much of learning is not the result of organized, deliberate instruction; it comes rather as a by-product of the participation of the young in the ways of living of their society. All of these ways educate, and from the standpoint of the developing child what we call "miseducation" is just as real as the other and more approved forms of learning. In this indirect and informal sense all adults are teachers, for the specialized but interrelated activities they carry on are the primary force in evoking and patterning the responses of the children of their community. Learnings acquired in this incidental manner frequently play a crucial part in the shaping of the basic emotional and intellectual dispositions of the young. It is only as we perceive the unremitting rôle of these community activities in the nurture of the immature that we grasp the meaning of this thing we call education.

But adults are not content to rely exclusively on these incidental and informal means for the education of their children. At an early stage in the development of their affairs they are led to organize and maintain a special institution—the school— to assume direct responsibility for the introduction of the young to their established and cherished modes of life and thought. The function of the school is to provide a selected environment and schedule of activities for the nurture of the young in those appreciations, outlooks, and behaviors considered most important and essential to the life of the group.

The functions, the responsibilities, and the prestige of this deliberately organized educational enterprise have grown, not declined, with the advance of civilization. Indeed, the more human beings discover and learn, and the more enriched and complex their ways of living become, the greater the tendency to rely upon the agencies of deliberate education. Today, the deliberate education of the young is recognized in all parts of the world as a primary human activity, and the school has become one of the major human institutions.

In this book our concern is with the *moral* nature of this undertaking in which adults evaluate and formulate their experience for the express purpose of the education of the young. It is our conviction that any agency—private or public, ecclesiastical or secular—that undertakes to select and mediate human experience in order to provide for the nurture of immature human beings is engaged in the most fundamental of all the moral activities of mankind. Nor is this moral approach to the tasks and problems of education a one-sided and partial way of looking at the work of the school. As used in our discussion, the term *moral* refers to both the ends and the means of this organized effort of the school to guide the process by which the young achieve the forms of their being, their thinking, and their doing. It is our conclusion that the most significant approach to any working program of education is to examine it from the standpoint of the values it seeks to cultivate in the young.

§ 2. *Education and Primary Human Faiths*

As we have already indicated, men everywhere reveal by their actual deeds that they regard the immature human being as the kind of creature who should go to school. This universal tendency to organize and support schools is a concrete expression of the basic human conviction that patterns of conduct and personality are not wholly predetermined, but are created, at least in some significant sense, by experience—that is, by that which human beings learn and become as a result of what they do and undergo. Faith in this capacity of man to learn, and to benefit from that which he learns, is implicit in every attempt of adults to plan and maintain an organized program of education.

Schools are also public testimony to man's faith in the possibility of control over his own destiny. They are founded because man believes that he has some measure of power to shape the course of his own ways of living. A school system is organized whenever a human group begins to become conscious of its own experience, and desires to select from the totality of its beliefs and practices certain things which it is concerned to preserve and foster by reproducing them in the lives of its young. In other words, the organization of a system of schools signifies the deliberate attempt of a human group to control the pattern of its own evolution. Through the responsible guidance of the experiencing and learning of their young, adults hope to make of them and of their society something different and more satisfactory than would eventuate if affairs were left to take their own course. Organized education is thus the antithesis of a laissez-faire practice; it is an activity that deliberately involves itself in the destinies of human beings.

In fine, the enterprise of education is grounded in two basic and interrelated faiths—faith in the modifiability of the human form, and faith in the possibility of controlling the human enterprise in the interest of cherished ends, or values. Man demonstrates by this universal tendency to found and support schools that he is not a fatalist. Were he really convinced that his preferences and efforts were without power to ameliorate his own estate, he would not progressively expand his investments in deliberate education. This increasing tendency to trust in the art of education is associated with a growing respect for the powers and potentialities of man. Implicit in the practice of the school is the faith that human effort, guided by intelligence, can make a real difference in the course of those things that matter most.

§ 3. *Education and Choice Among Life Alternatives*

The moral nature of education stems from the fact that schools are organized and maintained by adults, not by the children who attend them. Adults engage in deliberate education because they are concerned to direct the processes by which their children mature and learn to become participating members of their society. A manifestation of preference for certain patterns of living as opposed to others is therefore inherent in every program of deliberate education. Schools always exhibit in their purposes and their programs of study that which the adults of a society have come to prize in their experience and most deeply desire to nurture in their own children. Hence the curriculum of a school is an index to the values of the particular human group that founds the school. It is because some conception of what is humanly significant and desirable is implicit in all nurture of the young that we may say without exaggeration that each program of deliberate education is, by nature, a moral undertaking.

Our thought about education will be confused at its very root if we do not perceive that a school can never be a morally indifferent institution. Each school operates within a definite historical-social situation. This situation is marked by genuine life alternatives. Amid these plural and competing patterns of living, the school seeks to emphasize and to foster certain types of growth, and to hinder and to avert other types of growth. Were one invariant line of development alone open to the young, there would be no need for adult guidance. Thus, both lay and professional educational leaders misconceive the essential meaning of a school whenever they pretend to be neutral or indifferent to what happens to the children under their jurisdiction. In the last analysis, the success or failure of a school is measured in *moral* terms, that is, by what it does with and for the human beings entrusted to its care. All of the other functions of a school are ancillary to this primary responsibility of directing the growth of the immature members of its society.

Obviously, there can be important differences in judgment about what kinds of human behavior are so fundamental and desirable that they should be cultivated in the school. In view of our present limited knowledge of the process of human maturation and learning, there can also be legitimate differences about the best means of nurturing cherished attitudes, techniques, interests, tastes, outlooks and patterns of conduct in the young. But the fact that we still have much to learn about both the ends and the means of education provides no sound ground for the notion that we can educate, and at the same time avoid responsibility for making judgments about the kind of person, or persons, we want the immature to become. This elemental moral responsibility is inherent in each program of deliberate education, for the cultural selections and rejections inescapably involved in the construction and direction of an educational program necessarily have consequences in the lives of those who are nurtured in it.

This tendency to pattern the intellectual and emotional dispositions of the young is present in every type of educational program—democratic as well as authoritarian, secular as well as religious, scientific as well as humanist, liberal as well as vocational, individualist as well as collectivist. In sum, the making of choices that have to do with the destinies of human beings cannot be eliminated from that directing of experience and learning which is the distinctive function of the school. It is choice among significant life alternatives that is the essence of the *moral* act, and choice among values necessarily pervades those human actions by which the program of a school is organized and communicated.

§ 4. *Man Learns His Human Nature*

Although education is typically carried on by groups and in groups, its concern is with the individual human being. Irrespective of the ethical nature of our educational philosophy— that is, irrespective of its regard, or lack of regard, for the worth of human personality—when we educate we cannot ignore the individual human being. Learning is a process of the reconstruction of experience, and experience is always an affair of individuals. As many have emphasized, that which individuals experience is of their surroundings—both physical and social. And in our effort to modify a child it is important to take account of the group of which he is a member. But the individual human being is nevertheless the only center of behavior, feeling and thought. Hence there can be no general, or impersonal, effects of educational activity. Either the results of our educational activity register in the behaviors and dispositions of individual human beings or they do not register at all. Without definite modifications in the habits, the appreciations, the skills, the knowledge, the attitudes, the allegiances, and the dispositions of individual children, there is no education. It follows that any person who is not willing to assume responsibility for directing the growth and the reconstruction of the experience of immature human beings should not enter the work of education. This kind of moral responsibility is written into the very constitution of the undertaking in which adults essay to direct the experience of the young.[1]

The more knowledge that we accumulate about human beings and the process by which they develop, the more we are confident that the patterns of human nature are neither uniquely given at birth nor do they automatically develop by a process of the unfolding of a pre-formed self. Inherited factors set broad limits for the growth of the individual human being, but evidence from a variety of sources—biological, psychological, and anthropological—indicates that a wide range of possibilities lies within these native determinants. The manner in which these organic potentialities of the human infant will be synthesized into a mature human being is always conditioned by factors of culture and experience. William James did not exaggerate when he declared that many different selves are open to each individual at the beginning of life, "but to make any *one* of them actual, the rest must more or less be suppressed."[2]

---

[1] The discussion is phrased in terms of the school, and of adult interest in the education of the young. The same general principles apply however to the education of adults. Deliberate education, at any or all age levels, makes sense only as it denotes a conscious ordering of means to foster desired developments in the lives of individual human beings.

[2] William James, *Principles of Psychology* (New York, Henry Holt and Co., 1890), Vol. I, pp. 309-310.

Learning continues throughout life, but the early years are the formative ones. It is then that the basic intellectual and emotional dispositions are developed. During the early years of their existence, individuals acquire their characteristic modes of feeling, appreciation, and perception, as well as their governing principles of response to their fellow human beings. All of their subsequent learning tends to be assimilated to the patterns of personality gradually articulated and more or less integrated during this plastic and formative period. Hence in directing and ordering the experience of the young, we are not merely selecting the fields of subject-matter and life-activity in which they shall gain knowledge and competence, we are also inescapably sharing in that foundational process that determines the very mode of their personhood.

Bernard Shaw has contended that "the vilest abortionist is he who attempts to mold the mind of a child." [3] In this striking phrase he has summarized a view held by some of those who have been identified with the "child-centered" educational movement. Shaw, however, both mistakes and mis-states the issue. The primary fact is that the life and the mind of the child is necessarily molded, for it is through the nurture provided by other human beings that each child achieves its most distinctive human traits. Apart from this group nurture, were the child fortunate enough to survive, he would not achieve a type of existence much above that of other animals. It is through this association with others that the infant acquires the characteristics that we designate as mind. The actual choice therefore is not between a process of unfolding from within and a process of molding from without; it is a choice between alternative ways of having the human surroundings effect this molding of the child. The real question is whether the development of the child is to come as a by-product of the accidents and pressures of his own unplanned and unguided interactions with his sur-

_____
[3] George Bernard Shaw, *Man and Superman,* "The Revolutionist's Handbook" (New York, Dodd, Mead & Co., 1948).

roundings, or whether his growth is to come as the result of an experience in a special environment planned for this educational purpose. Schools are organized and supported because adults have faith that better results will be attained if the young grow to maturity in an environment that has been deliberately organized for the purpose of introducing them to the life and thought of their society. If we really oppose any and all molding of the life of the child, we should in consistency repudiate the whole enterprise of deliberate education because this patterning of the development of the individual is its basic purpose and justification. The actual moral problem therefore is not one of molding versus not molding; it is rather the problem of discovering the means by which the nurture of the child can be made a process of enrichment and liberation, not one of exploitation and enslavement.

§ 5. *The Obligation to Be Intelligent*

Viewed from the standpoint of their founders and supporters all schools are activity schools. A school, it should be noted, is not primarily a building, it is an organized program of human activity. It is an enterprise of purpose. Like other purposeful activities, it involves the selection and the ordering of *means* to attain projected and desired outcomes. As we have emphasized in the foregoing, these educational outcomes have to do with the lives of human beings. A program of education is therefore intelligent only to the degree that those who have constructed it are aware of the results they desire to attain in the lives of the young and have adapted their means accordingly.

A harmful fallacy is thus imbedded in the notion that teachers can do more satisfactory work if they simply seek the growth of each child and are not encumbered with definite ideas about either the outcomes they hope to attain or the means by which they expect to achieve these outcomes. Ignorance, vagueness, and aimless "busy-work" have no greater value in education than in other spheres of human effort. Certainly those who have faith in intelligence will believe that our prospect of getting satisfactory results will be greater if we know what we are about when we undertake this very important task of directing the experiencing of the young.

On occasion the educational ideas of Dr. John Dewey have been cited as authority for the view that education becomes *immoral* whenever it becomes conscious and definite about the results that it is seeking to achieve in the lives of the young. In *Democracy and Education*, Dr. Dewey did characterize education as a "process that has no end beyond itself" and he also said that since "there is nothing to which growth is relative save more growth, there is nothing to which education is subordinate save more education." [4] But in the same volume, Dr. Dewey indicated that for him growth meant not mere spontaneous activity, but activity that resulted in enriched meaning and in increased power of control. He also explicitly stated "that education will vary with the quality of life which prevails in a group." [5] He further affirmed that the "conception of education as a social process and function has no definite meaning until we define the kind of society we have in mind." [6] In an article written thirty-five years after the founding of his Chicago "laboratory school," Dr. Dewey declared in an appraisal of that educational experiment "that there is as much adult imposition in a 'hands off' policy as in any other course, since by the adoption of that course the elders decide to leave the young at the mercy of accidental contacts and stimuli, abdicating their responsibility for guidance." [7]

Believing as he does that the ideal of growth for each and every person can best be realized in a coöperative, democratic society, Dr. Dewey has devoted much time to the elaboration

---

[4] John Dewey, *Democracy and Education* (New York, The Macmillan Co., 1916), pp. 59-60.

[5] *Ibid*, p. 94.

[6] *Ibid*, p. 112.

[7] Katherine Camp Mayhew and Anna Camp Edwards, *The Dewey School* (New York, Appleton-Century-Crofts, Inc., 1936), p. 469.

of the definite moral implications of the democratic conception for the nurture of the young. He has emphasized that generalized democratic principles cannot really direct education unless we make the effort to translate them "into descriptions and interpretations of the life which actually goes on in the United States today for the purpose of dealing with the forces which influence and shape it."[8]

It is important for educators to recognize that education in and for democracy in no way lessens our responsibility for being aware of the values we are seeking to nurture in the young. Democracy is not a form of anarchy, it is a definite system of social and political life. The democratic way of life is indeed a distinctive mode of associated life and it makes its definite demands on its members. It therefore should have its own distinctive educational program. But a distinctive program of education is still a program, and the adults who are to introduce the young to the principles and the practices of democracy carry a definite and demanding intellectual and moral responsibility.

Democracy is not nature's own unique mode of life. It is the product of a long and costly human struggle, and its life of freedom, of shared responsibility as well as its basic principle of government of, by and for the people make demands on the individual that are ethically more, not less, exacting than the practices of authoritarian social and political systems. Nor is democracy inevitably fated to be the pattern of the future. The future of democracy depends upon the depth of our commitment to it, and upon what we are prepared to do to preserve it. Now all of this carries its implications for the way we should think of the function of education in a democratic society. Democratic attitudes, behaviors and values do not spontaneously unfold in the bosom of the child; he acquires them only as he learns them. The democratic way of life can renew itself only as the children of each successive generation reproduce in their own

---

[8] William H. Kilpatrick (Ed.), *The Educational Frontier* (New York, Appleton-Century-Crofts, Inc., 1933), p. 34.

lives its principles, its techniques, its disciplines, its loyalties and its responsibilities. Our schools must be clear about their part in all of this. It is a confused and misleading interpretation which holds that since democracy is a life of freedom based on respect for each person, we offend against its morality when we take positive steps to cultivate its distinctive attitudes and behaviors in the personalities of our young. Tolerance is a great virtue, but tolerance does not imply moral indifference. Tolerance, moreover, is but one of many values comprehended in what we call our democratic way of life, and educators can be intelligent about education *in* and *for* democracy only as they are intelligent about the various human attitudes and practices which make this life of freedom and tolerance possible. It is a dubious allegiance to democracy that leads one to be indifferent to its foundations, particularly those foundations that are constituted by the attitudes, the loyalties, the habits, and the dispositions of its citizens.

§ 6. *Ends and Means in Education*

It is also important for educators to recognize that a scientifically grounded pedagogy is no substitute for clear ideas about the values and purposes of education. The scientific study of both the nature of the child and the process of human maturation and learning is making indispensable contributions to the work of education. No teacher worthy of the name can afford to ignore these tested findings. But knowledge of these scientific findings does not in and of itself define our educational objectives. For example, knowledge of the fact of individual differences, and of the uniqueness of each child, does not relieve us of responsibility for making judgments about the way in which that inherited uniqueness is to find its appropriate expression within the context of our changing modes of life and thought.

Studies in human learning show that learning is an active, dynamic affair, and the leaders of progressive education have rendered an important service by developing an activity curriculum to provide more adequately for these dynamic aspects of the learning process. But "pupil initiative" and "wholehearted purposeful projects" are in no sense a substitute for adult guidance; they should rather be viewed as improved means of making that guidance more effectual. The more knowledge that we can get about the process by which the powers of the child ripen, the better we shall be able to plan the program of the school, but knowledge of "the human maturation sequence" does not justify a "hands-off" policy in education. As a matter of fact, such findings as we have about child development show that "the human maturation sequence" is by no means exclusively an affair of the biological organism; it is deeply influenced by environmental factors, and after the first years, the rôle of a culturally conditioned experience becomes primary in determining the further lines of personal growth. Confronted with plural and conflicting cultural patterns, educators cannot escape responsibility for choosing main lines of human development.

Those educators who have combined the psychological principles of child growth with the moral principles of democracy and have developed the conception that the supreme aim of education should be the nurture of an individual who can take responsibility for his own continued growth have made an ethical contribution of lasting worth. But acceptance of the objective of developing a person who can eventually take over his own education does not at all imply that the school should arrange its affairs so that each child, unhindered by adult guidance, will be left "free to develop in his own way." To attempt to do this is to negate the very purpose of deliberate education. We establish schools because we recognize that the child does not know the principles and the means of his own development, and because we also realize that the kind of scientific and humane conduct we call "mature" and which is presupposed in the principle of responsible "self-education" is not an original endowment. It is a genuine ethical insight that distinguishes intellectual and emotional maturity from mere slavish conformity to custom, but we err whenever we assume that what is prized

as "maturity" is the product of an unguided, spontaneous unfolding of an inborn pattern of human personality.

Although method is fundamental in the nurture of the
young, method, in and of itself, cannot determine the objectives
of our educational program. To define these educational objectives we must have a definite conception of the kind of person
we are seeking to develop. If that conception is to be more than
a formal abstraction, it must take account of the actual life conditions and relationships of the society in which the child is
to live, along with those more general principles of human conduct which men of many different societies have come to honor
because these principles have been confirmed by all that they
have experienced.

Education is grounded in respect for the achievements of
human beings. If man did not have regard for that which he
has learned and created, he would not organize schools to communicate his culture to his young. But in a democratic society,
education is also grounded in respect for each human personality.
It seeks the growth, not the enslavement, of the immature members of its society. Fortunately, these two basic values are not in
conflict; on the contrary, they mutually support one another. We
can manifest respect for the child and contribute to his progressive liberation through the procedures of deliberate education only
as we have respect for the knowledge and values that man has
derived from that which he has suffered and undergone. No
educational theory or method is to be trusted which opposes
respect for the child to respect for human experience and
knowledge.

In fine, education is a value-conditioned activity. The school
seeks to cultivate selected values in the young by means of both
the subject-matters and the methods that it employs in its program. In education, as in other human arts, our practice becomes intelligent as it grows, both in its awareness of the ends
that it is seeking to attain and in its mastery of the means which
it must use to attain these ends. The fact that these ends or

outcomes involve the lives of the immature deepens—it does not diminish—our responsibility to know what we are trying to accomplish when we undertake to educate.

§ 7. The Moral Nature of Deliberate Education

As we have emphasized in all the foregoing, deliberate education is never morally neutral. A definite expression of preference for certain human ends, or values, is inherent in all efforts to guide the experience of the young. No human group would ever bother to found and maintain a system of schools were it not concerned to make of its children something other than they would become if left to themselves and their surroundings. Moreover, in order to develop the preferred and chosen patterns of behavior, it is necessary to hinder other and incompatible kinds of growth. A school is ineffective as an educational agency whenever the emphases in certain aspects or departments of its work are denied or negated in other parts of its program. In education, as in other realms of human activity, the actual practices of a school are more potent than its verbal professions. Maximum results are achieved when both the declared aims and the actual deeds of a school are unified, and its children are reared in an environment that supports in its daily practices that which it affirms in its theory.

As we have already stated, the term *moral*, as used in this discussion, does not pertain to a restricted phase of the work of the school. The moral interest pervades the entire educational program. It is involved whenever a significant choice has to be made between a better and a worse in the nurture of the young. The moral factor appears whenever the school, or the individual teacher or supervisor, is *for* certain things and *against* other things. The moral element is preëminently involved in all of those selections and rejections that are inescapable in the construction of the purposes and the curriculum of the school. It appears, for example, in the affairs of the playground—in the kind of sports that are favored and opposed, and in the code of sportsmanship by which the young are taught to govern their behavior in the actual play of the various games. It appears in the social life of the school—in all of the behaviors that are approved or disapproved as the young are taught the manners— the conventional or minor morals—of their society. It appears in the school's definition of the delinquent and in its mode of dealing with him. It appears in the way children are taught to treat those of different racial, religious, occupational, economic or national backgrounds. It appears in the department of science: in the methods the young are expected to adopt in conducting their experiments, in their reports of what actually happened during the course of their experiments, as well as in the regard of the teachers of science for accuracy, for precision, and for conclusions that are based on objective data rather than on wishful thinking. It appears in the department of social studies: in the problems that are chosen to be discussed, in the manner in which they are discussed, in the historical documents and events that are emphasized, as well as in the leaders that are chosen to illustrate the important and the worthy and the unimportant and the unworthy in the affairs of man. It appears in the department of literature: in the novels, the poems, the dramas that are chosen for study, in what is considered good and what is considered bad in the various forms and styles of human conduct and expression. It appears in the organization and the government of the school: in the part that superintendent, supervisors, teachers, pupils are expected to play in the making and the maintenance of the regulations of the school. It appears in the methods of grading, promoting, and distributing honors among the children of the school. It appears in the celebration of national holidays: in the particular events that are celebrated as well as in the historical and contemporary personalities who are chosen to exemplify the qualities of citizenship and worthy community service. It appears in the programs for the general assemblies of the schools: in the various leaders from the community who are brought in to speak to the children. It appears in the way teachers are treated: the amount of freedom and initiative they enjoy, in the extent to which teachers are permitted to take part in the life of their community, and the degree to which the young believe that they are studying under leaders who are more than docile, routine drill-masters in assigned subjects. It appears in the way the community organizes to conduct its schools: in the provision it makes in its schoolgrounds, buildings, and equipment, in the kind of people it chooses to serve on the school board, and in the relation of the members of the board to the administrative and teaching staff. In sum, the moral factor enters whenever and wherever significant decisions have to be made about either the organization, the administration, or the instructional program of the school. All of these decisions, whether they relate to curriculum or to extra-curriculum affairs, exert an influence on the attitudes and the behaviors of the young.

Thus judgments about life values inescapably pervade and undergird the whole process of providing and guiding experience. More than many teachers recognize, a scheme of values—a structure of things considered significant, worthful and right—operates in their endless responses to the daily behavings of their pupils. Many of these educational values concern the very fundamentals of human existence. They have to do with such elemental things as the rights, the responsibilities, the beliefs, the tastes, the appreciations, the faiths and the allegiances of human beings. As we introduce the young to the various aspects of human experience—familial, economic, scientific, technological, political, religious, artistic—we inevitably encourage attitudes and habits of response in and to these affairs. In order to encourage, we must also discourage; in order to foster, we must also hinder; in order to emphasize the significant, we must identify the non-significant; and, finally, in order to select and focus attention on certain subject-matters of life, we have to reject and ignore other subject-matters. Were our values different, our selections and our rejections would also be different. The process of selecting and rejecting, of fostering and hindering, of distinguishing the lovely from the unlovely, and of discriminating the important from the unimportant, is unending in education. It is this process of choice and emphasis that defines what is meant by the term *moral* as it is used in this book.

As thus interpreted, the concept of the *moral* refers not primarily to the particular ethical quality of the life interests, outlooks, and practices involved in any given educational program, but rather to the more elemental fact that *choices* among genuine life-alternatives are inescapably involved in the construction and the actual conduct of each and every educational program. These choices necessarily have consequences in the lives of the young, and through them in the life of their society. Viewed from this perspective, education undoubtedly ranks as one of the outstanding moral undertakings of the human race.

CHAPTER II

Society and Education

THE purposes and the subject-matters of the school are not developed by a process of adult contemplation carried on in a social vacuum, nor do they arise spontaneously from the interests and activities of school children. They are invariably developed through the evaluative and selective response of adults to the traditions, the conventions, the life practices, and the changing conditions of their society. Thus a school is a very human institution. Its program is never formulated by "nature," by "history," by "the state," by "religion," by "science," or by any impersonal agency or process; it is always constructed by ordinary human beings whose value judgments and educational selections are necessarily influenced by factors of time, place, status, interest, belief, knowledge and custom. Both religious and secular programs of education bear the marks of the particular societies in which they have originated, as well as the definite cultural interests they have been designed to serve.

Search into the materials and the purposes of any school and you will come upon that which extends beyond the school. You will encounter the language, the literature, the practical and fine arts, the science, the institutions, the moral ideals, and the faiths of an historical, human group. You will find these things, however, not in the gross form in which they exist and function in the society that creates the school, but abstracted, sifted, classified, and graded into a curriculum for the nurture of the young. Considerations both of group welfare and of pedagogy play a part in this process by which the affairs of a human society are selected and transformed into a curriculum for the school. But no matter how drastically these life materials may be refined and rearranged in the subject-matters and activities of the school, they are always taken originally by somebody, for some definite purpose, from the totality of the ways of life and thought of a human society. As these group practices, interests, beliefs, and outlooks change, the program of the school also changes. In this basic sense education *is* a social affair. Educational choices are always, in the last analysis, social choices.

§ 1. *Human Interests and the Purposes of Education*

The historical and the comparative study of man's educational activities shows that the actual ends for which different societies, and different groups within the same society have chosen to educate have been many and various. As we emphasized in the first chapter, adults tend to make central in their program for the nurture of the young whatever they consider of major importance and value in their ways of life and thought. Even the needs and the possibilities of the young are always defined in terms of the particular mode of life that the adults who organize the school desire and expect the young to lead. It is therefore natural that educational purposes, materials, and methods have differed as widely as have types of human association, systems of value, and patterns of authority and leadership.

Military castes, for example, have resorted to education in order to fashion the young into efficient "bayonets" for their armed forces. Social and political despots have used education for the purpose of breeding devoted and docile "subjects" of their autocratic regimes. Revolutionary communists have organized schools to train the young in the ideology of the class-struggle, and to fashion them into "militant warriors" in the world-struggle to overthrow the existing capitalist system. Supernaturalists have elaborated school rituals and programs in order to nurture "devout believers" in a revealed plan of life and education. Literary humanists have made a curriculum of the "great-books" and have sought to develop the "gentlemen of culture"—the cultivated person who is possessed of "the conscience of truths valid for all and the will to undertake duties common to all." Experimental scientists have sought to develop the "man of the laboratory," equipped with the attitudes, faiths, and allegiances implicit in the objective experimental process of discovering and testing truth. Ardent nationalists have demanded a common system of schools devoted to the cultivation of the "patriot"—the obedient citizen whose final authority and supreme object of affection and loyalty is the fatherland. Absolute pacifists have founded schools dedicated to world brotherhood and the religion of humanity, and designed to create the "conscientious objector"—the person who instinctively believes that "all war is sin" and who will have no part in its organized slaughter of fellow human beings. Private enterprisers have propagandized for a school that will make each child into a "rugged individualist," committed beyond recall to the system of private ownership and the principle of "free" and "unregulated" acquisition. Liberals have sought a school system that would cultivate the "informed and critical mind," contending that the "enlightened citizen" is the only secure foundation for a humane mode of existence.

Diverse as the foregoing educational purposes and programs are, they have certain common features. Each of these educational programs defines some historical group's conception of basic life interests and meanings. Each has a conception of the kind of person it wants the school to produce, and its norm or standard for human personality is derived from its interpretation of fundamental group values and relationships. Each of these groups is concerned to construct a definite program through which its preferred and predominant pattern of living will be bred into the dispositions and the habits of the young. It has no thought of letting "the child develop in his own way," whatever that may be held to mean. Each expects that its teachers will be faithful in the work of communicating its chosen values to the young. Although the "ethical" quality of these programs varies enormously, they are all "moral" undertakings in the elemental meaning of the term *moral*: each has its governing principles of evaluation and choice in matters of taste, faith, allegiance, and human conduct.

§ 2. *Life Imperatives and Educational Programs*

Fortunately, the clash in purpose and program is not quite so sharp as the foregoing list of life interests and educational objectives suggests. The history of education shows that the predominant life-alternative, or value, favored by any particular cultural group, or sub-group, has seldom been the sole interest included in its total educational program. Militarists, tyrants, revolutionists, supernaturalists, literary-humanists, scientists, nationalists, pacifists, capitalists, and liberals: all, alike, live under the compulsions of the here and now. This means that each must take account of the stubborn requirements of human existence—collective and personal. In order to provide for these life-imperatives, adults have to do more than train the young in a single cherished and selected aspect of life; their educational programs must also provide some opportunity for the new-born to learn about the varied human arts and institutionalized practices that are essential to the maintenance of their society.

A militarist, for example, may be consumed by his interest in guns and soldiers, but in his total political and educational program he courts disaster if he ignores the need for bread, and that whole structure of economic and social institutions and relationships by which bread is produced and distributed. As a militarist he may have no regard for letters and science as such, but in the modern world an illiterate, and scientifically and technologically untrained army has little chance to survive in the ordeal of total war.

The supernaturalist educator may esteem salvation in the life beyond the grave above all other values, but he cannot afford to be indifferent to the mundane aspects of life. Most

parents will not accept discipline in the life eternal as a substitute for competence in reading, writing and arithmetic. They
also expect their children to learn geography, science, history
and civics as well as the doctrines that comprise the catechism of
the church. The curricula of church and public schools therefore have much more in common than one might suspect if he
has heard only the strictly theological defense of the religious
school. Supernaturalists are also children of their age; they are
not wholly immune to the "climate of opinion" in which they
live and think. Today, the tendency increases in their ranks to
reject asceticism and all forms of withdrawal from society as
modes of preparation for the life eternal, and to hold instead
that the best preparation for the next world is the most adequate
and meaningful living in the present.

So, also, for the literary-humanist: he may believe that the
"unkillable classics" constitute the only significant source of
human enlightenment, but when he designs his educational
program, stubborn realities will demand that he give some attention to our scientific and technological ways of thinking and of
making a living. When he builds his school plant, he will probably furnish it with the best of modern equipment. More than
he is aware modern influences will also pervade the classrooms of
his school—even the imperishable principles of the classics will
be taught and studied by those whose minds have been conditioned by the affairs of their own age and society.

The utilitarian-vocationalist may be passionately devoted to
narrow technical training in the interest of more efficient and
more profitable production, but the imperatives of the life of an
organized community—a community without which his whole
system of technology and factory production could not survive—
will require him to give place to many other life interests and
subjects in the curriculum of his vocational school.

The experimentalist may accord the attitudes and methods
of scientific inquiry the supreme place in his philosophy of life
and education. But when he undertakes to organize a school

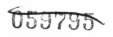

for the nurture of the young, he will find that the important and distinctive demands of family, economy, vocation, government, religion, and art will compel him to make educational provision for many human interests other than the disinterested pursuit of truth. All of the subject-matters of life can and should be explored by the critical and objective method of experimental science, but the method of science is in no sense a substitute for a direct experience of these varied subject-matters. Important and fundamental as is the interest in knowledge, it is by no means the only human interest, and it would be a very inadequate school that restricted its attention to the method of experimental inquiry.

The shift from an agrarian to an industrial-urban civilization has greatly strengthened this tendency to broaden the perspectives, the interests, the purposes and the subject-matters of the school. For most of human history, the young have learned the arts by which life is sustained, not primarily by instruction given in the school, but by direct and responsible participation in these productive activities under the supervision and direction of the adults engaged in them. In our highly articulated, specialized, and technological civilization, this ancient system of apprenticeship is rapidly disappearing, and with it is going much of the opportunity of the young to learn through direct sharing in the productive affairs of their community. In order to adjust to this transformed social and economic situation, the functions and the responsibilities of the school have been greatly expanded, and the period of schooling has been correspondingly extended.

It is only natural that this rich and diversified curriculum, open to all the children of the community, should have greatly altered the educational situation. One consequence has been a decline in the emphasis on the transmission of doctrines in the education of the young. In a school in which increasing attention must, of necessity, be given to the preparation of the young for the things that they have to do as citizens and as members of particular occupational groups, concern with mundane affairs tends to take much of the time that used to be centered on the study of doctrines and the memorizing of moral maxims. In our complex, technological society the school has been compelled to give major attention to the introduction of the young to those basic life functions upon which the general welfare depends.

§ 3. *The Democratic Conception and the Aims of Education*

The development of democracy has also eliminated certain historic types of educational purpose and program. In any society that is really governed by the democratic principle of the worth and dignity of each human personality exploitive systems of education are necessarily precluded. The democratic community negates its own moral foundations whenever it regards the child as a mere potential "bayonet" for its armed forces, as a mere future "hand" in its system of factory production, or as a mere instrument of any kind to be fashioned for the perpetuation of an established institution, or the interests of a special class. A society that is grounded in the conception that governments are instituted among men to promote "life, liberty and the pursuit of happiness," and which holds "that whenever any form of government becomes destructive of these ends, it is the right of the people to alter or to abolish it" cannot consistently support an educational practice that is designed to fashion human beings into the mere instruments of the state. The supreme moral trait of the democratic community is that it has no good other than the good of individual human beings.

Moreover, in a democratic society authority and leadership in education, as in government, are not supposed to be lodged in the hands of any ruling group—hereditary, military, ecclesiastic, or economic. It is the very essence of democratic theory that authority and ultimate control in all public affairs should be transferred from all such limited groups to the people as a whole. In accordance with this principle we have sought to organize a system of public schools in the United States in which the responsibility for the determination of the educational program would rest with the local communities, and with the various state authorities, not with the Federal government—that is, with the parents and their own chosen representatives on local school boards, not primarily with national or church officials. It has been our conviction that a school system thus responsive to the interests and the preferences of parents would tend to make the needs and the welfare of the child its primary concern. We have also assumed that schools which are controlled by the very groups whose children are enrolled in them could not easily be manipulated to serve the special interests of privileged classes. On the whole, events have justified this faith; the American school has been disposed to make the growth, not the exploitation, of the child its controlling objective.

But even in a democratic society the needs of the immature do not define themselves, nor do they remain constant in a world in which change is real. As we have already emphasized, in order to define desirable patterns of growth for the individual child, we must take account of the kind of life that we expect and desire him to lead. This pattern of life is not an isolated and private thing. It involves, to be sure, the individual child with his distinctive native endowment, but it equally involves the community with its public modes of life and thought. The deeper the regard of the educator for the worth and dignity of the child, the deeper his interest in the community should become. Any program of education tends to become abstract, formal, and therefore a mechanical routine whenever its purposes and materials are considered to be the property of a self-sufficient school, for this means that dynamic continuity between the work of the school and the life that goes on outside the school has been disrupted. A school best provides for the growth of the child when it maintains living interaction with the community of which he is a part.

§ 4. *Names and Realities in Human Conduct*

A theory of morals is of course implicit in the foregoing view of the relation of the program of the school to the ongoing affairs of its society. This moral theory holds, in the first place, that human rights and human responsibilities do not constitute a separate and fixed system, but that they are conditioned by the concrete ways in which a human group makes its living and carries on its whole schedule of interrelated life activities. This theory assumes, in the second place, that as knowledge grows and new means of control and modes of living develop, traditional patterns of human rights and duties may also have to be modified. In other words, this social conception of education is the correlative of a moral theory which holds that morals are related to human interests and evolving conditions of life, and hence are not absolute and transcendental, but empirical, institutional, and historical in nature.

It is easy to deceive ourselves and to conceal this empirical and social character of morals. All that is necessary to make morals appear to be unconditioned and immutable is to concentrate attention on moral terms or names, and to ignore the actual human relationships and behaviors that are denoted by these moral terms. Thus an educator may affirm that even revolutionary social changes are of no concern to him, for he knows that in each and every society a child should be taught to be unselfish, to be honest, to be chaste, to be loyal, and to make his behavior conform to all of the fundamentals of the moral code. There is, to be sure, a measure of truth in this educational affirmation, for in the course of its experience the human race has gained many ethical insights. But this emphasis on continuity and permanence in the moral life of man becomes harmful whenever it is taken to mean that new knowledge and powers of human control, and altered conditions of life, do not make necessary fresh appraisals of the behaviors that are to be considered authentic expressions of these traditional moral principles.

For example, changes in modes of production have in no way eliminated the importance of the distinction between the "selfish" and the "unselfish" in human conduct, but these economic changes are calling for a fundamental review of the rights of both the owner and the worker. Considerations of public welfare in our interdependent world are now demanding that the right of the owner to do as he pleases with that which he owns, and the right of the worker to leave his job when and as he desires, be altered. Now these are not superficial moral changes; they involve fundamentals in human relationships and behaviors in the economic sphere. The meaning of the concepts of "selfishness" and "unselfishness" must be revised to correspond to these new realities in our interdependent ways of making a living. So also in the realm of family relationships. The development of effectual contraceptive measures has aroused deep controversies about what should now be considered "moral" in this aspect of human behavior. The evidence indicates that a new standard is developing in this ancient sphere of the "moral," and already important church groups are strongly supporting on ethical grounds the principle of planned parenthood. Nor does the concept of "loyalty" in the realm of political affairs automatically define itself. World-wide totalitarian political movements have resulted in novel political affiliations and practices which have raised the most difficult kind of questions about the meaning of citizenship and the criteria by which "loyalty" is to be measured in contemporary political, educational and similar public undertakings.

In brief, unless education is to serve outmoded and reactionary ends, it must accept responsibility for defining the kind of behaviors which now should be associated with such traditional and basic moral categories as "honesty," "unselfishness," "chastity," "loyalty," "equality," "responsibility," and "freedom." The present has its deep continuities with the past, but it also has its significant discontinuities. The discontinuities, moreover, are as real as the continuities. Education, during this period of social transition and strain, will not promote democratic interests, if it seeks to make "moral absolutes" out of historic rights and forms of human conduct. To serve democratic purposes, education must play its part in the important task of moral discovery. It can do this only as it is willing to continue to examine and test its educational values by whatever we gain of new knowledge and also by that structure of human relationships and activities which is ever developing in the society outside the school. An unexamined morality is not fit to fashion the educational program of a democracy in this period of social transition. Apart from intelligent study of the changing affairs of its society, the school has no adequate means of determining the worth of its moral foundations. Recognition of the reality of change must be one of the fundamental principles in the philosophy of education of our period.

§ 5. *Basic Meanings in the Social Interpretation of Education*

Measured by all the crucial scientific criteria, human beings constitute a common *biological* family. All members of this human family share a basic organic inheritance. But *culturally* they are members of many different human societies. These societies, located in various parts of the world, are the products of a long development. They have their common features, but they also have their distinctive traits. Each of these societies, taken as a whole, is unique. The things which differentiate one human group from other territorial and cultural groups are no less real than those elements in its ways of life and thought that it shares with other human societies. It was this perception which led the Commission on the Social Studies of the American Historical Association to declare that:

Education always has a geographical and cultural location; it is therefore specific, local, and dynamic, not general, universal, and unchanging; it is a function of a particular society at a particular time and place in history; it is rooted in some actual culture and expresses the philosophy and the recognized needs of that culture. . . .

Although the basic biological equipment of man seems to be comparatively invariant and may therefore be expected to give certain common elements to education everywhere and at all times, human civilization has characteristics of neighborhood, region, nation, and more extended cultural areas, which lend unique qualities to every working educational program, however persistent and pervasive may be the universal elements entering into it.[1]

It is significant that the eminent members of this Commission of the American Historical Association decided to emphasize in their concluding Report that deliberate education should be viewed not primarily as a function of humanity in general, but rather as a function of particular human societies, each with its own individualized past, its own language and literary heritage, its specialized skills and modes of making a living, its distinctive structure of customs, laws, and institutions, as well as with its own unique beliefs, sentiments, moral outlooks, and conceptions of human excellence and of human destiny. For the historian, accustomed to think in the categories of time and place, societies are many, not one; dynamic, not static; individualized and evolving, not fixed specimens of an immutable human pattern. Individual human beings, in their actual psychological natures, are creatures of these historical cultural groups. They think, evaluate, and respond out of an intellectual and moral consciousness that is saturated and hallowed by the history and the achievements of their people. It is not surprising then that when these culturally conditioned groups of human beings undertook the deliberate nurture of their young, they should have created systems of schools which in their subject-matters and their purposes reflected the societies into which they had been born, and which had shaped the very forms of their own being.

But this argument from history is not decisive. The fact that education down to the present has been an undertaking

---

[1] American Historical Association, *Conclusions and Recommendations,* The Report of the Commission on Social Studies (New York, Charles Scribner's Sons, 1934), pp. 31-32.

which has varied with factors of time and place, does not in and of itself warrant the conclusion that education in our shrinking and closely integrated world should continue to be that sort of an enterprise. It is wholly fair to ask those who adopt the social interpretation of education to justify their position in terms not of historical origins, but rather in terms of present human values. Certainly a discussion of education and morals should be willing to meet this demand, for the deepest concern of morals is with what *should be,* not simply with the description of what *has been,* or *now is.* We shall therefore conclude this discussion of society and education by enumerating some of the considerations that make it desirable for us to continue to view education as a human undertaking in which factors of time and place are centrally important.

In the first place, this social theory of education is in harmony with the imperatives of educational practice. In spite of present cultural changes, no advocate of universalism in education has been bold enough to contend that the children of the United States should be nurtured in the Chinese language, or that the children of China should be nurtured in the English language, or that the children of these two countries should be educated in a new world-language. In other words, in the case of such basic interests as language and literature, it is generally recognized that stubborn historical factors make it both necessary and desirable that the program of the school be rooted in the cultural heritages of actual human groups. Even following the total military defeat of Japan and Germany, no one has recommended that the children of these two countries be educated in the language of one of the victorious Powers.

The situation is no less compelling when we come to the subject of history. Men in different parts of the world have had their own and distinctive experiences, and these diversified pasts are not dead; they constitute the very substance of the cultures in which men now live and through which they develop their objects of allegiance and devotion. History, moreover, is the past of the present, and to be significant must be explored from the perspective of some actual present. These perspectives are as many as are present human societies. Hence proposals for "objectivity" in the teaching of history have never assumed that the children of the world should be taught a colorless, universalized human history. These proposals for more impartial historical textbooks have recognized the necessity and the desirability of plural accounts of what human beings, organized in different societies, have done and undergone. The demand for objectivity in the preparation of school history books has therefore been the demand that these various cultural and national accounts strive to be more accurate and fair in their report of other cultures and other national groups, particularly in their interpretations of past transactions and conflicts with these groups. It has been accepted that it would mean impoverishment, not enrichment, were all of these individualized human records to be merged in one common, authoritative history of universal man.

The same considerations obviously hold for vocational education, for education in citizenship, for worthy home membership, and for the creative use of leisure time. Without taking into account the operating institutions and practices of its own society, the school would have no adequate means for the construction of its educational program in these vital dimensions of human experience.

Since the school, in one way or another, must make this reference to the affairs of its society, the adherents of the social interpretation of education hold that this evaluation of the life of a people should be made deliberately with public responsibility for whatever cultural selections and rejections are actually involved in the construction of its program. The ends of objectivity will be better served in education when choices among life-alternatives are recognized and avowed, not concealed or denied.

This social view of education, in the second place, can

help us overcome the tendency to *formalism* in the work of deliberate education. The constant temptation of the school is to permit its materials and schedules of activities, once they have been selected, classified, graded, and organized into a curriculum, to become an autonomous program of self-perpetuating interests and subjects. The school begins to die both emotionally and intellectually whenever it thus becomes imprisoned in an inherited curriculum and begins to turn its back on the society that it was organized to serve. To make the communication of meaning a living thing, the teacher must grasp the connection of his "subject" or sphere of human interest and knowledge with that which his people have suffered and enjoyed and with that which they now do and undergo. Education, moreover, is an affair of the young just as literally as it is an affair of the heritage of the group. These young are living as well as learning. They live by participating in the affairs of their family, neighborhood, community, and country. A primary aim of education should be to make this participation more meaningful by placing it in a wider historical and geographical and cultural context, and by helping the young to acquire the knowledge, the skills and the techniques which make this participation more effectual. Growth in meaning and growth in capacity for participation in the life of a human group are not effectually cultivated in a school which makes its own world a rival and a substitute for the world outside the school. An increasing number of educators perceive that both "subjects" and "children" become abstractions whenever they are dealt with as entities independent of the life of the community. They recognize that educators can become wise about the nurture of the immature members of their society only as they continue to grow in their understanding of that world *from* which the young come to school, *in* which they continue to live during the period they study as pupils in the school, and *to* which they must go to work out their own careers when their years at school have been completed.

The social conception of education, in the third place, can

help save us from the evil of utopianism in education. By utopianism is meant any projection of social and educational ends
which fails to take responsible account of actual cultural conditions, and hence evades responsibility for developing the concrete means by which its ideal ends are to be achieved. Whenever
we view moral ideals as absolute and unconditioned things, we
are apt to get involved in this kind of romanticism. Our country,
for example, is committed by both religious and political ideology
to the principle of the dignity and worth of "all men." To the
extent that we believe in democracy we are necessarily opposed
to all patterns of discrimination and enforced segregation based
on factors of religion, race, color, sex, class, or national origin.
But nothwithstanding our official democratic affirmations, the
plain fact is that the ideal of equality in the economic, political
and cultural affairs of our country is at present most inadequately
realized. Our historic system of property ownership often operates in present-day industrial society so as to favor a privileged
few at the expense of the many; our political system in its actual
operation in many states now denies Negroes elemental civil
rights; and existing American attitudes and practices tend to
subject the members of minority religious groups to a variety
of discriminations. Education in and for democracy must share
in the struggle to get rid of these inequalities. But educators can
assist in this important task of democratic, social reconstruction
only as they recognize that these discriminations are stubbornly
grounded in the past experience of the American people. That
experience still lives in characteristic mental habits. The pioneer
and agrarian experience of the American people, for example,
has disposed many of both farm and city to a firm faith in the
system of economic individualism, even though their own interests would now be better served in a regime of coöperative
planning. We misconstrue the nature of the present economic
problem if we do not appreciate the strength of this faith in individualism, and discern the ways in which it is often manipulated by minority groups that have a vested economic interest in

the maintenance of the *status quo*. Experience also demonstrates that racial attitudes and the group mores that underlie our segregated school system have deep roots in the past. It is apparent that education can serve as an agency for social progress only as it takes full account of these group attitudes and the factors in our cultural history which have produced them.

But to take account of existing attitudes and prejudices does not mean that we must weakly surrender to them; it rather means that our proposals for reconstruction should be so formulated that they will strengthen, not weaken, the forces that are striving to dissolve this legacy of discrimination. Democratic advance is undoubtedly a function of human courage as well as of intelligence, but no amount of courage will bring us nearer the goal of equality unless that courage is informed by the kind of understanding which comes from historical and social analysis.

Education frequently fails to enjoy the coöperation of many thoughtful people of genuine democratic interest because of its tendency to make vague moral slogans a substitute for analysis of the conditions with which it has to deal. Actually we know our moral ends only as we know something of the means by which these ends are to be attained. Because the social interpretation of education tends to focus attention on conditions and means it gives promise of developing a morality in education that will be free from the weakness of sentimental utopianism.

Finally, the social interpretation of education can help us discern the defects of traditionalism in education. By traditionalism is meant not sincere regard for the human past, but rather the social and educational view which assumes that we already have a completed system of truth concerning the essentials of human nature, moral values, and the patterns of human civilization, and which also assumes that this completed system contains the answers to whatever problems of human belief, human conduct, and social policy may beset us. On this basis, education becomes merely a process by which the young are indoctrinated with the truths of this closed, authoritarian system. Only those educators who are so immersed in a system of intellectual and moral abstractions that they are immune to the instructions of ordinary human experience, can thus convince themselves that change, and novelty, and moral uncertainty are not real factors in the experience of human beings.

In our period of profound social transformation and transition it is no contribution to the resolution of the problems of mankind to minimize the drastic nature of the adjustments which men must now make if they are to continue to survive. In later chapters we shall explore in some detail the nature of these adjustments and the importance of nurturing the young in a morality that is more consonant with the life imperatives and life possibilities of the new age we are now entering. Every resource in our intellectual and moral heritage will be needed to help us make satisfactory adjustments to these emerging modes of life, but we shall also do well to accept the fact that we are confronted with novel life conditions which call for real moral pioneering if we are to make our new powers of control over the physical environment serve the ends of a good life. Both the nature of our problems and the means for resolving them will be more adequately understood if old and young seek to educate and re-educate themselves in terms of the actual social situations in which they are now involved. A fundamental merit of the social interpretation of education is that it invites educators to view their task as a significant part of the total task of building a civilization that is in harmony with the deep moving forces in the modern world.

CHAPTER III

Substitutes for Mundane Evaluations in Education

WE HAVE emphasized, in the foregoing, that education is an activity inescapably conditioned by values. These values do not originate primarily with the young in the schools; they are developed by adults from that which they have experienced, and in terms of their conceptions of human potentialities and of what is humanly significant. Indeed, schools are maintained because adults have definite patterns of human living that they desire their children to acquire through a weighted and directed course of experiencing. It is this ineliminable rôle of choice among values—among genuine alternatives in human life and thought—that makes every program of deliberate education a moral enterprise. Since the formulation and the organization of a program for the nurture of the young necessarily entails an evaluation and interpretation of the particular society the school is organized to serve, factors of time and place are of central importance in education. Organized education is intrinsically a social undertaking, because the controlling purpose of the school is to prepare the young for their life careers as members of some actual human group.

§ 1. *The Search for the Universal and the Immutable*

Some educators reject this social theory of education. They are in accord with the view that education is a deliberate effort to shape the development of the young, and is therefore, by nature, a moral undertaking. But these educators recoil from the proposition that the norms for human life which undergird all nurture of the immature are necessarily derived by a process of social analysis and appraisal. These critics perceive that this social conception makes education a function of particular societies, and hence a human enterprise that varies with cultures, and with different periods in the same culture. They demand a more universal and permanent foundation for an undertaking that has to do with the destinies of human beings.

These educators are also opposed to a theory of education that makes the critical evaluation of the traditions and institutions of their society a necessary part of the task of education. Human interests and preferences, they contend, are notoriously subjective and relative, and educators need a more secure and universal basis for their educational work than can be supplied by a process of critical analysis of the subject-matters of ordinary human experience. Education will surely get involved in disruptive controversies, they assert, if its program for the nurture of the young has no more solid and authoritative foundation than can be provided by mere educational judgments about the important and the unimportant—the worthy and the unworthy— in the endlessly changing affairs of human societies.

These educators remind us that in this period of profound social change and transition the public is sharply divided. They emphasize that as yet no stable consensus has been achieved about the kind of reconstruction—intellectual, institutional, and moral—that is now required to re-order our common ways of living. They hold that since public education is an enterprise of the whole community, the school should be shielded from involvement in the present disturbed social situation, marked as it is by intellectual uncertainty and group conflict.

These critics of the social interpretation of education also recognize that they cannot evade the responsibility for providing an alternative method for the determination of the purposes and the content of the program of the school. They differ among themselves, however, about the nature of this substitute source, or plan, for the development of educational aims and materials.

"Supernaturalists" believe that this superior source is to be had in the declarations of revealed religion as authoritatively interpreted by the leaders of the Church; "classicists" hold that it is available in the teachings of the great books—books that have endured because they contain the insights of intellectual and moral leaders who have succeeded in going beneath the local and the transient to the deeper and more ultimate meanings of human existence; "essentialists" affirm that a more dependable source of educational values is given ready-made in the intellectual and moral findings of the "common sense" of mankind; still another group insists that this more stable source is provided by the original nature of biological man—a nature considered more fixed and fundamental than is exhibited in the varied patterns of living that men acquire as a result of their experience in different human societies.

In this and the succeeding two chapters, we shall consider a number of these alternative proposals. The examination of these substitutes for ordinary human judgment in the determination of educational programs will serve a dual purpose. It will show, in the first place, that the proposed alternatives are not real alternatives. Each of them involves, in one form or another, actual reference to historical systems of life and thought. Each is influenced by the behavior and philosophies of men existing in particular human societies. But each of these substitute methods refuses to assume open responsibility for the definite cultural evaluations and choices involved in that particular interpretation of human life which it makes the basis of its own educational program. Hence, in actual practice, each of these alternative plans relies on a procedure that is more subjective and arbitrary than is the cultural or social method of analysis which it condemns. Choice among life alternatives becomes responsible and objective not when it is denied or concealed, but when it is openly avowed and submitted to public inspection and criticism.

The examination of these alleged alternatives will serve, in the second place, to make clearer the actual meaning of the social interpretation of education. Many of the current criticisms of this social theory of education are grounded in misconceptions. They relate not to the essentials of the theory, but to inadequate educational views and practices which from time to time have been associated with it.

§ 2. The Alternative of Supernaturalism

The oldest of these alternatives to human judgment based on empirical social analysis is reliance on supernatural authority. For a long time in the Western world, education was predominantly under the control of religious agencies. During this period the purposes and much of the subject-matter of education were taken from the intellectual and moral tradition of the church with its supernatural sanctions. A variety of factors have operated to weaken the prestige of this supernatural tradition in modern life and education.

On the intellectual side, the most important of these factors was the rise of modern science and the resulting struggle for the right of freedom of the mind. The heart of this struggle was the demand that the process of inquiry be freed from external controls—more specifically from supernatural preconceptions and clerical censorship. Eventually, the empirical procedures of science gained a considerable measure of autonomy in the realm of knowledge. Today, efforts of supernaturalists to impose dogmatic views about the nature of the physical world when these views are known to be in conflict with scientific findings are repugnant to the intellectual and moral presuppositions of modern man. To be sure, the victory of the empirical over the dogmatic even in the realm of knowledge is by no means complete, for any effort to inquire into the nature and meaning of human experience is still apt to be suspect. We have in the United States, for example, a number of states in which acts of legislatures, not the results of scientific research, authoritatively define what shall be taught about the origin, the nature, and the development of man.

On the other hand, many church leaders are now included in the ranks of those who regard freedom of thought and belief a primary spiritual value. These religious leaders perceive that the freedom of each human being to make up his own mind on the basis of such evidence as is available is a basic presupposition of the spiritual conception that regards men as moral agents and, therefore, endowed with the ability to think for themselves and to act with responsibility. They are no longer content with any interpretation of respect for human personality that does not include as an essential part of its moral outlook, respect for the mind of the individual human being. Thus, today, church leaders often unite with secularists to oppose obscurantist efforts to dictate what men shall believe. These religionists hold that the interests of spiritual religion will not be advanced by any attempt to maintain pre-scientific outlooks in the schools through reliance on either ecclesiastical or governmental authority and power.

Even in the more restricted realm of "moral" conduct many areas of life have freed themselves from a control once directly exercised by ecclesiastical authorities. In a number of countries, including the United States, church and state have been separated, and when conflicts about community standards and personal or group rights arise, it is the civil, not the religious authority, which speaks the official word on behalf of the organized community. This shift in the seat of established authority is illustrated by the manner in which the government, acting as the agent for the whole community, now officially determines the rights of even the "conscientious objector."

In many spheres of human interest it is now commonly accepted that regulative principles must be evolved from within the context of the particular life activity in which they are to apply, not imposed from without by authoritarian deductions from a supernatural code. Modern life has become so complex, and its range of interests so diversified and specialized that an increasing number of religious leaders are disposed to abandon the whole claim of supernatural revelation to serve as a special road to human understanding and moral direction. For the most part, when clergymen now pronounce on social, economic, and political questions, they speak in the rôle of informed and interested citizens, not as the supernaturally sanctioned trustees of the moral interests of the human race. The irresistible movement of events has forced this readjustment. The effort to prescribe for the concrete and intricate human practices of the modern world by deduction from a closed, supernatural revelation was tending to become either an irrelevance, or an intolerable interference. In a world marked by wide diffusion of knowledge, by the vast and growing specialization of human activities, by a more rapid rate of social change, as well as by the spread of the democratic attitude, the moral authority and prestige of a system of supernaturalism began to disintegrate.

But this increasing respect for the empirical in many fields of human activity does not mean that the traditional claim of supernaturalism to a superior kind of "moral" certainty has been entirely withdrawn. Many still insist that in certain crucial areas of human experience reliance on supernatural direction is indispensable. The nurture of the young is often considered to be one of these special areas, and thus the struggle for the moral autonomy of education has not, as yet, been fully consummated.

§ 3. *"Primary" and "Secondary" Aims in Education*

This tendency to give over many particular areas of human interest to "mundane evaluations," but to assert that the ultimate meanings and purposes of life are not to be determined by empirical procedures is well illustrated in an article on education by F. J. Sheed, a prominent lay religious leader.[1]

Mr. Sheed declares that the purpose of education "is to fit human beings for living," and in order to do this, the educator must know "the right purpose of the living human being." He

---

[1] F. J. Sheed, "Education for the Realization of God's Purposes," *The Social Frontier*, Vol. I, No. 4 (January 1935), pp. 10-11.

further contends that "no one who knows what knowing means can pretend that he *knows* the purpose of human life as a result of his own examination of human beings and human history; he can claim no more than probability." Now the educator who attempts to shape the lives of the young on the basis of "probability" is guilty of "the tyranny of imposition"—the "imposition" of himself on the immature.

It is important to note the various steps in the process of reasoning by which Mr. Sheed reaches this conclusion. He starts with the commonly accepted proposition that all knowledge achieved by human procedures is "probable," not absolute, for it may be corrected by later investigations. But then he goes on to assert that since human knowledge is corrigible, not absolute, it is nothing more than a mere individual guess—surely a *non-sequitur* of the crudest sort. And thus having reduced empirical knowledge to the status of an ungrounded, arbitrary, private guess, he concludes that any "educator who proceeds to shape human lives according to his own guess is exercising a tyranny."

Many educators, Mr. Sheed argues, seek to escape this moral difficulty by restricting themselves to "secondary" educational questions such as the best way "to condition the child," "the best subjects to teach," "the best arrangements of society," "the validity of the profit motive," and the like. But no one of these "secondary" questions, he asserts, "can be answered intelligently, till you can say what man's purpose is. You do not even know (save on the most obvious questions) what is good or bad for man till you know the purpose of his existence." Mundane methods, therefore, "can never give certainty save in the lower grades of existence: and not always there." In order to get the master purposes for your educational program, you must be able to go beyond the deliverances of ordinary human experience. Thus, Mr. Sheed asserts:

> In fact, the only strictly scientific way to find out the purpose of anything is to ask its maker. He, if he be not a lunatic, will know what

he made it to do. If he (being a truthful person) tells you, then you know the thing's purpose. Otherwise you can only guess. The Catholic position is that man has a maker and that the maker has said what he made man for. Therefore—not of himself but by the revelation of God—the Catholic knows the purpose of man's life and, if he be an educator, he has the answer to what we have seen is the first question.[2]

In other words, the teacher cannot escape the "tyranny" of imposing arbitrary personal guesses and preferences on the young, unless he grounds his educational activity in a special supernatural revelation.

§ 4. *Supernaturalism and Factors of Time and Place*

As we have already indicated, we share Mr. Sheed's conviction that education is an undertaking that is concerned with the destinies of human beings. We also recognize that an inescapable moral responsibility is involved in the selection and organization of the basic modes of life and thought in which the young are to be nurtured. But we are not persuaded that resort to a special supernatural revelation actually relieves educators of the moral responsibility inherent in their educational function.

In the first place, many and conflicting systems of supernaturalism have emerged during the course of human history. Even within the religious tradition of the Western world these revealed systems of interpretation are many, not one. In a world of interacting cultures and different religious institutions and traditions whoever accepts the authority of supernaturalism is necessarily obliged to choose among these rival systems of revealed truth. Obviously this choice is a *human* choice, subject to all of the limitations of "experience" and "probability" that Mr. Sheed deplores. Should Mr. Sheed reply that no choice is really required, because he knows by intuition—by an infallible "inner light"—that his particular system of supernaturalism is true and self-evident, eminent students of human culture and

---

[2] *Ibid,* p. 10.

religion are prepared to show him that members of other religious groups, no less sincere and devout, are equally confident by "inner feeling" that the system of revealed moral truth in which they were born and reared is the only valid one.

Should Mr. Sheed affirm that his system is indubitably superior because it rests on the unimpeachable authority of an inspired Book, a superhuman Leader, or a venerable and trustworthy religious institution, these adherents of other historically grounded religious traditions will readily confront him with their own sacred literature, with their own superhuman leaders of miraculous birth, and with their own hallowed religious institutions and rituals. If in response to these rival claims, Mr. Sheed shifts the basis of his position and argues that "by their fruits ye shall know them," he will be on firm ground—the ground of shared human experience—but he will have gained this more secure base by appeal, not to the internal authority of his supernatural system, but to the empirical deliverances of ordinary fallible human experience. Without this appeal to something more public and shareable than the distinctive sanctions of his own inherited system of supernaturalism, it is difficult to see how Mr. Sheed can expect a hearing for his view of the purposes of the living human being from any of those groups who have not been habituated from infancy to the doctrines of his Church.

In other words, real communication can begin between partisans of rival absolute systems only as each is willing to abate the claims of his own transcendental absolutes and participate in the processes of ordinary human experience and discourse. One of the factors which is transforming the basis of moral authority is the growing recognition that in a world that is now interdependent we can hope to achieve community only if the members of the various religious systems recognize that no one of these systems automatically provides the warrant for its own superiority. Dr. Northrup has called attention to the fatal flaw in any remedy for our present difficulties that invites us to accept the dogmas of any one system of supernatural truth:

> The very number and diversity of conceptions of what the good and the divine is, give the lie to any such diagnosis, and to the ever present proposal that a return to the traditional morality and religion is the cure for our ills. All that such proposals accomplish is the return of each person, each religious denomination, each political group or nation to its own pet traditional doctrine. And since this doctrine (or the sentiments which it has conditioned) varies at essential points from person to person, group to group, nation to nation, and East to West, this emphasis upon traditional religion and morality generates conflicts and thus intensifies rather than solves our problems.[3]

Mr. Sheed's discussion also discloses a second major difficulty in the plan of relying on supernaturalism for the construction of educational programs. He frankly admits that we live in a world different in many respects from that which existed when his supernatural code was delivered to man. In order to educate today, we have to make decisions about many complex human situations that are not explored or even mentioned by the religious sources upon which he relies for ultimate moral guidance. Mr. Sheed seeks to meet this difficulty by dividing human experience into two parts—one composed of problems of the "primary" sort, the other, those that are "secondary." These "secondary" problems are to be resolved by the use of ordinary human methods and intelligence, but the over-all moral orientation in the "primary" matters of life is to be given by supernaturalism.

Obviously this adjustment marks a radical shift and contraction in the historic claims of supernaturalism. Many of the most crucial moral and educational problems of our time arise in what Mr. Sheed calls the "secondary" grade of existence—the sphere of the institutionalized practices of man. He is constrained to remove these problems from direct supernatural regulation because painful experience has demonstrated that the adherents of the revealed systems have no common mind about the impli-

---

[3] F. S. C. Northrup, *The Meeting of East and West* (New York, The Macmillan Co., 1946), p. 6.

cations of their religious doctrines for these perplexing affairs. Supernaturalists, for example, divide sharply among themselves on such living issues as the pattern for our economy, the form and functions of our government, the desirability of untrammeled inquiry, the rights of the worker, the rights of minority religious and racial groups, the nature and justification of war, the obligations of citizenship, and the moral worth of fascism and communism. Even in the more conventional and restricted field of the "moral" these differences among supernaturalists about the meaning of the inherited code are fundamental. They are split, as we have indicated, into warring camps about "planned parenthood." Some declare that the whole conception "is contrary to the laws of God and nature"; others are equally convinced that it is a practice that is grounded in the basic religious principle of respect for human personality. Their differences about the organization and control of education are equally fundamental.

As a result supernaturalists have come to be on guard against easy and dogmatic deductions from their revealed code. Often premature pronouncements by Church leaders on controversial moral issues have had to be reconstructed, or abandoned, in the face of stubborn human preferences and the findings of ordinary human experience. Hence there is now a marked tendency among supernaturalists to maintain the "prestige" and "purity" of their "first" principles by refraining from defining their specific implications for changing life conditions. But "purity" of this kind is gained at the heavy cost of evasion and moral barrenness—it tends toward a morality that separates the realm of ends from the realm of means.

Certainly education cannot discharge its daily responsibilities if it remains on this lofty but barren plane. Educators must respond not with glittering generalities, but with definite encouragements and discouragements, with concrete approvals and disapprovals, as the young, under their guidance, live and learn and progressively mature their habits of thought and behavior.

A supernatural morality which preserves its prestige by refusing to deal with the world of particulars of a changing human existence is too abstract and vague to help teachers at the point of their most critical moral need.

Actually all educators—supernaturalist and humanist—do take account of the changing human scene in which they carry on their educational activity. This is unavoidable since it is from this world that the young come to school, and it is in the context of its mundane affairs, not in some secluded and sheltered retreat, that they ultimately work out their careers as human beings. As we have already stated, we believe that reference to group practices is apt to be less arbitrary, and more objective and morally significant when it is made consciously and openly, not surreptitiously, and with full responsibility for whatever judgments are made about the "values" and the "disvalues" inherent in these social practices. An element of strength in the social interpretation of education is that it deliberately seeks to make educators aware of the rôle of human preference and judgment in the whole process by which schools are organized and conducted. Such awareness is essential to a morality that aspires to be reflective, not merely conventional.

§ 5. *The Meaning of Cultural Relativism in Education*

For those who have adopted the ways of scientific and historical study there is a third major difficulty in the absolutism and intransigence of the supernaturalist. Scholars in the field of religion have applied these modern methods of criticism to the moral traditions of religion. As a result of their historical and comparative study many of these scholars have reached the conclusion that religion itself is an historical affair, an aspect of human experience that is also conditioned by factors of time and place. They find that the moral principles of all the different religions have been deeply influenced by the folkways, the knowledge, and the life interests and problems of the particular human groups in which they originated. As Santayana suggests, the voice of the religious prophet is a voice from a human, not a supernatural, world:

> There is a sort of acoustic illusion in it; the voice that reverberates from the heavens is too clearly a human voice. Is it not obvious that the reports contained in this revelation are not bits of sober information, not genuine reminiscences of a previous life, not messages literally conveyed from other worlds by translated prophets or visiting angels. Are they not clearly human postulates. . . . Human nature includes intelligence, and cannot therefore be perfected without such an illumination, and the equipoise which it brings; and this would seem to be a better fruit of meditation upon the supernatural than any particular regimen to be forced upon mankind in the name of heaven. Not that the particular regimen sanctified by Platonic and Christian moralists is at all inacceptable; but they did not require any supernatural assistance to draw it up. They simply received back from revelation the humanism which they had put into it.[4]

In brief, the message of religion is one form of the message of human experience. The pronouncements of each religious prophet carry the marks of the culture and the age in which he lived. This recognition that all moral principles and patterns for human living have thus emerged from within the context of experience has been construed by some to imply that these principles have no real authority. As Becker indicates, certain cultural relativists have carried this view to extreme lengths:

> All the assured traditional foundations of law and morality seemed to be crumbling away; and, as usually happens in periods of intellectual reorientation the new ideas were apprehended and made use of in their crudest and least defensible form. It was readily supposed that if reason was an instrument biologically developed to serve the interests of the organism, its pronouncements could never be disinterested; that if truth was relative, nothing could be really true; that if morals varied with the customs of time and place, any custom that got itself established was moral, and one system of morality as good as another; that if ideas were inspired by individual or class interest, the success of an idea in promoting individual or class interest was the only test of its validity.[5]

---

[4] George Santayana, *The Genteel Tradition at Bay* (New York, Charles Scribner's Sons, 1931), pp. 44, 46-47.

[5] C. L. Becker, *New Liberties for Old* (New Haven, Yale University Press, 1941), pp. 136-137.

But the perception that moral principles are the product of human experience can be made to support a very different and more defensible conclusion. It can provide the foundation for a very positive moral orientation. Certain ethical principles have become firm and clothed with authority because they have been tested and confirmed by the actual experience of human groups living in many ages and in many places. As we have emphasized, human experience has its continuities as well as its novelties. Ideas and ideals may be related to particular human groups in the sense that they developed in the matrix of the life experiences of these groups, and yet have a meaning and a validity that transcends the groups that gave them birth. If there are common elements in all forms of human existence and human association, it is entirely possible that significant general principles can be derived from the things that men suffer and enjoy in a diversity of cultural environments. The actual histories of the various cultural groups seem to show that this is the fact. Moral and religious traditions are many, not one; they have their differences in outlook and emphasis, and these differences are real; but they also have their similarities and these similarities are also real. Thus Becker who devoted his life as an historian to the study of the actual social, political, moral and religious systems of man asserts in the face of tendencies toward extreme ethical relativism that it is a fallacy "to suppose that because truth is in some sense relative it cannot be distinguished from error, or that the margin of error cannot be progressively reduced." He finds ample support in the ordinary experience of man for a number of basic moral affirmations:

Whatever success men have had since the Stone Age in lifting themselves above the level of brute existence has been the result of the slowly developing capacity of reason to distinguish fact from illusion and to prefer the values that exalt the humane and rational qualities of the human personality to the values that deny and degrade them.

To have faith in the dignity and worth of the individual man as an end in himself, to believe that it is better to be governed by persua-

sion than by coercion, to believe that fraternal good will is more worthy
than a selfish and contentious spirit, to believe that in the long run all
values are inseparable from the love of truth and the disinterested search
for it, to believe that knowledge and the power it confers should be
used to promote the welfare and happiness of all men rather than to
serve the interests of those individuals and classes whom fortune and
intelligence endow with temporary advantage—these are the values which
are affirmed by the traditional democratic ideology. But they are older
and more universal than democracy and do not depend upon it. They
have a life of their own apart from any particular social system or type
of civilization. They are the values which, since the time of Buddha and
Confucius, Solomon and Zoroaster, Plato and Aristotle, Socrates and
Jesus, men have commonly employed to measure the advance or the
decline of civilization, the values they have celebrated in the saints and
sages whom they have agreed to canonize. They are the values that
readily lend themselves to rational justification, yet need no justification.[6]

Time-tested principles such as the above, are, to be sure,
no substitute for a reflective morality which has respect for experience and for the reality of the changes which constantly take
place in the ongoing life of man. An empirical morality must
take full account of the salient features of changing life conditions with their new resources, new possibilities, new obstacles,
and new compulsions. These altered modes of living cannot be
automatically assimilated to inherited rules of human conduct;
they frequently call for important readjustments in our historic
attitudes and behaviors. But evolving life conditions are not
totally unique; they have their continuities with what men have
hitherto experienced. A morality which slurs or denies these
continuities is as dogmatic and misleading as is an absolute,
closed supernatural system which ignores the fact of change,
and the adjustments in life that change demands.

Education has suffered much from those dogmatic relativists
who have assumed that, in a world of change and uncertainty,
each life-situation is so unique we must deal with it without
reliance on that which man has learned and preserved in his
moral heritage. Actually no teacher ever approaches any problem
of human conduct with a mind empty of all moral presuppo-

[6] *Ibid*, pp. 148-150.

sitions. There is a vast difference, however, between a customary morality and a reflective morality—between an appreciative and critical use of moral principles and the unconscious and automatic reliance upon tradition. The responsible teacher should neither be "emancipated from," nor "enslaved by" these moral traditions. His educational activity should be informed by the wisdom that this moral inheritance can engender, when it is accepted, not as a body of ready-made rules to be applied automatically to all life situations, but as a summary of the fundamental meanings that men have developed in and through their experience. As a matter of fact, the real life situations which call for re-evaluation and fresh moral assessment in the work of the educator are generally constituted by some discordance between inherited moral practices, and the new perspectives and life circumstances that have resulted from the growth of knowledge, from expanding powers of human control, and from altered modes of human activity and relationship.

No social theory of education can be viewed as satisfactory that concentrates attention on the contemporary to the exclusion of that which men have discovered and funded in their moral traditions. One of the strengths of the democratic conception in the work of education is that democracy is a human faith and movement, unencumbered by supernatural preconceptions, which comprehends the essential meanings of our moral heritage. The totalitarians of both the right and the left with their disregard for human personality have shown us that this democratic moral heritage is not something that we should take for granted.

The dispositions and allegiances of democracy do not unfold automatically in the natures of the young. Human beings can and have been nurtured in conflicting types of human outlook and conduct. As we have emphasized, the young acquire the sentiments, the faiths, the attitudes, and the allegiances of the democratic way of life only as they are nurtured in them. The development of these enduring emotional and intellectual dispositions is a responsibility of any school that purports to serve as the educational agency of the democratic community.

A defensible social interpretation of education will therefore take due account of the spiritual meanings of democracy and the implications of this democratic heritage for the deliberate nurture of the young. There is every reason why this regard for the spiritual inheritance of man should be congenial to a *social* conception of education. A human society is something that has not only a present, but also a *past* and a *future*. It is *human* precisely because its present is involved in both a past and a future.

CHAPTER IV

Nature and Education

IN HIS celebrated essay on Nature, John Stuart Mill declares that in all ages there has been a tendency to make *"naturam sequi*—follow nature"—a fundamental principle of morals.[1] "That any mode of thinking, feeling, or acting, is 'according to nature'," he asserts, "is usually accepted as a strong argument for its goodness." "If it can be said with any plausibility that 'nature enjoins' anything, the propriety of obeying the injunction is by most people considered to be made out; and conversely, the imputation of being contrary to nature is thought to bar the door against any pretension on the part of the thing so designated, to be tolerated or excused; and the word unnatural has not ceased to be one of the most vituperative epithets in the language."

"Nature" when thus adopted as the source and the criterion of the norms for human conduct, is not viewed as the totality of all that exists, including the realm of human art and culture. On the contrary, the term "nature" is restricted, as Mill emphasizes, to signify "the spontaneous course of things when left to themselves" or "that which takes place without human intervention." Mill is scornful of the attempt of moralists to derive the standards for human behavior from "nature" when it is defined so as to exclude the self-conscious and purposeful existence of man in society. He holds that the maxim "follow nature is palpably absurd and self-contradictory" because "the

---

[1] John Stuart Mill, *On Liberty and Other Essays*, The Modern Reader Series (New York, The Macmillan Co., 1926), pp. 152, 153.

very aim and object of action is to alter and improve nature." "If the artificial is not better than the natural," he asks, "to what end are all the arts of life?"

But despite the strictures of Mill, and of many others who have written in the same vein, the notion persists that the fundamental patterns of behavior are given in "nature" and that they can be known if men will only put aside their preconceptions and receive with a humble heart the instructions that "nature" has to give. Although deliberate education is a human art, not a laissez-faire practice, educators have also been numbered among those who have cherished the hope that the universal and permanent directives for the nurture of the young could be found in the original and spontaneous occurrences of "nature." Wordsworth has expressed this faith in the moral superiority of the ways of "nature" as opposed to the ethical judgments of man.

> One impulse from a vernal wood
> May teach you more of man,
> Of moral evil and of good
> Than all the sages can.[2]

Even scientists, devoid of all tendency thus to idealize nature, have shared the belief that study of the biological order of existence could provide the primary patterns for human activity. An eminent psychologist used to tell his students that the purpose of educational research should be to discover the answers to those problems about the constitution and behavior of man which, once they were attained, would hold for the work of education in all cultures and all periods. Obviously, this theory of educational research has its definite presuppositions. It assumes that a basic human nature underlies the variety of behaviors exhibited by human beings in the different historic cultures, and it also assumes that research will eventually be able to uncover this deeper and more permanent human nature and make it serve as the determining source of our educational programs. Nor is this theory without its points of strength. Appar-

---

[2] William Wordsworth, in *The Tables Turned.*

ently there has been little change in the biological nature of man for thousands of years, and the biological unity of all human beings is a well established scientific fact. The findings of both biology and psychology clearly support the principle of the organic brotherhood of man. Biology affirms that all of the so-called "racial" or "nationality" groups must be viewed as members of the same human family since they can intermarry and bear fertile children. While the results of tests of mental ability show that there is no evidence in psychology to support the notion that we can divide human beings into "superior" and "inferior" groups on the basis of "racial" characteristics such as the color of skin, the texture of hair, the slant of eyes, or the structure of skull.

But the foregoing theory presupposes more than the mere biological unity of mankind; it also assumes that for the purposes of education, biological nature *is* human nature. Its conception of educational research is grounded in the faith that the scientific study of the human organism can give us all essential knowledge of human nature and behavior—that is, knowledge not simply of man's biophysiological equipment, but also of his basic needs and powers, his primary likes and aversions, his drives, his enduring interests, and his invariant principles of growth and learning. In other words, this whole approach to education is pervaded by the assumption that man is basically a creature of biology, not of human association and culture, and that the essential characteristics of human beings are given in the structure and the functioning of the biological organism.

In the previous chapter, we have described the failure of the attempt to derive the purposes of education from a source alleged to be above and beyond the mundane life of man. In this chapter, we shall review the considerations which have convinced many that the effort to discover in biological "nature" a more adequate, certain, and universal source for education than is provided by the diversified and changing patterns of social life is likewise doomed to failure.

§ 1. *The Dual Approach to the Norms of "Nature"*

The search for nature's own original and invariant patterns of behavior has taken two main forms. One line of investigation has sought the elemental ways of nature in the characteristics of living creatures other than man. Sub-human animal forms appear earlier than man in the evolutionary series and therefore their behaviors have been assumed by some to be more representative of the elemental principles of nature. In the pursuit of this lead innumerable studies have been made of the behaviors and the modes of learning exhibited by reptiles, fish, chickens, rats, monkeys, apes, cats, dogs, and many other animal forms.

The second line of inquiry has sought the norms of "nature" in the activities, the sensitivities, the mechanisms, the drives, the interests, and the patterns of growth of the human infant. From the moment of birth through the years of early childhood daily and systematic observations have been made of the behaviors, the learnings and the growth of children. Their perceptions, their movements, their manipulations, their aversions, their satisfactions, their eating and sleeping schedules, their responses to adults and to other children, as well as their general characteristics of development and learning have been noted, classified, and recorded. In order to make these observations more objective, the reports of trained observers have been supplemented by the extensive and the ingenious use of mechanical instruments such as the camera, the moving-picture, the sound-recording machine, and the like.

Both types of investigation have been carried on with such industry that today psychological research institutions and child-study clinics have large storerooms literally packed with the data they have accumulated on the behavior of "nature" in the world of the animal and the world of the human infant. Beyond all question, much of primary importance for our understanding of human behavior and learning has been derived, and will continue to be derived, from these studies of animal and infant behavior. As a result of these investigations older dualistic conceptions are being superseded, and more adequate principles of interpretation and methods of analysis have been developed which all further responsible study of human behavior will have to take into account.

But the net outcome of these studies has not strengthened the notion that the prototypes for human conduct and the final norms for education are to be found in these sub-human or pre-social behaviors. On the contrary, these researches have vastly weakened, if indeed they have not destroyed, the very foundations of this assumption. The evidence which has been gathered does not support the preconception of those who hold that the simple and instinctive behaviors which appear earliest in the evolutionary sequence are more real and causally efficacious than the complex and purposeful behaviors which are characteristic of the life of man in human society. The search for an underlying and governing system of original or instinctive responses has resulted in quite unanticipated findings. The evidence which has been gathered supports the conception of a flexible native human endowment that can develop through experience and learning into a wide variety of human interests, drives and activities. Nor have these research studies confirmed the idealizations of the "nature romanticists." These findings do not show that the "spontaneous" occurrences at the pre-human or pre-reflective level of existence are all good, harmonious, and perfectly ordered for the well-being of living creatures; nor do they show that the life made possible by human art and culture is in any real sense artificial and inferior.

§ 2. "Nature" on the Nature of Behavior

One of the major results of the study of the behavior of the biological organism is a more adequate view of the characteristics of the life process. Living at all levels—plant, animal, and human—has been found to be literally an affair of environment as well as of organism. Our conception of biological behavior will be grounded in error if it assumes that the organism is a discrete and segregated thing. Every living thing, to be sure, has its distinctive characteristics and it is so organized that it strives to preserve its own identity. Indeed, the defining trait of the animate as contrasted with the inanimate thing is that the former seeks so to interact with its surroundings that its distinctive and organized pattern or system of activity will be maintained, while the latter does not. But the biological organism does not maintain its vital interests through a process that seeks to protect the organism by separating it from its surroundings.

On the contrary, each organism is so constituted that it lives in and by means of its environment. Its elemental functions involve a continuing coördination of internal processes with external conditions or events. Breathing, for example, is a function both of air and lungs, nourishment involves food and digestive tract, perception is an affair of stimulating objects and organic sensory equipment, walking implicates both ground and locomotor organs, while manipulation is a process that involves movable things as well as organic structures that can grasp and carry. There is abundant evidence to show that the structures of each living creature have developed in and through its functioning in a determinate environment. Forms of being are evolved in the process of doing and undergoing. The internal needs of the organism are demands for external materials and energies; physiological drives are manifestations of tensional tissue-conditions, and these tensional conditions arise because of an imbalance or lack in the relations of the living creature with its surroundings. Indeed, behavior is typically sourced in these disturbed relations, and it moves to achieve a more satisfying adjustment with environmental affairs.

Even when new organic forms arise through mutation, the environment still has its decisive part in determining whether they shall continue to exist. Only those forms survive whose structures are congruent with essential environmental features.

The record shows that many species have perished because they did not possess, or could not develop, the kind of structures required for successful functioning in their particular environments. In a real sense, the environment inherits and adapts each variety of living thing to its basic conditions. Those forms that are unable to make the necessary adaptations are gradually eliminated.

In sum, to understand the organism—its structures and its behaviors—it is necessary to understand things other than the organism. It is necessary to understand the features of the environment in which the organism lives, and without which it cannot live. Nothing biological and nothing psychological can be learned about the nature of living things except as we observe them in the context of the definite environments which have inherited and evolved them. It is in and by means of some particular environment that each living form carries on its activities; it is from this environment that it derives the means of its livelihood.

This is the first lesson "nature" has to teach those who would learn her ways. Life is a process in which organism and environment are inextricably bound in together. All efforts to discover the nature of behavior must begin with this vital dependence of the living thing on its surroundings. Behavior is not exclusively a subcutaneous affair; it is never spontaneous in the sense that it is not conditioned by environmental factors. In brief, all biological activities are in the nature of transactions between a sentient creature and its surroundings.

Empirical study of the various living forms shows, in the second place, that the process of living is intrinsically selective or adjustive in character. It is selective because that "nature" each living creature experiences as actual environment is marked by a plurality of conditions. From the standpoint of the life interests of the biological organism these surrounding conditions are not homogeneous. Some are friendly and supporting, others are hostile and menacing. For example, foods that nourish and rebuild the body, and germs that breed disease and death are equally characteristic of the natural surroundings. The living creature, as we have indicated, is so organized that it seeks to maintain its individuality. It has its vital interests and preferences and it is therefore predisposed by its biological nature against the rôle of the neutral. It seeks certain conditions, it strives to avoid other conditions. All living creatures struggle to make these life-sustaining adjustments, for "nature" taken as the totality of surrounding conditions makes such adjustments the condition of survival. Although most living forms have no conscious recognition of the ends or goals implicit in their striving, in a rudimentary sense all living may be said to be a selective or goal-seeking process.

Each living form, moreover, is not infinitely plastic or elastic. It has limits beyond which it cannot be coerced or strained by environmental forces if it is to continue to exist. It lives in the midst of a complexity of conditions that makes the achievement of good and the avoidance of ill a real, not a sham, struggle. Existence is uncertain, and outcomes are not assured. The behavior of the organism is therefore essentially adjustive in tendency. The qualities of the varied experiences the sentient creature has had with environmental affairs tend to be retained in its organic feeling states. By virtue of this organic sensitivity —native and acquired—the living creature senses—discriminates —the bearing of surrounding things on its own welfare and the welfare of its kind. The very existence of the higher animal forms depends upon their ability to learn to make these distinctions, and to direct their behavior accordingly. Thus, adjustment is an elemental principle of life.

This is the second lesson "nature" has to teach. For nature is not one, it is many: it is not fixed and certain, it is changing and hazardous; it is not an abode specially designed for the welfare of living creatures, but it is a complex of conditions sufficiently favorable to have permitted these creatures to evolve and survive. It follows therefore that "nature" taken as a totality has no norms for living things, because from the standpoint of their life interests, natural processes and events divide into affairs that are favorable, and affairs that are harmful. Hence the necessity for selective response is one of the deepest instructions which nature has to give the living creature. For the human form, survival itself is not a function of a ready-made system of behavior, it is contingent upon its ability to learn to discriminate, to adjust, and to control. These learned adjustive powers are necessities, not luxuries; the existence and welfare of human beings depend upon the various arts by which natural conditions are utilized, transformed, and controlled for human purposes.

We have indicated that living is an affair of organism and environment, and that the life process is a process of adjustment. Empirical studies show, in the third place, that it is within the matrix of these adjustive acts that *learning* originates. Learning has two main modes: the development of appreciation, and the development of control. Living creatures grow in their appreciation of the qualities or the life significance of things through their interactions with them; they also grow in their ability to adjust to things and to manipulate them on behalf of their own vital interests. The learning of both appreciations and skills is achieved in one and the same interactive or adjustive process.

Many of the animal forms, as we have seen, are much better equipped by native endowment than is the human infant. This original superiority pertains to their sense of the value of things as well as to their ability to behave with reference to them. They are apparently equipped by inborn and preformed behavior patterns to do many things that the human being can do only after experience and learning. Learning, however, is by no means confined to man, nor is learning in man always a self-conscious process. The biological organism is so constituted that it necessarily learns from that which it does and undergoes. Hence the behaviors of the mature form are not the exclusive property of inherited determinants; they are also the properties or functions of all that is wrought in these hereditary factors through that which the creature does and undergoes. The qualities of these things that have been experienced as harmful as well as those which have been found to satisfy life needs are both, to some extent, preserved in the subsequent feelings and habits of the biological organism. The living form, through continuous interaction with its surroundings, develops attitudes of avoidance and acceptance along with increased ability to adapt its responses to the significant features of its environment.

We misconstrue the process of learning and habit formation, however, if we regard it as a mere fixing through repetition of specific reaction patterns. The organism learns to improve its responses by taking progressive account of the characteristics of the affairs that are involved in its activities. As certain psychologists have indicated, if the practice that yields learning were a process of sheer repetition no improvement in performance could result from it. The individual, moreover, is not a simple aggregation of specific responses. Behavior is typically the response of the whole organism to its surroundings. Habit, therefore, is not primarily a fixed and automatic response to a specific stimulus; it is more in the nature of an acquired art of dealing with the significant traits of environing materials. We learn as we grow in the "feel" and in the mastery of the varied conditions with which we have to do. Learning signifies new capacity for adaptation on the part of the organism, but that capacity is also regulated by the character of environmental affairs.

It would be a mistake, however, to assume that learning always results in growth of power. The organism can make mistakes in that which it accepts and retains as in line with its own welfare. Although it learns through its own trials and fumblings, associated as they are, with organic satisfactions and dissatisfactions, not all of the resulting acquired behaviors are really advantageous. There is a real "wisdom of the body" in the sense that the organism is equipped by constitution to discriminate much that is harmful from that which is beneficial. Were this not the case, it would not continue to live, for the environment as a totality is not concerned with its well-being. But the biological organism is not infallible. It can make errors in its discriminations between the good and the bad. These mistakes may result in the learning of inferior and even harmful patterns of adjustment. The greatest limitations of the organism at the level of animal behavior is its inability to perceive and consciously retain those dynamic connections between conditions and outcomes which make possible the reshaping of environmental things to make them serve as tools. As a consequence animals develop little in the way of tools or culture, and they are largely limited in their environmental manipulations to what they can do in and through their own organic structures.

Empirical study has also discovered that learning is not a process in which new traits and behaviors are merely added or superimposed upon an inherited system of responses that continues to function in its original form. Learning is a process of reconstruction, not of addition. In a real sense, the organism becomes that which it learns. Hence the developed creature is not a compound of two sets of drives and behaviors, the one inherited, and the other acquired, although the conventional use of the terms "nature" and "nurture" tends to make it easy for us to get this view of the case. Habit is not a "second-nature," as some have asserted. Habit is the nature that inherited propensities assume as they are modified and organized in definite ways by the life experiences of the individual organism. This holds for drives and interests and "satisfiers," as well as for action patterns. In short, the "nature" of the biological organism is not an original structure that persists unchanged beneath the varied learned behaviors of the living creature. These developed behaviors define the real nature of the living form.

This is a third lesson that "nature" would have us learn. The inherited nature of a creature of feeling and action is not immutable—it is whatever it becomes through the process of living and learning. It is the notion that learning is simply a process of adding something to an original and fixed hereditary pattern that partly accounts for the tendency to search for the real norms for living in the behaviors of the biological organism. These original or inherited behavioral characteristics are no more natural or real than the traits into which they are fused by the interaction of the organism with its surroundings. The organic cries of an infant are not more real than the meaningful speech of an adult.

There are indeed many things that the human organism cannot become—its potentialities are definitely conditioned by its biological inheritance. But the fact that the biological nature of man is not infinitely plastic provides no ground for the denial of the full reality of whatever transformations are wrought in it by that which it does experience and learn. It is a materialistic metaphysical dogma, not the findings of empirical study, that underlies the notion that the earlier and more primitive in behavior is more natural and real than the later and more complex. Could "nature" speak, it would have the right to ask us not thus to demean it. Nature is equally exhibited in whatever comes to exist. It certainly is not least well represented by those creative developments which occur at the level of the self-conscious, purposeful life of human beings. We turn now to consider how the adaptive processes of animal forms become transformed into the behavior that we define as mind.

§ 3. *Nature and Mind*

In the facts associated with the emergence of mind, "nature" manifests another principle of cardinal importance that is often ignored by those who would have us turn from the study of the life of man in society in order to discover the norms for education in the "spontaneous course of things." Nature asks us to remember that it is not static, but dynamic, and that in the "spontaneous course of things" which is the essence of "nature," novel events occur or evolve. Indeed, in that state of affairs we designate as "nature" nothing is more real than change and development. In the course of the evolution of living things, human mind, deliberate invention, and culture eventually appeared. Although they emerged relatively late in the evolutionary series, mind and culture are natural, not artificial; they are as natural as atoms, organisms, sunsets and stars. It is therefore not the ways of "nature," but culturally conditioned habits of thought that lead us to assume we have to seek "non-natural" principles to explain these later and more complex developments in the process of evolution. The phenomena of mind and culture do not signify an abrogation of the processes of nature, they rather signify a dimension of nature becoming aware of its affairs and seeking through the natural but conscious life of man to direct events on behalf of chosen ends or values. In other words, if we are prepared to follow the knowledge we now have about the nature of "nature," we must abandon the man-nature, mind-body dualisms of pre-evolutionary thought and be ready to view human nature and reflective thinking as emergents within the nature process.

John Dewey has pioneered in the development of this non-dualistic, evolutionary view of human thought and culture. He contends that thinking like all other human behaviors is not a subcutaneous activity; it is rather a particular kind of functioning of organism and environment—a functioning no more subjective, artificial, or unnatural than breathing or eating. William James once described the distinguishing "mark and criterion" of mind as "the pursuance of future ends and the choice of means for their attainment." [3] Dewey holds that we find anticipations of this distinctive mental behavior in the life activities of the higher animal forms. By "higher animal forms" are meant those creatures that are equipped with distance receptors such as the organs of sight, smell, and hearing, and with locomotor organs that make it possible for them to move about in their surroundings. Given these sensory and motor equipments, the behavioral field —the environment that enters significantly into the vital activities

[3] William James, *Principles of Psychology* (New York, Henry Holt and Co., 1890), Vol. I, p. 8.

of the living creature—becomes transformed. Responses no longer consist of a mere succession of reactions to the qualities of things as they impinge on the skin surface of the organism. Objects distant in space—for example, the prey that the hungry animal is seeking to capture and devour—become more potent in arousing and directing the activity of the animal than those things with which it has immediate body contact. This response to things distant in space is equivalent to response to that which is future in time. Activities now divide into two kinds—preparatory and consummatory—and this development introduces a real time-dimension into the interactions of the living creature with its environment. Through repeated trials the earlier or preparatory acts leading up to a desired or eventual outcome are shaped into a regular series or organization of acts.

Thus a sequence of acts, by means of learning, gradually gets integrated into a serial whole—in this series the component acts are not discrete, they are phases of a larger organized activity, and each promotes the forward movement of the total act by making its own efficient and distinctive contribution to what has to be done in order to attain the desired outcome. In animals, some rather elaborate action-patterns, such as nest-building, for example, are apparently "instinctive"—that is, they are latent or pre-formed in the inherited equipment so that they function under appropriate circumstances with little or no learning from experience. Many such sequences of acts, however, are learned through the recurring trials of the animal form, and in this process of fumbling, organic and environmental factors collaborate to mold efficient habits of response. The more the resulting behavior approaches the pattern of a real series, the more is order or "rationality" implicit in it—that is, acts assume the character of means efficiently ordered or organized to achieve outcomes.

This variety of learning is frequently called "trial and error" learning. Some contend it would be more aptly described as "trial and success" learning, since the successes are apparently more potent than the failures in the development of the total pattern of response. Although the data show that trial and error learning is typically a function of the whole organism in interaction with its surroundings, and therefore not so atomistic and mechanical as once assumed, it is nevertheless clear that acts can be organized into an orderly sequence leading to a desired consummation, without the creature involved in the process having any conscious awareness of the connections that are being developed in its habits of response. Even with human beings much learning is undoubtedly at this biophysical—non-ideational —level. In brief, acts can become ordered by the processes of nature, even though no mind directs the ordering.

Thus far our discussion has referred exclusively to the behavior of the individual animal form. Certain animals, including men, carry on their struggle for existence in groups. This group life further prepares for the emergence of mind—the kind of existence that is consciously purposeful. The life of mind— the kind of behavior that has become intellectual in quality and which involves the use of symbols—began to develop as human beings became aware of the significance of certain factors present in their coöperative group activities.

Mead holds that it was in the context of the conjoint activities of the group that language—the use of significant symbols —first emerged.[4] He finds the "natural" event that is the forerunner of this more significant or meaningful behavior in the signalling acts of animals. This signalling behavior is illustrated by the "conversation of gestures" that ensues when two dogs approach each other in hostile attitude. The growls, the successive body postures, and the shifting positions of the one, function as signals or stimuli to direct the responses of the other, even though these particular physical manifestations are a mere "organic overflow," in the sense that they are not produced by either dog with conscious intent. Mead describes this reciprocal

---

[4] George Mead, *Mind, Self and Society* (Chicago, The University of Chicago Press, 1934), Part II.

adjustment of the movements and attitudes of the two dogs as a "conversation of gestures." He considers it a kind of conversation because the acts of each dog influence those of the other, but interaction is "non-significant" because neither animal is aware of the rôle that its gestures play in evoking the responses of the other. Although the behavior of each is stimulated by that of the other, neither animal participates intellectually in the developing situation. It does not intend—mean—to arouse the responses its own acts call forth in the other form.

Organic gestures become "significant symbols" when the creature that makes the stimulating gestures perceives their effects in the behaviors of other forms, and, having once grasped this relationship, deliberately repeats his gestures under appropriate conditions in order to elicit these definite responses from his fellows. Consciousness of self as agent thus arises as the living form acquires this ability to anticipate. In order for one individual to turn his gestures into deliberate instructions to others, he must first be able to comprehend the significance that his sounds or movements carry for the behavior of other human beings. It is thus in the context of social or group behavior that meaning and consciousness of self originate. Our gestures acquire meaning when we apprehend the connection between what we do and say and the adjustments our movements and utterances arouse in the behaviors of others. Our gestures may be said to be informed with significance and meaning when they carry for us the same behavioral values that they have for our fellow human beings. Conscious awareness is thus a function of this internalization of the patterns inherent in the external social situation. This internalization is made possible by the use of symbols. A symbol is a gesture, a sound, or a mark that stands for some external event, condition, process, or behavior.

Language is thus the bridge between the unconscious course of things in "nature" and the self-conscious life of man. But language is a natural development. It is as natural as the conjoint behaviors of human organisms in which it originates.

Meanings are properties of group behavior and are shared by those who speak and understand the language of the group. Language is a natural development from the signal reflexes of animals, but it is not to be identified with them, for it is an intercourse that has become charged with meaning. As one writer has observed:

> Speaking or talking is not reducible to mere utterance, or to signal reflexes. Signals become signs, sounds become words, speaking or talking comes into being, when the behavior intends to elicit a response, and the response, on its side, is meant to be such. Speech takes its character from being the common endeavor of at least two centers of activity engaged in the act of intercommunication. It implies reciprocal cross-reference and joint anticipation which, when acted out, result in a conjoined undertaking, regulated, as to each partner, by his participation in the partnership. . . . Speech is thus in its very essence a coöperative venture. It is a social act. It involves at least two persons. Together they accomplish one of the miracles of nature—the communication of meaning.[5]

Although the gestures that are basic in language-communication can be made in various ways, it is not difficult to discern the reason for the almost universal reliance on vocal gestures. The spoken word does not involve the use of those organs that are required either for locomotion or for the holding and the manipulation of things; little physical energy is involved in human utterance, and sounds can be organized into innumerable combinations and therefore provide for subtlety and flexibility of expression. The spoken word, moreover, has the advantage that it gives the person uttering it much the same physical cue that it gives to others. But vocal sounds are not language. There is nothing "psychical" nor "mental" in mere vocalization. We misconstrue the whole nature of language, if we do not perceive that words—oral and written—gain their intellectual significance because they represent, function as signs of, or symbolize things other than themselves. The world of meaning is not a purely private and subjective affair, nor does it involve mysterious

[5] Abridged from M. C. Otto, "Speech and Freedom of Speech," *Freedom and Experience*, edited by Sidney Hook and Milton Konvitz (Ithaca, New York, Cornell University Press, 1947), p. 83.

reference to a transcendental realm beyond ordinary human experience; it has its origin in the public, objective world of adjustive, social acts.

Not all signs are gesture signs. Things can also function as signs, and as a result of our interactions with things they can become characterized by meaning. Natural things are involved in other things, and they have their characteristic ways of interacting and correlating with these other things. Thus physical things or events can operate as signs of absent and future occurrences or conditions. A dark shadow under the surface of the water, for example, can operate as a sign of a submerged rock and the possibility of a boat sinking because its bottom has been ripped open; or a black cloud and a distant rumbling sound can become the sign of approaching rain, and, by the use of concepts made possible by symbols, rain can signify mud, mud the possibility of skidding, and skidding the need for a change in the plan for an automobile trip in order to avoid clay roads; or, again, spots of a certain shape and color on the skin may serve as a sign of unseen disordered organic conditions that demand prompt attention. To be sure, the affairs of the environment can take on this rôle of functioning as signs only in the presence of an organism capable of observing and retaining these natural connections and sequences, but that does not make the realm of meaning a mysterious and exclusive property of the individual human organism. As is the case of other behaviors, the kind of functioning that signifies and has significance—the functioning that is mind—is an activity that implicates environment as well as organism. Without the environment that is our natural abode, no signs; and without signs, no mind. Any educational program, therefore that plans to deal with the intellectual aspects of human experience will have to take account of more than the individual human organism; it will have to concern itself with the physical and cultural environment in which the behaviors that are mind are elaborated.

§ 4. *Nature and Culture*

An environment of objects—of things plus their meanings or implications for human experience—is what is meant by culture. These objects that constitute culture are of two kinds. They include, in the first place, all of those environmental affairs or conditions which as a result of the interactions of a human group with them have been transformed into *objects*—that is, into things that have had their potentialities or consequences funded in them so that responses to them are made in terms of these eventual and anticipated properties. Seeds, for example, are responded to not simply as things of a sensed shape and color, but as things that can be eaten, and as things that can be planted in the ground, and which, in time, will sprout into plants that will assure a future food supply.

But culture also consists of tools. These tools are of two sorts. They include all of the physical things from chipped stones to engines and airplanes that have been refashioned and reorganized from natural materials into agencies that increase the power of man to utilize and to control his environment. These instruments of physical control have evolved from within the context of the purposeful acts of man. Indeed, a tool may be defined as anything that can operate as an agency of control and added power in a sequence of means organized to attain a desired outcome. There are, however, social as well as physical tools. Social tools include all of the traditions, customs, laws, institutions and conventions by which a human group has come to organize and to regulate the life activities and relationships of its individual members. These social tools have also developed from within the means-consequence continuum; they are the result of the effort to achieve group ends by coördinating and regulating the activities of individuals and various subgroups.

The attributes and the abilities that we prize as distinctively human are due in no small part to the fact that man lives in this culturally transformed, and educationally more potent, environment. As the child matures in this cultural environment his responses are directed by "weighted" stimuli—by stimuli that are charged with the meanings which his human group has acquired from that which it has suffered and undergone, from that which it has appropriated from other human groups, together with those meanings it has discovered through its deliberately controlled efforts to get knowledge of the behaviors and the connections of things. Without his superior organic endowment, man would never have got started on the enterprise of the development of culture—but once he began to remake "nature" into culture his own powers of understanding, of prediction, and of control began to expand. Nature was in a real sense rationalized as it became progressively instrumentalized through the activities of man.

Language was the most significant human invention. Symbols are the greatest of all tools for they are the indispensable means of that conscious existence that is the source of all deliberate inquiry and invention. With the development of significant symbols, the response of the living creature to its environment is transformed. Activity is liberated because it is no longer bound to things physically given in the immediate surroundings. Symbols make possible the construction and use of concepts, and these concepts make available for purposes of thought and invention the behavioral values of things that are distant in space and time. As some have suggested, this development so modifies the behavioral field that it literally becomes "superorganic" in character—man henceforth lives in a world of meaning. Through symbols he becomes a creature of memory, imagination and foresight.

Nor is the extension of the environment in space and time the only significant result of this development of language. The power of attention is also transformed—it is no longer a function of organic tensions that wax and wane with the immediate condition of the physiological organism. Human attention can now be focused and sustained by these accumulated "objects" of the cultural environment, and by the new interests and drives that these cultural meanings breed in man. In the behavior marked by meaning and self-conscious awareness, situations of tension in which responses are confused and blocked can be turned into intellectual problems, and man can attend to these problematic life-situations for prolonged periods as he gradually elaborates and tests means for dealing with them. Thus the life of mind—the response to the significance and the possibilities of things—introduces new dimensions, new values, and new dynamics into human experience. Empirical study of the order of the social and the mental shows that this order of behavior cannot be reduced to the physical, or the biological, nor can it be explained or understood by principles wholly derived from within these pre-human levels of existence.

Take, for example, the elemental biological need for food. We have indicated how this need denotes an imbalance in the relation of the individual organism with its surroundings, and that this imbalance, or lack, is manifested in the cravings of the physiological organism. These disturbed tissue-conditions drive the living creature to seek satisfaction from its surroundings. It continues its restless search until its needs are met, but once these organic cravings are satisfied, the tension disappears and the interest of the organism lapses or shifts to other things.

Although man is a creature of culture, he is nonetheless a biological organism with his imperative life needs. In common with all other animal forms, he requires food if he is to continue to live. A secure and adequate diet is therefore a primary human need and interest. So universal and basic is this need that the most inclusive organization man has developed—the United Nations—has appointed a Commission on Food and Agriculture to consider what can be done to provide the whole human race with a more satisfactory food supply. But the motives that prompt the very distinguished members of this Commission to undertake this fundamental task are many and various—it is simply impossible to reduce them to the tissue-needs of their own bodies for food. Indeed, many of the interests and drives which underlie the work of the members of this Commission are far removed from their personal biological needs—they are the complex products of the particular life careers they have had as members of a human civilization.

The members of this Commission on Food and Agriculture are motivated, for example, by their interests in science and all that the quest for truth and power of control signifies in the life of man, by their regard for the welfare of human beings, many of whom they have never even seen, by their desire to share in the development of a world organization that will make it possible to eliminate war, by their concern for the approval of their fellow human beings, and by many similar sentiments and interests nurtured in them by their life in human society. They will continue to work on this problem of the United Nations when their individual needs for food have been met, and, at times, they may become so absorbed in their investigations and conferences that they will stay by their projects long past the point where the physiological demands for food begin to assert themselves. To say this is not to suggest that the members of this Commission have attained a level of intellectual and moral existence that supplants the life imperatives of the biological order, but it is to say that these biological needs are now so implicated in interests that appear only at the level of culture that they are characterized by a significance that spreads far beyond the individual creature needs of the animal order. Indeed, conditions might well arise in which men on this Commission, in order to satisfy interests that they have achieved as members of a human civilization, would be prepared voluntarily to risk their own physical well-being and continued existence in order to forward the cause to which they are devoted. In sum, the motives and interests which human beings acquire by virtue of their participation in a human society are not of a lower grade than those motives and interests that are found at the biological level of existence. Even historical materialists recognize that the level of subsistence—the conditions that men will consent to endure—are culturally as well as biologically determined.

The cultural order of human existence is, to be sure, continuous with the biological. But so is the biological continuous with the physico-chemical order of existence. Scientific study of affairs at the biological level of existence began to make progress once it was recognized that this level of behavior has its own irreducible traits, and constitutes a new dimension of behavior continuous with, but distinct from, the physical. Biologists were eventually convinced that the behaviors of living things could not be fruitfully explored by the exclusive reliance on categories and principles of interpretation derived from the simpler physico-chemical level of behavior. The adoption of this methodological principle did not deny the continuity of the biological organism with physico-chemical energies, but it did affirm that the synthesis of these energies into a living creature signifies the emergence of a new phenomenon, and that the characteristics of biological behavior are fully as real as those of inanimate things.

The same principle holds for our study of man. Undoubtedly the characteristics that man has acquired by virtue of his membership in a human society have their physiological or biological correlates. It is difficult to see how any learning could be preserved if it did not involve some change in the biological organism. But this does not at all imply that the significance of these distinctively human traits can be defined in purely biological terms without reference to the cultural world of meaning and value in which they originated. Much of our psychology has been guilty of this fallacy of reduction. It has assumed that a thing cannot be related to another thing without being that thing: that the nature of a thing is found in that from which it has evolved, not in its own distinctive traits—a principle which if literally accepted would deny the reality of all emergence or evolution.

This fallacy of reduction was implicit in the physiological behaviorism of Watson. He correctly perceived that thinking required as an essential condition the use of language, and that language involved the organs of speech. Watson then plunged to the conclusion that thinking was merely a kind of internal manipulation carried on by the vocal organs. In this subcutaneous and mechanical explanation of human thought, he overlooked the vital part played by continuous and conscious reference to the external world in the process of thinking. In other words, he ignored the rôle of things operating as signs, and the importance of responsible reference to these objective events and processes if the symbols that denote these environmental things are to be used in ways that are genuinely significant.

The same tendency toward reductionism is found in Freud with his emphasis on the primacy of sex in human behavior. Here again we have the assumption that the earlier biological drive is the *real* factor, and that all later developments through learning from the life of man in society have no genuine novelty, but are mere disguised and indirect expressions of this primitive drive. It is true that the sexual nature of man—the principle of love—gets stretched in the Freudian interpretation so that it comes to be identified with a wide variety of concrete behaviors, but always there is the presupposition that these later and more complex developments are nothing but expressions of an original and unchanged sex drive as it is repressed and thwarted, but never modified, in any important sense, by the experience of man in a human culture. The possibility that man by virtue of his life in a human group might achieve new interests, new purposes, and new drives is discounted by the reductionist assumption that the earlier—the biological—defines the ultimate for the human being.

A changed point of view in the study of man is beginning to develop. It is increasingly recognized that whenever the order of the social is thus reduced to the biological, we have not explained, but have rather explained away, the very factors that create the distinctive subject-matter of a psychology of human personality. The processes that are distinctively human and rational appear only at the level of the social. It will therefore require a social, not a simple physiological, psychology to do justice to them. Education will receive more concrete aid from psychology when it frankly accepts responsibility for the study of the behavior of men as members of actual human societies. It will find that this human behavior is conditioned by values, and that a scientific study of man cannot be at all adequate if it eliminates the rôle of values from the scope of this study of the human.

§ 5. The Human Organism and Education

A long series of studies in infant behavior has underlined the conclusion that the human organism cannot tell us how to educate. The norms for human conduct and human development are not given in the native endowment of the human organism, nor do they develop by the mere unfolding or maturing of inborn patterns or faculties. The evidence is strong that acquired characteristics are not biologically transmitted. The superiority of the human organism, moreover, lies not in its preformed action patterns, but rather in its remarkable capacity for learning and in the superior stimuli provided by the social environment. It is because we ignore the unremitting influence of the cultural environment in guiding the perceptions and responses of the young that we tend to assume that much is inborn which is in reality learned. As we have already indicated, the human form at birth is less able to care for itself than are the offspring of many of the sub-human animal forms.

Consider, for example, the matter of language: Dr. Thorndike who always sought to do full justice to inherited factors says that language "may be prepared for in the genes only by a

proclivity to move the mouth parts in a great variety of ways." [6]
The data clearly show that so far as native equipment is concerned, English, Chinese, German, Russian, Choctaw, or any other language, are all alike wide-open possibilities for the newborn child. The mother-tongue of the parents becomes the mother-tongue of the child because his surroundings encourage him to learn it, and apparently for no other reason.

What holds for language also holds for so-called racial and nationality traits. Children born of white parents can and have become Chinese in personality characteristics when reared in the culture of China, and Chinese children can and do become American in outlook, sentiment, and loyalty when reared in the American culture. Nor does the organism have inborn propensities that enable it to discriminate between the systems of life that we call democratic or authoritarian, individualistic or socialistic, scientific or magical. Even "feminine" and "masculine" natures, or temperaments, are not the inevitable psychological correlates of biological constitution. From her studies in three simpler societies Margaret Mead declares: "I was innocent of any suspicion that the temperaments which we regard as native to one sex might instead be mere variations of human temperament, to which the members of either or both sexes may, with more or less success in the case of different individuals be educated to approximate." [7]

In sum, "the ways of nature," if we mean by those ways merely that which is exhibited by the behavings of things outside the life of human beings in society, cannot tell us how to educate. The biological order simply does not contain many of the fundamental criteria by which we necessarily make those value discriminations that are crucial in the nurture of the young. In order to get these criteria we have to go to nature as it has

[6] E. L. Thorndike, *Human Nature and the Social Order* (New York, The Macmillan Co., 1940), p. 302.

[7] Margaret Mead, *Sex and Temperament in Three Primitive Societies* (New York, William Morrow and Company, 1930), pp. xxi-xxii.

evolved in the order of the social, for it is in that order that man becomes human. And education is an affair of human beings not of mere biological organisms; it has to do with values that appear only at the level of conscious, purposeful human life.

CHAPTER V

The Alternative of Classical Humanism

THE view that education is a mode of social action and interpretation, necessarily conditioned by factors of time and place, has been repudiated by a group of educators led by Dr. Hutchins of the University of Chicago. Although higher education is the special interest of the members of this group, they have grounded their program for the reconstruction of higher education in a general theory of the nature and purpose of education at all age levels. These educators are not impressed by the fact that the historical and the comparative study of education shows that the purposes, the materials, and the methods of the school have varied with the folkways and the thought-ways of different cultural groups. The crucial point, they assert, is not what education has been up to the present time, but rather what education must become if it is to realize the full humanity of man.

According to this group, when education is rightly understood, its primary task will not be viewed as the maintenance of a program for the purpose of introducing the young to the ideals, the customs, the changing institutions, and the practical activities of their own society. Human standards should signify something more fundamental and permanent than the rationalizations of the mores found in the different cultural groups, and truth should signify something more universal and invariant than the shifting opinions of historically conditioned men. In brief, the supreme concern of education is with the moral, not with the mores; with truth, not with mere human opinion or preference; and with man as man, not with man as the member of this or that nation or society. Now the trait that distinguishes man from all other living creatures is the power of reason, and hence the cultivation of the intellect defines the central function of education. No program of education can be considered worthy of man that permits its interest in the local, the vocational, and the empirical, to substitute for the development of the rational powers of the young.

This capacity for reason may be nurtured in the immature human being by two basic processes. First, by the cultivation of his own latent rational faculties. This can be accomplished, moreover, without getting involved in controversial social issues, through the training of the young in special disciplinary studies such as mathematics, language, logic and rhetoric. But this strengthening and sharpening of the rational powers must be supplemented by the study of first principles. Mastery of these first principles is indispensable to rational thought for it is by their use as governing major premises that individuals are able to explore and to command the particulars of their existence.

Nor are we without an adequate source of these first principles. They are to be sought, not in the native impulses of the child, not in the accidents of history and culture, not in the coöperatively developed and tested findings of the various empirical sciences, not primarily in the doctrines of alleged systems of supernaturalism, but in the nature of ultimate Being as interpreted by right reason. These deliverances of reason about the laws of natural and human existence are stored in the teachings of those inspired leaders whose writings have been accepted by men everywhere as classics. These great works have demonstrated by their ability to persist and to continue to enrich human thought that they have a genuine timeless quality. Indeed, a classic may be defined as a book that is contemporary in any period. Taken together these classics constitute an authoritative moral and intellectual tradition for the whole human race. It is in this universal humanist tradition that the education of the young should be rooted.

§ 1. *Reason and Education*

Dr. Hutchins has boldly outlined the foundations of this more rational and universal program of education in his book, *The Higher Learning in America*.[1] He declares that the "one purpose of education is to draw out the elements of our common human nature," and that "these elements are the same in any time or place." The most basic of all these human attributes is the capacity for reason, and when education is rightly understood, "it will be understood as the cultivation of the intellect." A worthy program of education will be concerned with "the attributes of the race, not the accidents of individuals," with the characteristics of "man as man" and with that which "connects man with man." It follows that "the cultivation of the intellect is the same good for all men in all societies."

Now an education that is concerned with the development of man as a rational creature will not be interested in "educating a man to live in any particular time or place," or "to adjust him to any particular environment." Differences in habits and customs, in social organization and educational administration, according to Dr. Hutchins, are mere details, and these details should not be permitted to shape the materials or the purposes of the nurture of the young. "The heart of any course of study designed for the whole people will be, if education is rightly understood, the same at any time, in any place, under any political, social, or economic conditions."

One of the weaknesses of contemporary education is that it has so broadened its interests that its primary functions of the training of the mind and the nurture of the young in first principles have been subordinated to innumerable practical and social affairs. Organized education would do well to leave the

---

[1] Robert M. Hutchins, *The Higher Learning in America* (New Haven, Yale University Press, 1936), Chapter 3.

getting and the directing of experience to other institutions "and emphasize in education the contribution that it is supremely fitted to make, the intellectual training of the young." Physical education or "body building," and moral education or "character building," as well as the "social graces," along with training in the techniques of the various trades and professions should be excluded from the school. All of these interests have their due and necessary place, but it is not the responsibility of the educational institutions of a society to provide for them.

The curriculum therefore "should be composed principally of the permanent studies." These are the studies best able to "draw cut the elements of our common human nature"; they also "connect man with man," and "with the best that man has thought." "We have then for general education a course of study consisting of the greatest books of the Western world and the arts of reading, writing, thinking, and speaking, together with mathematics, the best exemplar of the processes of human reason."

It is obvious that the foregoing theory and program of education elaborated by the Hutchins group raises some very basic educational questions. These questions have to do both with that which is possible, and with that which is desirable in education. For example, is it possible for any group of adults to select "the greatest books of the Western world" without taking some account of contemporary events, interests, knowledge and values? And why, if this educational program is designed to serve the interests of men of all nations, races, and religions, should the great books be restricted to the classics of the *Western* world? Or, again, is it possible for contemporary teachers and students to explore the meanings of the "great books" without permitting the perspectives of the present to influence that which they find in these formulations of the leaders of other ages and societies? Do the findings of educational psychology support the view that the intellectual powers of the young can be satisfactorily developed by reliance on a method of formal discipline in an educational program that deliberately divorces the theoretical from the practical, and the intellectual and moral from the social and the vocational? Moreover, does not this program of intellectual training necessarily rest on an authoritarian foundation? Is it desirable in a democratic society to restrict the purpose of education simply to the cultivation of the intellect, and if it be assumed that this is desirable, by what concrete means should we seek to attain this result? To put the question in more definite form, what, if any, part do the procedures of science have to play in the nurture of the rational powers of the young? We shall examine these and related questions in this chapter, but we shall begin with a consideration of the factors in the contemporary situation that led to the elaboration of this theory of education. Fortunately, we do not have to resort to speculation in our effort to do this, for Dr. Hutchins has set forth in some detail the tendencies in the existing social and educational situation which were of concern to him when he developed his plan for education.

§ 2. *The Cultural Roots of the Great Books Curriculum*

In the first part of *The Higher Learning in America,* Dr. Hutchins makes it quite evident that his bold program for educational reconstruction is in the nature of a reaction to the current scene in American life and education. In other words, although Dr. Hutchins undertakes to formulate an educational program to meet the needs of all men in all societies, the primary stimulus to his educational thought is not the condition of humanity in general, but rather the deplorable state of affairs existing in the confused, divided and uncertain America of the decade of the depression before the beginning of World War II. His book is grounded, not in the contemplation of the nature and condition of universal man, but in a passionate protest against what he considers to be the materialism, the mass mediocrity, the narrow specialism, the anti-intellectualism, and the discord of the contemporary social and educational American scene.

His program is also quite explicitly a value-conditioned affair. Dr. Hutchins pretends to no neutrality in the realm of values and morals. He is definite about the things that he is for; he is even more definite about the things that he is against. He is deeply opposed to the tendency of the leaders of American education to respond to what he condemns as the shifting, surface demands of the general public. According to Dr. Hutchins, the American public has many weaknesses. It is obsessed by the love of money. It has a narrow utilitarian bias that leads it to demand a vast program of vocational education. In this constantly expanding vocational program our educational institutions are expected to train farmers to feed and care for chickens, pigs, horses, and cows, to teach mechanics how to repair and care for automobiles, to train journalists to edit newspapers, businessmen to manage commercial enterprises, aspiring young lawyers to win cases, laborers to organize and manage trade-unions, domestic workers to cook and to sew, and even to instruct prospective housewives in the best ways to rear babies, to make good use of the consumer's dollar, and to furnish and decorate their homes.

The American public also has a mistaken notion of the meaning of democracy. This leads it to ignore the fact that one-third of the young, according to Dr. Hutchins, "cannot learn from books," and prompts it to demand "free education" for all, irrespective of their "ability to profit by it." This false conception of democracy also prompts the public to interfere with the management of education: to demand that the subject-matters and the methods of the schools and universities be regulated by representatives of the lay community, by alumni, by legislatures, and by trustees. The result of all this is that the educational institutions in the United States are, on the whole, badly run.

These incessant demands from pressure groups of one sort or another are transforming our educational institutions into public-service stations, and the disinterested search for truth and first principles is being submerged by the growing tendency to provide more and more information that will help people do better the wide variety of ordinary activities in which they are daily engaged. This tendency to help people "adjust" to the immediate circumstances in which their lives are set has led the schools to exalt empirical knowledge. And thus it comes about that empiricism "having taken the place of thought as the basis of research" now takes "its place, too, as the basis of education." And since the "facts" that a "practical" people want to learn about their life pursuits, must "be as immediate and useful as possible," we have sunk into an "anti-intellectualism" in education "which denies, in effect, that man is a rational animal."

One may reject Dr. Hutchins' low estimate of the intellectual and cultural potentialities of the occupations of everyday life, and still recognize that there is much of substance in some of these criticisms of current tendencies. But this searching analysis of weaknesses and wrong emphases in contemporary American affairs does not prompt Dr. Hutchins to try to develop a concrete socio-educational program for the purpose of dealing with these affairs. His discussion also fails to emphasize that some of these undesirable group attitudes and tendencies are bred into the lives of Americans by the presence of false interests and goals in the habitual and outmoded practices of the individualistic, pecuniary economy under which they now conduct their life affairs. Since he believes that an educational program should "draw out the elements of our common human nature," and since he further assumes that "these elements are the same in any time or place," it is apparently unnecessary for him to accept responsibility for this type of analysis and appraisal of the actual operating institutions of his own society. He holds that education makes its contribution, not by the development of a program that takes account of the real resources and difficulties of its society, but by giving its attention to the cultivation of the generic traits of man as a member of the human species.

Hence, although the first half of his book is given to a description of the present American social and educational situation, he turns his back on that situation once he begins to make his positive proposals for the reconstruction of education. Indeed, Dr. Hutchins seems to assume that the farther he can remove his program from everything that now exists in American life, the more ideal and valid it will be.

This, of course, is an old human practice—it is sometimes characterized as the practice of constructing utopias. The principle by which this is done is also now well known. Utopias are often built, not by really forgetting the here and now, but by unconsciously assuming that the opposite of what man now experiences and suffers must be the very essence of the ideal. Dr. Hutchins builds his utopian educational plan by employing this procedure. As the head of a university he has become weary of alumni who measure a college by its winning football teams, of parents who insist that their children be cultivated in the social graces, of "moral" reformers who demand that their particular conception of character training be made primary, of narrow vocationalists who seek to get practical results without taking the trouble to master the bodies of knowledge that underlie these utilitarian practices, of ambitious youngsters who seek a short-cut to pecuniary success through the learning of the mere "tricks of the trade," of a positivistic scientific practice that centers its attention on the mere accumulation of information rather than on the development of basic principles and genuine intellectual grasp, of sheer busy-work so often found parading as genuine scientific research, of pressure groups who insist that instructors teach only that which is in harmony with their vested interests, of patriotic citizens who get legislatures to pass laws prescribing loyalty oaths and defining what shall and shall not be included in the curriculum, and of boards of trustees who are disposed, on occasion, to substitute personal interests and prejudices for hard won standards of scholarship in the evaluation of the worth of teachers. From all of these undesirable things, Dr. Hutchins would deliver American education. We turn now to examine his specific proposals for educational reconstruction.

§ 3. *The Training of Human Reason*

Dr. Hutchins contends that education can get the desired emancipation, if it has the courage to do two things: first, to withdraw from the social, the contemporary, the vocational, and the empirical, and to give its attention instead to basic principles as defined and developed in the great books of the human race; and, secondly, to refuse to carry responsibility for the direction of the whole experience and the all-round development of the young, and to center its attention instead on the training of intelligence. As we have seen, he holds that the school can develop the rational powers of the young through the systematic exercise of their mental faculties in such logically exact and non-controversial disciplines as grammar, rhetoric, logic, and mathematics. Hence it can and should reject those empirical procedures that seek to develop meanings and to cultivate mind in the young by providing opportunity for them to grasp connections between that which they do and undergo as they interact with their varied physical and social surroundings. In sum, Dr. Hutchins advocates a program of education that will treat man as a being endowed with reason, not as a mere creature of feeling and action seeking to become intelligent about the behaviors of things and persons in the particular environment in which he lives.

Were we to attempt a comprehensive analysis of Dr. Hutchins' program of education many points would have to be explored. Here our primary interest is with his contention that education should be devoted to the universal, and the immutable; not to the local, the contemporary, the empirical, and the changing Many basic propositions that seem to him to be self-evident are far from self-evident to many other students of human nature, behavior and learning. Certain of the moral assumptions implicit in his program of education have also seemed to many educators to be more in accord with the practices of an authoritarian than a democratic society.

Social psychologists and anthropologists find it difficult to accept Dr. Hutchins' view that human nature is given at birth and is not conditioned, in any significant respect, by factors of culture, experience and learning. Many suspect that these educational ideas are really grounded in the traditional dualistic view of man as a metaphysical soul, and not as a unique emergent in a bio-cultural evolutionary process. Educational psychologists also have serious difficulty with his notion that the intelligence of man can be trained and developed without actual experience in the particular fields of subject-matter and activity in which it is to operate. Most of them have long since given up the principle of "formal discipline" that Dr. Hutchins makes the psychological foundation of his educational program. They no longer believe that the human mind is composed of special faculties, or reasoning powers, that can be matured and sharpened by a process of training in a course of selected disciplinary studies, much as our muscles can be developed by special exercises in the gymnasium. Experimental tests fail to verify this doctrine of formal mental discipline, and scientific students of human behavior have little confidence in a theory of learning that does not meet the test of actual experiment. Dr. Whitehead has spoken of the dangerous error involved in this theory of intellectual training:

> With good discipline, it is always possible to pump into the minds of a class a certain quantity of inert knowledge. . . . But what is the point of teaching a child to solve a quadratic equation? There is a traditional answer to this question. It runs thus: The mind is an instrument, you first sharpen it, and then use it; the acquisition of the power of solving a quadratic equation is part of the process of sharpening the mind. Now there is just enough truth in this answer to have made it live through the ages. But for all its half-truth, it embodies a radical error which bids fair to stifle the genius of the modern world. I do not know who was first responsible for this analogy of the mind to a dead instrument. For aught I know, it may have been one of the seven wise men of Greece, or a com-

mittee of the whole lot of them. Whoever was the originator, there can be no doubt of the authority which it has acquired by the continuous approval bestowed upon it by eminent persons. But whatever its weight of authority, whatever the high approval it can quote, I have no hesitation in denouncing it as one of the most fatal, erroneous, and dangerous conceptions ever introduced into the theory of education. The mind is never passive; it is a perpetual activity, delicate, receptive, responsible to stimulus. You cannot postpone its life until you have sharpened it.[2]

Many educators are also deeply troubled by the assumption of Dr. Hutchins that the schools need not undertake to provide for the course of experiencing of the young, and that their responsibility should be restricted to the single objective of the training of the intellect, excluding among other things all responsibility for "character building." These teachers believe that one of the central purposes of the American school should be the nurture of the young in the dispositions, the attitudes, the practices, and the allegiances that constitute the moral foundations of our democratic way of life. Moreover, they consider the notion that a school program can be so conducted that it will not have consequences in the characters of those involved in it is far from self-evident. They know of no evidence that supports this view; on the contrary, their experience shows that learnings are never single, and that habits, meanings, feelings, insight into principles, appreciations and attitudes all develop in one and the same process. These teachers therefore are convinced an educational system can be moral only as it accepts responsibility for all of the consequences—emotional, intellectual, behavioral— that it produces in the lives of those under its direction. Nor is it at all clear that a school will best cultivate the intellectual interests of the young if it seeks to separate the theoretical from the practical, the development of principles from the actual observation of events, the growth of cultural appreciation from the development of vocational interests and skills, or the grasp of meanings contained in books from the natural and social affairs

---

[2] A. N. Whitehead, *The Aims of Education and Other Essays* (New York, The Macmillan Co., 1929), pp. 8-9.

to which these meanings refer. It is possible that Dr. Hutchins' conclusion that real intellectual interests cannot be developed in one-third of our children is due, in part, to his assumption that intellectual training is something that is carried on by the exclusive use of literary symbols without reference to actual life conditions and processes. The world of the mind is real, but as we have seen, it is not an autonomous world divorced from the ordinary experiences and the environments of men.

Many, including the author, who are friendly to the use of the classics in the education of the young are also doubtful that creative abilities can be fostered by a reliance on books alone. They recall that the classics were written by men whose minds were developed, not simply through the study of the ideas of others, but primarily through their own first-hand and creative responses to the actual conditions and problems of their time. As Dr. Woodbridge has emphasized, there is a basic weakness in the humanist tendency to rely wholly on these great literary formulations of the past. Whenever this is done, he contends, we tend "to shut human life up in books, making these books authoritative and forgetting that the men who wrote them wrote, not out of contemplation of the past, but out of the richness of their own experience." [3]

§ 4. *The Inescapable Rôle of Human Preference*

Nor does the "great books" conception really relieve us of responsibility for evaluating the life affairs of some actual human society when we undertake to develop a program for the education of the young. Reference to the interests and values of the present inevitably enters into the construction of the "great books" curriculum. In the first place, not all of the books of the past are or can be included in any given course of study. As a matter of fact only a very small fraction of even those books widely recognized as "great" can be used in the work of any

---

[3] Frederick E. Woodbridge, *Nature and Mind* (New York, Columbia University Press, 1937), p. 90.

single school program. Selection therefore must operate in the determination of the special list of books included in any particular educational program. This selection is always made by human beings whose interests and perspectives are invariably conditioned by their life experiences. That which is taken from the heritage of the past is necessarily viewed and evaluated "over the shoulder of the present." Dr. Arthur Murphy has defined some of the prejudices which were present in the minds of those who chose the one hundred books for the curriculum of St. Johns College, the college created by the Hutchins group.

It may seem trite at this point to refer to the teachings of Thomas Jefferson, but since none of his writings are included in the "best books" at St. Johns, it is perhaps advisable to remind our traditionalists of their pertinence to this issue and to suggest that those who wish to instruct their students in the meaning of free institutions would be well advised to consult them. For if we are really going to return to our tradition in these high matters it is surely of particular importance to see that the tradition in question is authentic, and our own. . . .

It is a pity there was no room for *Walden,* or the *American Scholar,* or *Leaves of Grass* among the "unkillable classics" at St. Johns. There is a native tang to them and a native integrity from which an understanding of our tradition could profit much and for which no amount of undergraduate study of Plotinus (in translation) is likely to serve as an adequate substitute.[4]

But the rôle of selection does not end with the choice of the "great books" which are to be included in the curriculum. Selection also operates in the teaching and study of these books. Few would consider everything contained in the classics to be in harmony with the authentic humanist tradition—for example, the unquestioning acceptance of the pattern of a slave society by Aristotle, and the pre-scientific views of nature contained in many of the most revered classics. Nor will all those who use these books in the classroom give the same weight to their contents. Different conceptions of relevance, importance, and value

---

[4] Arthur E. Murphy, "Tradition and Traditionalists," in *The Authoritarian Attempt to Capture Education* (New York, King's Crown Press, 1945), pp. 22, 23.

will pervade the minds of the instructors who interpret, as well as of the students who study, this heritage. These personal frames of reference are inescapably influenced by the practical and the intellectual interests of the society in which both instructors and students have been reared, and they tend to shape the general pattern of their responses to these educational texts. Indeed, unless the examination of these writings from the past is made a part of a general study of the actual cultures in which these classics were written, and to which they were a response, the danger of an irresponsible play of contemporary outlooks and prejudices becomes very real. Thus to emphasize the manner in which contemporary interests and perspectives are involved in all use of the classics for educational purposes, does not at all imply that there is not much of importance to be learned from these classical formulations. But the inescapable operation of present perspectives and values in the selection, the interpretation, and the study of these works does very definitely support the conclusion that the classics are in no real sense a substitute for the use of the living and the contemporary in the education of the young. Indeed, many would affirm that the achievement of a broad human perspective which is informed by a real sense of the relative value of all things, is one of the most important results to be gained from the study of the classics.

The effort of the Hutchins group to derive the norms of education from the alleged traits of ultimate Being is, of course, but a special instance of the general effort to get the patterns of education directly from the patterns of things in nature. As we have already indicated, all attempts to erect the ways of nature into moral absolutes suffer from a fatal defect—namely, the inevitable tendency for men to read into "nature" the things that they have come to value most deeply as a result of their experience. Consider, for example, some of the conflicting interpretations different human groups have given the doctrine of "natural law" or "natural rights." Economic individualists have exalted the principle of "natural rights" in order to make secure the right of private ownership along with the freedom of the owner to do as he wills with that which he owns, whereas collectivists have appealed to the principle of "natural law" to justify the right of the community in the interest of equality to socialize the ownership of productive property; conservatives have construed the doctrine of "natural law" to involve the sanctity of established legal and economic institutions, whereas revolutionists have appealed to "nature's law" and "the inalienable rights" of man to justify the violent overthrow of the established order; ecclesiastics have stressed the moral law of "nature" in order to uphold the primacy of church over state, whereas secularists have introduced the principle of the "law of nature" to uphold the right and the authority of the whole community over the interests of all sub-groups or assocations; Roman Catholics have employed the concept of "natural law" to demonstrate the need for a universal moral and religious institution to administer and apply this moral law, whereas Protestants have used the concept of "natural rights" to confirm the principle of religious freedom, the inviolability of private conscience, and the need for religious toleration; supernaturalists have utilized the concept of the moral order of "nature" to support the revealed doctrines of their religious tradition, whereas empiricists have appealed to "nature" as an authority superior to that given in the pronouncements of supernaturalism—today in the field of education, the leaders of the Roman Catholic Church claim that the right of the Church to enroll all of its children in its own system of parochial schools is a "natural right," subject to no review or restriction by any agency whatsoever, while many adherents of the common school system maintain that there is a "natural law" which underlies the "right" of the whole community, acting through its agency, the government, to have its due part in the nurture of the young. In sum, the "laws of nature" have been construed to support whatever men deeply want in their struggles with their fellow human beings, and after the rival versions of the principles and purposes of "nature" have been given, there still remains the problem of how to regulate our common affairs so as to bring the maximum of order, security and meaning into them. There is no reason to suppose that the effort of the Hutchins group to derive the program of education from the metaphysics of ultimate Being will meet with any greater success than these other efforts to get "nature" to justify that which can only be ethically justified by a study of the actual consequences of social policies in the experiences of living men.

§ 5. *Universalism and Utopianism*

Finally, the fundamental thesis of Dr. Hutchins that the attempt to adjust a man "to any particular environment is therefore foreign to a true conception of education" is beset with difficulties of the most serious nature. We live in a world in which the unpremeditated and unplanned processes of history have given us not a single world society, but a world composed of many different human societies. Our world is peopled, not by *man*, but by *men*—Englishmen, Frenchmen, Germans, Mexicans, Norwegians, Russians, Chinese, Japanese, Hindus, Egyptians, Americans, and so on. Each of these historical groups has its own language, literature, history, customs, institutions, works of art, techniques, sentiments, faiths and loyalties, as well as its own revered heroes, holy-men, holy-places, holy-days, and other cherished memories. Dr. Hutchins suggests that these cultural differences are details, and that the important thing for education is the fact that men are all members of the same human species, and that "all societies have generic similarity."

It is on this shaky premise that he grounds his case for a universal program of education—a program deliberately designed to ignore all that distinguishes men because of their nurture and participation in the life affairs of different human societies. Surely this is the most extreme kind of adventuring in utopia-building. The educational proposals of Dr. Hutchins ask us to ignore all of the stubborn realities of human history; all of the differences in interest, desire, taste, need, appreciation, outlook, and allegiance that these historical cultures make in the members of the human species who are reared in them. As we have emphasized, men are literally creatures of culture and history as well as of biology. An educational program that slurs the particular and the actual in these individualized human societies as a consequence of its concern with the universal, necessarily becomes sentimental in its recommendations. It severs responsible connection with the definite life conditions, interests and motives that are required to make any human program for improvement more than a paper program.

The utopian tendency in the thinking of Dr. Hutchins is illustrated by his recent effort "to frame a world constitution." The same preference for abstract principles over analysis of concrete historical conditions, and the same tendency to make a paper plan substitute for the development of a responsible program for dealing with world forces as they actually exist, is found in the Preliminary Draft for Global Federation prepared by a Committee under his leadership. Apparently some of the members of the Committee were conscious of their failure to come to grips with the resources and difficulties in the contemporary world situation for when they submitted their report they stated:

> That the 'conceivable circumstances' for the rise of a world republic are not at hand, the Committee knows full well. Paramount among those circumstances should be the willingness of Russia, but not of Russia alone, to surrender sovereignty. To create these circumstances is beyond the power of any individual or group and this Committee is not a guild of miracle workers.[5]

The Hutchins group would also have done well to have announced frankly that their educational program as well as their political program was in the nature of "a proposal to his-

---

[5] "A Proposal to History," Printed in The Saturday Review of Literature, Vol. xxxi, No. 14, p. 7.

tory," and to have admitted that it would require "a guild of miracle workers" to make it an operating reality in the actual here and now. Unfortunately, many reactionary forces have found it easy to manipulate the formal educational concepts of the Hutchins group so as to make them justify a return to pre-scientific and authoritarian practices in American education.

But the recognition of the inescapable rôle of actual existing societies in the making of educational programs need not blind us to the fact that mankind is entering a new era, and that local, national and regional cultures are now real parts of an interpendent world. The development of some kind of world organization to meet this changed cultural situation has become the essence of practical politics. Efforts to develop this world organization will be successful to the extent that they take responsible account of these actual life conditions with their altered schedule of human needs and human possibilities. Education has its own important part to play in turning present critical human needs into dependable human capacities for meeting these new life conditions. This will involve among other things the cultivation in the young of wider appreciations and more inclusive loyalties. But these more universal human interests and perspectives will not be developed by an educational program that ignores the fact of existing national societies, and the varieties of outlook and allegiance and devotion which these societies breed in their members.

Statesmanship in education today involves the construction of educational programs that will continue to be related to the ways of life and thought of actual human societies, but which will also take account of the world civilization that is coming into existence. These educational programs will have to be integrated with political and economic and cultural programs that are de-signed to achieve world order and world community through the widening of the practices, the meanings, the shared interests and the loyalties of the members of these different national societies. The road to world order, security and peace must utilize, not ignore, the national and regional cultures and communities which the long processes of human development have created. Insofar as a universal human society defines a desirable human goal, it is something to be achieved, not to be assumed. Nor is it at all clear that world order and security necessarily involve a homogenous and standardized world community. Education for human brotherhood, peace, and economic, scientific and cultural coöperation still has to decide within what framework of cultural diversity and unity the interests of man can best be developed in our interdependent world.

CHAPTER VI

Parents and Teachers in a Period of Cultural Transition

IN OUR discussion thus far we have sought to describe some of the generic traits of deliberate education and to define their implications for a general theory of education. In this chapter we shall begin to deal more specifically with the problems and tasks of American education. Before undertaking this analysis, however, we shall bring together in summary review some of the basic concepts already considered in the previous chapters. It is on the basis of these principles that we shall make our interpretation of the present task of American education.

Our discussion of education and morals is grounded in four basic and interrelated conceptions. It holds, in the first place, that man achieves his human attributes through a process of experiencing and learning. The organic endowment of man is undoubtedly superior in many respects to that of other animal forms, but this superior biological inheritance in and of itself does not provide the sufficient condition for the emergence of human personality. As we have emphasized, it is group nurture, not organic constitution, that furnishes the individual with language and thereby makes it possible for him to attain the capacity for reflective thought. It is also membership in a particular cultural group, not original nature, that provides the history, the traditions, the customs, the literature and the arts which contribute the very stuff of the intellectual and moral consciousness of the individual human being. Each human being also has his governing principles of interpretation for both physical and human events, and the evidence shows that these explanatory principles are learned, not inborn. Whether the methods and attitudes of witchcraft or the methods and attitudes of science become the possession of an individual depends upon the life practices and assumptions of the culture in which he matures. Nor are ultimate objects of personal belief, allegiance and devotion inherited—a child becomes a Buddhist, a Confucianist, a Musslim, a Jew, a Roman Catholic, a Protestant, a Christian Scientist, a Materialist, or an Ethical Humanist because of the particular religious community and tradition in which he is reared. In brief, man gets his mental equipment by virtue of that which he learns in and through a human environment.

Our discussion is grounded, in the second place, in the perception that all organized education is in the nature of a moral undertaking. Adults found schools because they desire to mold the development of their young through the direction of the course of their experiencing. All efforts to guide the growth of the immature necessarily involve some conception of the kind of persons we want them to become, and this, in turn, presupposes some conception of the kind of life we expect them to live. Choice among alternatives in human personality and in modes of group living is therefore ineliminable in deliberate education. These preferred and chosen patterns of living, moreover, must be definite if they are to be of use in education. Vague moralizations that do not contain definite implications for group and personal behavior cannot be of any real service to teachers who are daily confronted with the necessity of fostering and hindering concrete patterns of human development. Our educational activity becomes morally responsible as it becomes aware of the pattern of values that pervades the organization and the activities of the school. All of the ways of the school are educative, for all of them help determine the course of the experiencing and the learning of the immature.

Our discussion is grounded, in the third place, in the conviction that the development of the program of the school inescapably involves an evaluation and interpretation of the ways of life and thought of its society. We misconceive the nature of the school whenever we assume that its program for the nurture of the young is an autonomous and self-regulating affair. The master purpose of the school is to prepare the young for responsible and resourceful living, and the school cannot effectively discharge this function without deliberate reference to the society in which the children live. It may well be, as some have asserted, that the most meaningful living in the present is the best preparation for adult responsibilities, but this desirable emphasis on the worth of the present experience of the child in no way alters the fact that the ultimate test of the school is what it does to prepare the young for life opportunities and responsibilities.

Now cultural interpretation and selection are foundational in all efforts to prepare the young for competent living. Consider, for example, one of the most basic of all the modes of preparation in the school—the attempt to equip the young for adult responsibilities by helping them to view the present in terms of the past from which it has evolved. We misconstrue the nature of history if we do not recognize that selection among human interests and human events plays a central rôle in the organization of any program for the study of the past. The department of historical studies always has to decide what institutions or movements of the present are of such importance that the young should devote their time to the study of their development. Moreover, the patterns for the interpretation of historical events in any given sphere do not automatically define themselves. The emphasis in the writing of history texts has changed profoundly with the growth of secular interests and activities. It has also changed now that the democratic struggle of the common people against the powers and privileges of aristocratic classes has become involved in the world-wide struggle of the liberal-democratic forces against the forces of revolutionary Communism. What holds in the instance of history also holds for the determination of programs to nurture the young in literature, science, civics, and the practical and fine arts. Each aspect of the work of the school tends to change as the life conditions, the problems, and the opportunities of its society change.

Nor is this process of cultural appraisal and selection ever completed in a world in which knowledge grows, and the conditions of life and the interests of people do not remain fixed. The shift from the conditions of pioneer, agrarian America to those of industrial-urban America have been accompanied by transformations in the length of the school year, in the vast numbers now enrolled in secondary schools and higher educational institutions, as well as in the scope and variety of subjects now included in the curriculum of the school. The emergence of the atomic age is calling for still further revisions in the program for the nurture of the young. Education is inextricably involved in the developments of its society, for it is in the context of these developments that we must undertake to define the kind of person we want the immature to become, as well as the particular forms of experiencing that are required to nurture this type of person.

Our discussion is grounded, in the fourth place, in the realization that the process of cultural interpretation and evaluation inherent in the work of the school becomes both more important and more complex and difficult in a period of cultural transition. By a period of cultural transition is meant a period when changes in life conditions have become so fundamental and extensive that historic outlooks and practices are no longer competent to organize and regulate the group activities upon which the existence of a people depends. In such a transitional period the re-examination of established norms and institutionalized practices becomes imperative, because adults realize that they cannot equip the young for life responsibilities if they continue to base the program of the school on an inherited system of living that is being progressively undermined by deep moving social forces. There is nothing morally or educationally admirable in the resolution to cling to an historic social system once the postulates of that system fail to verify when repeatedly put to the test of group action.

The process of cultural appraisal and interpretation not only becomes more important in a period of social transition; it also becomes more difficult. This is the case for two reasons. Psychologically human beings are so constituted that it is not a simple matter for them to become objective and critical about the modes of life and thought which have molded the very minds through which they think and evaluate. But this ability to project more adequate patterns of life and allegiance is precisely what is required if our schools are to educate, not miseducate, as they attempt to prepare the young for the new world in which they will have to live.

Nor is the difficulty exclusively intellectual; it is also social and practical. The problem is not simply one of developing adequate new patterns for human living, it is also one of developing an informed public opinion that will sift and support plans for social reconstruction. The achievement of a new consensus is not easy, for the initial phase of a period of social transition is generally marked by a decline in the unity of outlook of a people. Social inertia, old habits, as well as the propaganda of vested interests prompt many to defend the historic arrangements and to resist as subversive all effort to inquire into them and to modify them. At the same time, the life needs of the members of many groups, who feel themselves threatened by social developments, drive them to demand early and drastic action. It is within this situation of intellectual uncertainty, and of group tension and conflict, that the schools must continue to try to nurture the young. It is not surprising that in a democracy, the criticism of the public school grows in volume and intensity when the unity and the security of the public is disturbed by the movement of events. Education becomes confused and uncertain, because the society of which its program is an expression is also confused and uncertain. Clarification and agreement about the purposes and the content of the school involves a correlative clarification and agreement about the purposes and the patterns of the civilization of which the school is a part.

§ 1. *America is Entering a New Age*

This discussion of education and morals is also grounded in the conclusion that our country has entered upon a period of transition and revolutionary transformation. For more than a generation powerful forces have been operating to change the traditional bases of American life. The changes in our own culture are part of a larger movement that is being felt in all parts of the world. As a result of these developments in the basic conditions of life, many of our historic postulates no longer verify when put to the test of actual experience. We are disturbed as a people because so many things have happened and are continuing to happen which are contrary to the habitual assumptions by which we have been trained to interpret and to order our domestic and foreign affairs.

Although the pressure of events has forced us to depart in actual practice from many of our historic faiths and principles, we have not succeeded in developing a new intellectual and moral orientation to take the place of the one that is now disintegrating. Having failed to achieve a stable consensus about the framework for the America of the future, we are confused, divided, and uncertain. On the one hand, our command over nature which has so vastly increased our powers of production tends to nurture in us a sense of great, new life possibilities; on the other, our precarious control over many of the conditions under which we now live, along with our devastating power of material and human destruction, breed in us the fear that we may be plunged into social disorders and wars that may culminate in the end of democratic civilization itself.

Education at all levels is deeply involved in this situation.

Since the close of World War I a sharp controversy has been carried on by American educators about the implications of these changing affairs for the purposes and the program of the school. For a time many contended, as we have seen, that the crisis in our culture was no concern of the educator as educator. They argued that the teacher should attend to his own business, the education of the young; that he should stick to his own last, the school; and that he should leave the building of a new social order, if one were really required, to social experts working in coöperation with the duly elected members of our federal and state governments. But as the crisis has deepened, these voices have gradually been stilled. Today it is widely admitted that the transformations in our modes of living are so fundamental and pervasive that education would become an irrelevance should it try to ignore them. Slowly the conviction has grown that the American people are entering a new age, and that our schools must accept moral responsibility for undertaking to nurture a human being prepared to live in this new age—a person no longer patterned in the pioneer individualism of a self-sufficient agrarian America, but one who is equipped to live in a world marked by global interdependence, by control over the energies of the atom, by a disturbing and expanding scientific method and mentality, and by a more socialized and coöperatively planned system of democracy.

Most educators now affirm that the analysis and the description of the characteristics, the imperatives, the threats, and the possibilities of this emerging America is an essential part of the educational task. The realization is also growing that the schools must educate the young in an altered conception of social welfare and in a reconstructed pattern of human rights, responsibilities, and loyalties if they are to be equipped to share in the preservation and the further development of our democratic civilization. Many now recognize that bold institutional adjustments are required to resolve the problem of lag in American culture. The Research Committee on Social Trends, appointed by President Hoover, described this problem of cultural lag—the problem of the uneven rate of change in the interrelated aspects of our culture—as the deepest weakness in present-day American society. The Committee declared:

A nation advances not only by dynamic power, but by and through the maintenance of some degree of equilibrium among the moving forces. . . . Not all parts of our organization are changing at the same speed or at the same time. Some are rapidly moving forward and others are lagging. These unequal rates of change in economic life, in government, in education, in science and religion make zones of danger and points of tension. It is almost as if the various functions of the body or the parts of an automobile were operating at unsynchronized speeds.[1]

Unfortunately, the American people have certain traits which tend to complicate the problem of dealing with the lag in our culture. We are disposed to welcome change in the material and technological aspects of our culture—indeed, changes of this kind are considered in line with progress. We also hold in high esteem our scientific discoverers and our mechanical inventors. On the other hand, we tend to resist change in our institutional arrangements, and we are prone to ridicule and to condemn those who try to invent more adequate institutional means of providing for the human side of our industrial and urban civilization. As a consequence it is difficult in this period of social transition to achieve a solid consensus that will consistently support necessary reconstruction in historic institutional forms. This problem, of course, is not restricted to the American people; it has become the problem of democratic civilization everywhere. It is grim truth, not a mere rhetorical phrase, which asserts that the fate of mankind is literally at stake in the struggle now being waged between the forces of social invention and education and the forces that make for cultural lag.

In their efforts to serve as agencies of social progress in this period of acute cultural lag, the schools have encountered opposition from repressive groups of both the right and the left.

---

[1] The Research Committee on Social Trends, *Recent Social Trends*, Vol. I (New York, McGraw-Hill Book Co., Inc., 1933), p. xiii.

Vested interests on the right, making use of their extensive control over the press, the radio and other means of public communication, have waged an incessant campaign of propaganda
against proposals for institutional reconstruction. The purpose
of this propaganda has been to make the American people believe
that our material and cultural progress as well as our basic democratic freedoms depend upon the maintenance of the open-market system in which the private owner can adventure for profits,
unhindered by protective social legislation and the regulative
agencies of the government.

Revolutionary groups on the left have also sought through
the exploitation of the needs of under-privileged groups to sabo-
tage all efforts at social improvement by means of education, by
the organization of the major functional groups, and by peaceful, political action. These revolutionary groups—operating as
the conspiratorial agents of the world Communist movement—
have tried to cultivate the defeatist view that the democratic
state and its related cultural agencies, including public education, are simply the tools of the capitalist owning class, and that
it is utopian to assume that the needs of the common man
can be met by reliance upon these traditional means of American democracy.

Fortunately, the majority of the American people have refused to be duped by these two opposed systems of propaganda
which, although at polar extremes, nevertheless tend to feed
each other. Most Americans retain their faith in democratic objectives and in democratic means, and they realize that new public policies and new institutional forms are required if our
country is to utilize for the common good its present material,
technological, and human resources. They refuse to believe that
America cannot maintain its freedoms and at the same time
organize an economy able to sustain a high level of production.
They are aware that the dogmas of laissez faire are repudiated
in action by the very groups that praise these dogmas in their
campaigns of propaganda. But the American people have not

as yet reached firm conclusions about the implications of these
economic and social changes, nor have they stably defined the
directions in which reconstruction should move.

Of one thing we may be sure: the prospect of the schools
serving as agencies of enlightenment and human progress at this
historic turning point in the life of our country would not be
at all promising were either the reaction of the right or the left
to gain control. Our democratic theory of public education is in
deep-seated conflict with both of these obscurantist tendencies.
If the ways of democracy prevail, the rôle of the school will not
be determined by either of these intolerant and repressive groups.
It will be determined, instead, by what the great bulk of the
American people—the parents of the children in the schools—
really want their schools to do at this time. And the program of
education that the parents desire for their children will be determined, in the last analysis, by two factors: by the values they
cherish, and by the concrete meanings they discern in the altered
conditions that now confront them.

We turn, therefore, to an analysis of some of the major
changes that have taken place in the life conditions of the
American people. It is in this new America, already in process
of formation, that the children in the schools will have to live
and to work out their destinies. Any education fit to be called
education cannot escape from the honest effort to prepare the
young to live in this new world. In a very real sense the schools
of a democratic society must always be oriented to that which
is coming into existence, for it is in the context of this evolving
world that the concrete meaning of its basic principle of "the
greatest good for the greatest number" ever has to be redefined
and reënacted.

§ 2. *The Dynamic Nature of Contemporary Civilization*

Through the development of experimental science man
has finally discovered a method of making discoveries, and in
modern technological procedures he has institutionalized the

process of making inventions. As a result of these developments,
we live in a technological civilization that differs from all other
in its vastly accelerated rate of social change. Education must
take due account of the dynamic character of an industrial
society that is based on science and the systematic application
of scientific discoveries to its ways of living. Capacity to adjust
to changing situations is a life imperative in an industrial civili
zation. Nowhere has the force of these developments been
greater than in our own country. In the world of business and
government, as well as of the universities, the research labora
tory has become one of our most characteristic institutions. The
records of the U. S. Patent Office show the effect of this system
atic effort to promote the making of inventions. During the five
year period of 1851-55 a total of 6,000 patents were granted
whereas in the five-year span of 1926-30 the number of pat
ents had grown to 219,000. Thus in seventy-five years the rate
of making inventions had increased more than thirty-six fold
The activities of World War II greatly stimulated this effort
to strengthen the technological and scientific abilities of the
American people.

Although much of this interest in invention has been re
lated to the improvement of material production, the conse
quences of these inventions have spread to all aspects of our
culture—to life occupations, to the pattern of group relations
to modes of communication and transportation, to the organiza
tion of business, banking, labor, and agriculture, to government
and politics, to family life, to recreation and entertainment, to
art, to education, and to religion. The President's Research Com
mittee on Recent Social Trends enumerates 150 different social
effects of the introduction of the telegraph, the telephone, and
the radio.[2]

It is now clear that it is *knowledge*, along with "necessity,"
that is the mother of invention. As knowledge increases and the

_____
[2] *Ibid.*, pp. 153-56.

intellectual resources of a people are strengthened, the rate of inventions is stepped up and a culture becomes more dynamic. Professor Whitehead has pointed to the revolutionary implications of this accelerated rate of social change for the whole human enterprise and particularly the nurture of the young

> Our sociological theories, our political philosophy, our practical maxims of business, our political economy, and our doctrines of education, are derived from an unbroken tradition of great thinkers and of practical examples, from the age of Plato in the fifth century before Christ, to the end of the last century. The whole of this tradition is warped by the vicious assumption that each generation will live substantially amid the conditions governing the lives of its fathers and will transmit those conditions to mould with equal force the lives of its children.
>
> We are living in the first period of human history for which this assumption is false. . . . The note of recurrence dominates the wisdom of the past, and still persists in many forms even where explicitly the fallacy of its modern application is admitted. The point is that in the past the time-span of important change was considerably longer than that of a single human life. Thus mankind was trained to adapt itself to fixed conditions. But today this time-span is considerably shorter than that of human life, and accordingly our training must prepare individuals to face a novelty of conditions. But there can be no preparation for the unknown.[3]

Although the momentous moral and educational conclusion that Whitehead draws from the dynamic nature of life conditions in an industrial society is essentially sound, it must be qualified in certain respects. In the first place, the new rate of social change in no way invalidates the historic effort to organize a democratic society that will be grounded in an ethic which respects the integrity and the worth of human personality. In the second place, although it must be admitted that we cannot define the future in comprehensive detail, it does not follow that we have no understanding of the nature of the world now taking form. On the contrary, we can define with considerable confidence some of the main features of a new civilization that science and technology are bringing into existence. We face novelty and uncertainty, but we also face stubborn new condi-

---

[3] Alfred N. Whitehead, "Introduction," in Wallace B. Donham, *Business Adrift* (New York, McGraw-Hill Book Co., 1931), pp. xviii-xix.

tions of life that have to be taken into account if democratic civilization is to survive. The study of these changed life con-ditions and their implications for democratic values is an impor-tant part of the present human task. Finally, the school has shown that there can be a very important "preparation for the unknown." This preparation is achieved not by habituating the young to routine behaviors, not by preadjusting them to a fixed social situation, but by providing opportunity for them to have experience in the actual analysis and resolution of genuine problematic life-situations. If the school can help the young achieve a perspective from which to interpret changes now tak-ing place, and if it can nurture resourceful individuals equipped with the methods, the techniques, and the emotional and intel-lectual attitudes required to confront and overcome problems as they arise, it still has indispensable work to do in the preparation of the young to live amid the changing affairs of a dynamic society.

But the foregoing reservations do not touch the main point raised by the statement of Professor Whitehead. As he points out, man has entered a new order of human affairs—an order marked by a dynamism that challenges the historic presupposi-tion of "recurrence." Unless we are willing to repudiate science and invention, we must conceive of education as something other than the indoctrination of the young in a completed system of human living; education must strive to prepare the young to live in a world that will be marked by continued research and in-vention, by the development of new tools, by changing modes of production, and by the novelty and complexity of living con-ditions that these scientific and technological forces bring into existence. A morality that neither ignores nor deplores the reality of change, but which is prepared to make it a part of its life outlook, is now a foremost human need.[4]

---

[4] A masterly analysis of the implications for education of this accelerated rate of social change is given by Professor William H. Kilpatrick in his *Educa-tion for a Changing Civilization*.

§ 3. *The Problem of Human Survival*

A second change in the conditions of human existence is no less revolutionary in nature. Throughout human history territorial and cultural groups have relied on war as their ultimate resource for the resolution of their conflicts with their neighbors; we are entering a period when man, if he is to survive, must find an alternative to this ancient institution of war. Two factors have operated to bring about this new human situation. Improved means of transportation and communication have literally turned the whole world into a neighborhood. In our closely integrated and interdependent world, a war started anywhere by anybody may quickly spread to become a world conflict in which the whole human race is involved. With the end of human isolation, the problem of the organization of conditions for human security has become a planetary affair.

But advances in science and technology have not only developed an interdependent world; they have also revolutionized the character of war. We no longer have confidence in any attempt to regulate and to humanize war, for war has become a total thing. In modern, technological warfare the historic distinction between civilian and soldier has been destroyed, and entire populations now mobilize their full strength—material, technological and human—in the desperate struggle for sheer survival. Man's increasing command over nature has put awesome powers into his hands, including mastery of the energies of the atom. Those who know most about the destructive potentialities of these new weapons are the ones who are most deeply disturbed. Scientists have left their benches in the research laboratories in order to organize educational movements to persuade us that there is no real security to be had by an exclusive military defense against these scientific instruments of destruction. They warn in ever more urgent pronouncements that we must either develop a system of government competent to organize the world for peace, or be ready to revert to a new dark age.

Unfortunately, a functioning world authority is today a human need, not a developed human capacity. The peoples of the earth live in and through national states. These nations are not simply the ultimate political facts of the present world; they are also stubborn economic, cultural and psychological facts. Men are creatures of these nation-states. We yearn for security through collective means that have supplanted the ways of war, but we show by our concrete deeds that our first line of allegiance and defense is our own nation, not the system of world organization we call the United Nations. We may deplore, but we shall do well not to ignore, the reality of this national feeling and attachment. It is the nation—the motherland —that breeds the mentalities, the hopes, and the fears that govern our lives. We cannot eliminate the rôle of the nation in the psychological and practical life of man merely by declaring that modern man is obsolete, and that the day of humanity and of world law and government has dawned.

But neither can we ignore the reality and the horror of scientific war in our interdependent world. The creation of the new institutions—economic, political, cultural, and military— which will make possible the development of a real world organization is now the first task of statesmanship. These institutions can come only as the peoples of the earth are prepared to coöperate for common ends. The nurturing of the new understandings, the broader loyalties, the more inclusive sentiments and outlooks now defines a crucial part of the work of education. World organization requires a new human mentality; education working within the context of the various cultures must do its part to develop this new mentality.

§ 4. *The Good Life and Our New Powers of Production*

An increased capacity for production is a third characteristic of the new world in which we now live. The recent war demonstrated the vast productive potential of our country when the efforts of the American people are inspired by common purposes. During the first three years of the war we increased the total productive plant of our nation by one-half and at the same time we doubled the national output of goods and services. All of this was accomplished notwithstanding the fact that over ten million of the most productive members of our society were withdrawn from civilian pursuits and put into the armed forces of the country. Since the close of the war we have continued to maintain an unprecedented level of production and employment; the haunting fear remains, however, that our economy is without adequate controls and that we may soon plunge into depression and mass unemployment.

This demonstrated capacity for production calls for a revision of all former conceptions of what is humanly possible and desirable. It marks the beginning of a new day in the life of man. Both in industry and in agriculture man is well on the way to the solution of the age-old problem of production, providing he can organize an economy that can maintain the incentives of the worker, and at the same time so administer distribution that full employment and a steady consumer demand can be sustained. Nor is there anything materialistic in emphasizing these new productive powers. These powers of production, properly organized and directed, can mean increased resources for human living. They can be made to provide better homes, better food and clothing, more adequate medical care, finer communities deliberately planned to serve the ends of human living, and richer educational, recreational, and cultural opportunity for all.

In previous ages men have dreamed and outlined more ideal societies, but always these dreams have broken against the stubborn fact of the inability of a community to provide adequate life necessities for all of its people. Today these means are within the reach of man; so far as production is concerned, it is possible to plan for a society that will be free from the coercions and the degradations of poverty. The organization of an economy that can make this potential plenty an actual plenty, and which will preserve the liberties essential for a humane and creative experience, is now an urgent human need. The organization of a stably productive America is organically connected with the problem of developing a democratic world-order. Only an America marked by production and full employment can enjoy the unity and strength required to lead in the task of world reconstruction.

Here, again, education has its important rôle on the social frontier: it must do its part by attempting to develop the understandings, the desires, the interests, and the attitudes that are the human correlatives of a system of coöperative, planned production. Neither reactionary nor defeatist movements should be allowed to deter us from sharing in this task of the democratic reconstruction of our historic political and economic system. Education should be particularly on its guard against those economic groups who deny in their private practice what they praise in their public propaganda—against those who clamor for full production through a system of free and unregulated competition, but who constantly move in their own sphere of private enterprise to control and curb production by a system of monopoly control.

§ 5. *Power Production and Economic Interdependence*

The acceptance of the fact of human interdependence is a fourth imperative of our power age. Our new capacity for production has been attained through a division of processes, a specialization of functions, and a concentration of power in giant industries which have transformed the historic bases of American life. Gone never to return is the situation of a century ago in which the vast majority of our people enjoyed a rugged independence in a society mainly composed of self-sufficient farms. This pioneer America also contained a vast frontier of rich and undeveloped land—the great domain of the West into which people of the more crowded and settled regions could move whenever life circumstances made this desirable.

Today the frontier has disappeared and we live in a closely integrated corporate society. In present day America only about one-fifth of our people live on farms, and practically all of these farms are so specialized in their production they have lost their earlier self-sufficiency. For better or worse, life interests are now so tied together that human beings are dependent upon one another for their very existence. Region is dependent upon region, farm upon city, city upon farm, and the workers of both farm and factory upon the skilled services of professional groups. Our interdependence is increasing, not lessening. Today if owners choose to shut down their factories, if meat packers refuse to operate their packing houses, if farmers fail to bring their stock, grains, fruits, vegetables, and dairy products to the market, if miners refuse to go underground to mine coal, if railroad crews refuse to run their trains, if doctors and nurses refuse to care for their patients, if teachers stay away from their classes, if policemen and firemen leave their posts, the very means of human existence and welfare are disrupted. Indeed, the life activities of millions can be upset if the telephone girls abandon their switchboards, or the operators of the elevators in apartment and office buildings go on strike. In our fragile, interdependent world even a heavy snowstorm can plunge the population of a whole region into the most serious plight by interrupting the ordinary public services of telephone, electricity, sanitation, and transportation.

The fact of interdependence will not be denied by anyone who is at all acquainted with the network of interrelated activities through which modern man lives. We tend to forget, however, that we are attempting to operate this corporate and functionally coöperative society on the basis of an individualistic system of rights, freedoms, and responsibilities that was developed in an earlier and simpler social situation—a situation in which the individual family was largely a self-sufficient unit and in a position of direct control over the factors that affected its food, its shelter, its security, and its opportunity for productive employment. In present-day America these fundamentals of existence depend upon arrangements that extend far beyond the will of the individual, of the single household, or even of the local face-to-face community. Whatever controls are now exercised over these basic matters are exercised by voluntary organizations and by governmental agencies that are literally continental in scope.

Our social and educational policies must take account of this shift in the locus of control if American democracy is to continue to flourish. Our historic attitude of rugged individualism must be supplanted by a socialized mentality that is grounded in an adequate recognition of this fact of human interdependence. Effectual respect for human personality is not shown by any social system that in its pattern of operation deprives many human beings of their chance to have a part in the productive work of their society. Unemployment is a spiritual problem as well as an economic problem, and democracy can meet it only as it provides economic security and opportunity for all of its people.

As leaders of social and legal thought have indicated, the corporate form of property ownership and management—the dominant form in industrial America—has split the historic atom of property.[5] It is now possible to own and profit from that which one does not manage or control. This split between power and control—between responsibility and function—must be overcome if we are to live in a healthy society. Increased socialization of these vast productive enterprises is required to make them serve the common good. Sincere friends of democracy can differ about the forms this socialization should assume, but they cannot differ about the urgent need for it.

Nor can there be any real question that a new form of

---

[5] Adolf Berle and Gardiner Means, *The Modern Corporation and Private Property* (New York, The Macmillan Co., 1933).

economic and social power, the power now exercised by the trade unions, must also be brought under a greater degree of public direction. One can recognize that these organizations of workers are a primary resource of democracy at the present time, and yet realize that their methods of control and operation need to be modified so as to take more adequate account of the life necessities of a society of interdependent human beings. Fortunately many of the younger and abler labor leaders already share this point of view. They are prepared to unite with other functional groups to create a national system of coöperative planning.

All of the foregoing implies that a new social morality which redefines the rights and the responsibilities of both individual human beings, and of voluntary economic organizations, is required in this emerging order of associated human living. Individuals must not be expected to carry responsibilities which presuppose a control over their life affairs which they no longer enjoy as isolated individuals or as members of family and neighborhood groups. Our democratic way of life will not survive if the rights of property are held superior to the rights of persons, and private owners are protected in historic rights which, under the altered conditions of today, place the means of livelihood of hundreds of thousands of human beings under the arbitrary control of a few individuals. Without a real share in the control over the means of their existence, a people cannot be economically secure; without economic security a people cannot long continue to be culturally and politically free.

In sum, the historic notion of an automatic, self-adjusting economic and social system is an anachronism in the corporate life of our industrial society. Neither the economic nor the moral results of the practice of laissez faire support the assumption that the social good is best cared for in a regime in which each individual devotes himself to the relentless pursuit of his own gain. The exploitation and waste of our natural resources—land, forest, and mineral; the recurring and deepening crises in our unplanned and uncoördinated economic system; the irrationality of mass unemployment and want in the midst of potential plenty; the inadequate provision for health, education, and social welfare services; the rural and city slums, the inequalities in the distribution of wealth and income—all of these and other anti-social results demonstrate that we deceive ourselves when we assume there is a pre-established harmony, and that "self-love and social are the same." The extent to which the economic foundations of our democracy are already eroded is shown by the fact that during a year of the depression one-tenth of one per cent of the families at the top received approximately the same income as the forty-two per cent of the families at the bottom of the scale.[6]

In our concrete practices in industry, banking, labor, agriculture, and the various professions, as well as in the expanding functions of government, we have already departed in many ways from the official doctrines of economic individualism. We are handicapped, however, in our effort to deal with the new life conditions because we have adopted no alternative over-all conception of human welfare. The American people are in urgent need of a new social orientation to define the general direction in which reconstruction should move, and to serve as the moral foundation for the evaluation of specific proposals for adjustment. Actually the choice is no longer one of our historic individualism versus a system of coördinated control; events have already settled that question, for our industrial society cannot function without some measure of control. The real issue is what forces are to exercise the control, and the scope and the purposes of the control. Education has its due part to play in the development of this basic social orientation. Without a changed conception of human interests, rights, and obligations, we cannot bring about by democratic means the required reconstruction of our system of economy and government.

---

[6] Report of the Brookings Institution on *America's Capacity to Consume*, (Washington, D. C. 1934).

§ 6. Religious Outlooks and New Life Perspectives

Some of the foregoing developments have also had an effect on the deeper intellectual and moral frames of our civilization. Religion is involved in these developments, for religion is an affair of both human reason and faith, and of human vision and aspiration. The earlier optimism about the ease with which the transition to new life attitudes could be made has disappeared. Many now recognize that the attempt to meet the changed situation by dividing human experience into two realms—one, scientific and practical; the other, moral and religious—has failed. Attitudes and methods used in one sphere inevitably expand to pervade the other. Minds that are habituated to the presuppositions and methods of experimental science do not find that they can abandon these modes of thinking for the authority and presuppositions of supernaturalism when it comes to the determination of more ultimate meanings. A leading theologian has described this change in our mental outlook:

> To call things supernatural is no explanation of them according to the modern scientist, for to explain is simply to point out the natural connection between phenomena. The new general attitude has become so instinctive and so much a part of our world-view that most of us never think of interpreting extraordinary any more than ordinary occurrences in other than a naturalistic way. Fairies, witches, ghosts, angels and demons, once freely assumed to account for all sorts of phenomena, have simply dropped out of the mind of the average modern man and no longer play a part in his experience. Not that their existence has been disproved, but that they have become superfluous.[7]

But mentalities that are hallowed by religious associations tend to persist, and today we are not nearly so confident as many were a generation ago that religion will soon renew itself by a process of internal criticism and adjustment to the intellectual and ethical tendencies of the new age. Certain modernists now unite with orthodox fundamentalists to deplore the secularist

---

[7] Arthur C. McGiffert, *The Rise of Modern Religious Ideas* (New York, The Macmillan Co., 1915), p. 36.

tendencies of a society whole-heartedly committed to the principles of science and democracy. These modernists have learned that the growing faith in the power of man to develop his own directing moral principles, along with the spread of scientific inquiry to all realms of experience, including the realm of human personality, morality, and religion, carry far-reaching implications for classical religious outlooks. It is becoming increasingly apparent that the effort to achieve a new religious orientation in harmony with modern habits of thought entails a more drastic reconstruction than many had anticipated. Modernists shrink from this reconstruction and are involved in deep conflict as they seek to reconcile their contradictory outlooks and allegiances. Many believe that the new religious orientation will have to assume a bolder position.

> The new religious orientation represents a logical extension and development of the Judaeo-Christian tradition. It bears somewhat the same relationship to modernism that modernism bears to fundamentalism. Modernism has departed substantially from the world view, the intellectual methods, and the ethical values of the earlier Christian tradition, but it has halted halfway in going modern. It accepts science up to a point, but it holds on to a considerable number of conceptions which are part and parcel of an intellectual system which is no longer authoritative—no longer even respectable.[8]

It is too early to predict how long the present retreat from the methods of science and the values of democracy will continue. Much will depend upon the ability of democratic forces to rehabilitate our impoverished and war-torn world. For the moment the re-assertion of supernaturalism is setting a real problem for public education. Deep as may be our regard for the spiritual values enshrined in our religious tradition, we should not blind ourselves to the reality of the conflict between the supernatural elements in that tradition and the empirical attitudes and principles that permeate so many aspects of present human experience. We shall continue to develop intellectually

---

[8] Edward H. Reisner, *Faith in An Age of Fact* (New York, Farrar and Rinehart, 1937), p. 5.

and emotionally maladjusted people so long as the total educational influences of our culture perpetuate this split between the head and the heart—between modern man's tested methods of achieving knowledge and control and his ideal objects of aspiration, allegiance and devotion.

§ 7. *Education and the Need for a New Orientation*

In the foregoing, we have sought to map some of the major value choices that now confront American education. In literal truth we live in a transitional period. We inherit a tradition of supernatural authority with its closed system of absolute moral law; we live in a civilization that is increasingly committed in all aspects of its life to the methods and attitudes of science, and one which is so dynamic in nature that it compels continuous adjustment to novel conditions. We inherit a moral and religious tradition that emphasizes the weakness and unworthiness of man and his inability through his own effort to discover or do the good; we live in a democratic society that makes respect for human personality its first principle, and which has faith in the principle of self-government and the moral right of a people to fashion and refashion the laws, the institutions, and the standards that are to direct its activities. Historically, our country has followed a policy of security through national means and we are still jealous of our national sovereign right to control our own destiny; we live in an interdependent world possessed of instruments of death that make human survival contingent upon developing an authoritative world-wide mutual security system that will offer mankind a real alternative to the ancient practice of war. We have been nurtured in a mentality of scarcity, and we have been trained to believe that production is the basic problem; science and technology have so transformed the means of production that we stand at the threshold of an economy of abundance, and the creation of a system of distribution that will maintain employment and permit us to use our productive powers defines a crucial economic and moral need. Our pioneer experience has bred in us a rugged individualism, a faith in the right of private property and enterprise, a trust in the beneficence of an automatic self-adjusting economic system, and a fear of strong government and the positive state; we live in a corporate, technological civilization in which family is dependent upon family, occupation upon occupation, farm upon city, city upon farm, region upon region, and nation upon nation, and in this interdependent world some deliberate form of planning, coördination and over-all control is a necessity if our democratic way of life is to be preserved.

As one writer has suggested, we have been as a people walking backwards for many decades. We have sought to make adjustments to inexorable new conditions behind our backs while continuing to hold fast to the old dogmas and slogans. American democracy must cease trying to escape the new age; it must deliberately confront its problems and seek a new social and moral orientation. If education is to play a creative rôle during this period of transition to the new order of human relationships and activities, it must do its part in the development of this orientation. The outcome of the struggle of American democratic forces to clarify life attitudes, and to develop an informed public opinion that will support an adequate program of social reconstruction is of world-wide moment, for the United States has come out of the war possessed of a power that for at least a period is unmatched. The welfare of all humanity is involved in the use our country makes of this power and leadership.

§ 8. *Parents and Teachers*

We are convinced that the character of the program of education which the schools will provide during this time of transition will be determined ultimately by what American parents want for their children. Any effort on the part of a national political movement or party to dictate the program for the education of our young would meet with immediate and powerful resistance. Much as federal aid is needed to equalize educational opportunity throughout our land, all of its supporters demand it be provided in such a manner that the control over the purposes and the content of the school program will remain with the local community. So long as we continue in the democratic pattern, we shall strive to keep our schools from becoming mere propaganda instruments of the State.

Much has been written during the recent battle for the schools about the responsibility of the teaching profession. Its responsibility is very great, particularly in protecting the schools from the pressures of reactionary groups that seek to make the schools abandon their function of inquiry and evaluation, in order that they may serve as the agents of their own interests. The teachers, however, can maintain a pioneering rôle only as they enjoy the confidence and the coöperation of the parents. Once teachers lose the confidence of the parents of their community, there is little that they can do in and of themselves. Teachers need a stronger and more ably led professional organization, but it is both utopian and undemocratic to assume that a powerful teachers' organization, working separately, can take over the direction of the school. The initiative of the teachers can prevail only as it is supported by the understanding and the will of the parents. A first responsibility of teachers therefore is to keep parents informed about what is really involved in controversies about the school so that they may make wise judgments about basic educational policies, as well as about the kind of lay leaders that should be chosen to serve on the board of education.

Fortunately, the teachers in our country do enjoy to a remarkable extent the confidence of the parents. The fact that our teachers do not constitute a class apart, but come from the very groups whose children are in the public schools accounts in part for the esteem and support they receive. But the deeper reason for public confidence in the teachers is that they have demonstrated over the years that they are disinterested—disinterested in the sense that their first interest is the welfare of the child. It is because parents are convinced that the teachers share their own concern for the well-being and growth of their children that they are ready to back them in that which they seek to do. This confidence of the public is well-earned, for teachers on the whole have never tried to manipulate the young for ulterior sectarian purposes of their own. Through lack of adequate organization, teachers have failed, on occasion, to resist the demands of noisy minority groups, but even in these situations the parents have understood that the teacher's first loyalty has been to the children, not to those who would exploit them.

But the welfare of the child does not automatically define itself. Here again American education has been supported by a splendid tradition. From the beginning, our schools have been on the side of inquiry and knowledge, not of suppression and ignorance. The work of teachers has been supported by the faith of the American people in intelligence, by their conviction that the welfare of the individual in the long run is bound in with an educational process that is concerned to develop his understanding, his power to choose, and his power to evaluate critically that which results from the choices that he makes. It should not be too difficult, if educators go about it in the right way, to put any special group—patriotic, economic, ecclesiastical, or political—on the defensive whenever it seeks to dominate the school in order to prevent it from helping the young to understand the characteristics of the world in which they live. The right of the child to learn, and to come to know through that which he learns, is a right that parents are prepared to support whenever they are convinced this right is being subordinated by pressure groups more concerned about their own special interests than they are about the welfare of children.

The right to inquire and to analyze are basic rights, but candor demands that we point out that all inquiry into a culture has its standards of importance and relevance, and that all analysis necessarily involves emphasis. Indeed, it is no exaggeration to state that *analysis is emphasis*. This can easily be demonstrated by the discussion of this chapter in which we have sought to focus attention on basic characteristics of present-day American civilization. Our analysis has involved selection. It has also involved interpretation. We have emphasized, for example, the interdependent character of our industrial civilization, and we have also emphasized the anarchy and insecurity that result from seeking to operate this new society by reliance on individualistic outlooks and practices that are the product of earlier pioneer, agrarian America. Others with different interests and values can and do make a different kind of analysis. Some of them, for example, call attention to the expansion of the functions and controls of government, and they contend that it is the interference with the natural law of supply and demand by a government bureaucracy that constitutes the present menace. Still others take quite a different point of view. They assert that our troubles are due to the moral failures of individuals and that these troubles will disappear if individuals will cleanse their hearts and learn to love their fellow men. Parents must recognize that no educational discussion, either by textbook or by teacher, can ever be free from these historic and social presuppositions. Whatever objectivity in teaching may mean, it cannot mean the absence of values and a point of view. These are operative in each and every effort to introduce the young to our ways of living.

Obviously, it is important to give the young, with due regard for different age levels, a chance to know of these alternative and conflicting points of view. It is this which distinguishes democratic from authoritarian systems of education. But education is something more than the mere multiplication of alternative ways of considering a problem. Education, in order to be education, has to accept responsibility for helping the young to perceive which of the various factors involved in a situation are really crucial. Even when it seeks, as democratic education should, to encourage the child to make his own analyses and emphases, it still has to distinguish the superior from the inferior—the grounded from the ungrounded—in these interpretations worked out by the pupil. Values necessarily pervade the intellectual and educational processes of man. They cannot be extruded from any study—anthropological, historical, economic, political, sociological, psychological, ethical, or religious—of human affairs.

But in a democracy we are committed not only to the life of intelligence, we are also committed to the principles of a social system that respects all human beings and that aims at real equality of opportunity. Indeed, we believe that the free life of intelligence is dependent upon the maintenance of this kind of social system. In other words, education in and for democracy is education in and for a system of living that has its basic pattern of values. Consider, for example, the problem of race relations in the United States. Democratic education today must do more than merely call attention to the practices of discrimination and segregation which mark and mar American culture; it must also nurture in the young a basic moral disposition and outlook with which to view and judge these discriminations. No school that is committed to democracy will organize its classrooms, its laboratories, its social affairs, its athletic contests, or its recreational programs, so as to deepen these attitudes of discrimination. On the contrary, it will do what it can, taking due account of existing mores, to weaken and to eliminate them.

In a period of transition parents and teachers must examine the bearing of historic American attitudes and practices on this foundational system of democratic values. It is from the standpoint of these democratic values that they must decide the nature of the problems that now press for solution. It is also from the perspective of these same values that they must define the characteristics of what will be accepted as solutions to these problems. It is in terms of this program of democratic living that we should seek to define the life attitudes and habits which are to characterize the young as they enter upon their life responsibilities in the new world that is in process of formation. Only as parents and teachers can coöperate in explorations of this searching kind can we expect to have a school that will help meet the needs of our democratic way of life.

In the second part of this book we shall undertake a more detailed analysis of a number of these problems of value and education. Our discussion will necessarily have to be selective. It will attempt to deal frankly with some of the most fundamental and controversial issues before American education.

PART TWO

Education
and the Values of
Democratic Civilization

CHAPTER VII

The Morality of Primary Experience

FROM the standpoint of morals, the deepest cleavage in education is between those programs of education that regard human beings as ends in themselves, and those that regard them as mere means for the preservation or the promotion of some favored institution or fixed system of life and thought. The morality of democracy is distinguished from that of all authoritarian systems precisely because it is grounded in this principle of the dignity and worth of each human being. Our discussion of education frankly adopts this democratic point of view. It is concerned not with the demonstration of the superiority of the democratic way of life, but rather with the implications of its values for the conduct of education at this time.

As we view it, the democratic pattern is opposed to all exploitive systems that are organized to train the young in a predetermined rôle. It matters not whether the rôle be that of a subject for the established state, a conscript for the armed forces of a nation, a bearer of children for the fatherland, a serf bound to the land of his lord, a mere hand in the factory, or a disciplined agent of a totalitarian system of world-revolution. Educational programs of this sort are undemocratic, not simply because they are designed to perpetuate an inequitable economic and political system, but because they are also deliberately constructed to train the immature as animals, not to nurture and liberate their full potentialities as human beings. An educational program manifests respect for the individual as an end in himself only as it is committed to the development of his ability to think.

Without respect for the mind of the individual, there can be no adequate respect for human personality.

§ 1. *Deliberate Education and the Ethic of Democracy*

The democratic criterion has far-reaching educational implications. Not all of the educational programs that profess allegiance to the supreme worth of human personality measure up in their practices to this avowed democratic standard. A school may even be a "child-centered" school, yet fail to manifest this basic respect for the child. If a school construes the pedagogical doctrine of "interest" to imply approval of mere impulsive or random activity on the part of pupils, rather than the effort to secure their whole-hearted participation in activities that enrich meaning and increase their capacity for control of life-affairs, its program is not really in accord with the democratic conception. We show respect for the child in the school, not by indulging or coddling him, but by enlisting him in significant undertakings that result in the development of his resourcefulness as a human being.

Even programs of so-called "moral education" fail, at times, to exhibit this regard for the nurture of intelligence which is an essential part of any educational program that has genuine respect for the individual human being. Whenever concern for a "revealed" code prompts those who serve as its trustees to try to transmit the code by a process of indoctrination that involves the withholding of pertinent knowledge, the young are not treated as ends in themselves. To treat a child as an end, means so to conduct his education that he will progressively grow in his ability to make up his own mind about that which he shall believe, and about that which is to be considered worthy of his allegiance. Measured by this standard, alleged interest in the ultimate welfare or future salvation of the child does not give adults the right to deprive him of the opportunity to develop a mind of his own. One of the deplorable features in the present confused situation is that certain groups, purporting to have the spiritual interests of man at heart, are trying to impose special programs of "moral education" on the public school that actually involve an abridgement of the processes of historical and critical study. There is nothing "spiritual" about suppression, and it is difficult to see how the moral life of a democratic community will be strengthened by a program of "moral education" that strives to keep the young in ignorance about any aspect of human experience. A faith that fears knowledge cannot be counted on the side of the forces that are working to develop a democratic civilization based on respect for all men.

Nor are those groups who desire to indoctrinate the young in outmoded historic outlooks and institutionalized practices, the only ones who offend in these matters. Revolutionary groups may also organize authoritarian programs for social change that fail to measure up to the searching democratic criterion of respect for human personality. Leaders of movements for revolutionary change may proclaim that their aim is the welfare of the masses, but whenever they try to win their adherents, not by persuasion based on enlightenment, but by a process of disguised manipulation, they do not manifest this basic regard for the worth of the individual human being. Any program of education ceases to treat individuals as ends in themselves once its concern about a particular social outcome or goal—revolutionary or reactionary—overrides its desire to provide people with the knowledge they must have if they are to be in a position to evaluate the cause to which they are invited to commit their lives. So far as democratic educational values are concerned, a program of animal training remains a program of animal training, irrespective of whether it is organized to breed militant warriors for a new social order, or to train docile defenders of the status quo.

In brief, democratic education believes in the nurture of human personality. It holds that the nurture of human personality involves as its very essence the nurture of mind, and that the nurture of mind is incompatible with any attempt to inculcate beliefs and attitudes by a process that involves the deliberate withholding of knowledge. Such a process of suppression and indoctrination can breed a "mind in the individual," but it cannot nurture "individual mind"—the kind of mind a person must have if he is to be equipped to carry on his own education. We cultivate individual minds only as we nurture individuals who have the capacity for moral responsibility; that is, the capacity to coöperate in the development of life purposes as well as the capacity to evaluate the consequences that flow from their life activities. Any program of education that is committed to the development of individual minds is democratic in character—it necessarily has regard for the capacity of men to inquire, to evaluate, and to take responsibility for their own actions. Similarly, any program of education that seeks to restrict the development of mind is undemocratic in nature, no matter how much it may profess to believe in the worth and dignity of human personality. Such a program fails to satisfy the basic moral criterion of democracy, namely, that individual human beings be treated not as mere means, but as ends in themselves.

§ 2. The School and the Cultivation of Mind

Deliberate education, like all other purposeful human undertakings, is an affair of *means* as well as of *ends*. Unless our educational means are suited to our ends, we will not get the results in the lives of the young that we really intend. Even among educators who wholeheartedly accept the democratic conception that the development of personality through the nurture of mind is the supreme educational objective, there remain sharp differences about the kind of school program required to achieve this moral objective. These differences relate to both the method and the content of the educational program. They grow out of conflicting views of the nature of mind and of the process by which mind develops in the young. Associated with these different theories of mind are different conceptions of the nature and method of reflection, and of the relation of reflective thinking to the events of primary experience.

The adherents of the "old" and of the "new" education both affirm that education is a discipline of mind, but their respective views of how mind is to be disciplined, or cultivated, vary enormously. The "traditionalists" assert that mind is best trained through a process of formal discipline, and many of them are in accord with the declaration of President Hutchins that the school should leave "experience to other institutions and influences and emphasize in education the contribution that it is supremely fitted to make, the intellectual training of the young."[1] The "new" educationalists, however, have a very different view of the educational need. They contend that mind is developed in and through significant functioning in life situations, and that the program of the school therefore must provide opportunity for primary experience—that is, for rich and varied interactions with the world of persons and things.

Obviously, differences about the means of education as fundamental as those that divide the traditionalists from the new educationists, or the experimentalists, are more than mere pedagogical differences; they necessarily extend beyond matters of pedagogy to basic differences in conception of what is desirable in education. In a real sense this controversy about educational methods and purposes is a moral controversy; it is grounded in conflicting interpretations of the intellectual and moral nature of man, and in rival views of the means by which the most distinctive human attributes are developed in the young.

This controversy about the nature of mind and the best means for its nurture has its special significance for education in a democratic society. The democratic mode of human living presupposes a society whose members are equipped to share creatively—intellectually—in both the formulation and the evalu-

---

[1] Robert M. Hutchins, *The Higher Learning in America* (New Haven, Yale University Press, 1936), p. 69.

ation of the common ways of living. Education for the growth and the liberation of mind is therefore a basic value in a democratic civilization. Hence in the enterprise of democratic education, no problem has more fundamental moral implications than the determination of the means by which the school shall accomplish its intellectual task. In a democracy, one of the most searching questions to be raised about any particular educational program is the conception of mind imbedded in it. Intelligence may not be the sole ground of morality, but without intelligence men do not become responsible moral agents.

Thus the place given to primary experience in the program of the new education signifies something more fundamental than the mere introduction of a new pedagogical device into the work of the school. It really signifies a new moral approach to the nurture of the young, for this emphasis on primary experience is associated with a reconstructed functional theory of mind. Indeed, the deepest meaning of the new educational movement lies in its effort to develop an educational practice that is in harmony with this functional conception of mind—a conception that accepts without discount the evidence and the perspectives of organic evolution.

§ 3. Experience and Meaning

For those who accept the evolutionary account of the genesis of man, it is evident that man must have been a creature of action and feeling long before he achieved the capacity for reflective thought. Nor can an empirical thinker today seek to explain the development of mind by resort to the historic mind-body dualism. The evolutionary conception, for example, has bred an outlook and a mode of interpeting human personality which has dissolved the very foundations of the dualistic presupposition inherent in the following account by T. H. Green:

It will be found, we believe, that this apparent state of the case can only be explained by supposing that in the growth of our experience, in the process of our learning to know the world, an animal organism, which has its history in time, gradually becomes the vehicle of an eternally complete consciousness. What we call our mental history is not a history of this consciousness, which in itself can have no history, but a history of the process by which the animal organism becomes its vehicle.[2]

For the evolutionist, "the history of the process by which the animal organism becomes the vehicle of mind" is not the story of "an eternally complete consciousness" descending from some transcendental realm in order to make its abode in a human organism; it is rather the record of the manner in which the sentient organism becomes progressively aware of its own interests, and of the principles implicit in the habits which regulate its interactions with its surroundings. The transformation of the habit patterns of the living creature into the consciously purposeful activities of the human person is a great transformation, and we properly celebrate the rôle of symbols in making possible this transformation, for it is this evolutionary development which marks the emergence of mind. But the world of symbols is not an independent, self-sufficient world; nor is the realm of mind a realm of rational principles and concepts unrelated to the doings and the undergoings of ordinary experience. On the contrary, symbols have intellectual significance precisely because they do represent—symbolize—the values of things and organic acts in the world of natural existences. It is only as these verbal forms preserve for a human group that which it has learned about the way in which things are actually involved in one another, that they become charged with meaning. Symbols are important in the development of mind because they convey to man the import of things that are other than symbols. Words—oral or written—have no intellectual significance whatsoever apart from these life contexts.

Thus, if we accept the evolutionary point of view, we must recognize that *things* are prior to *symbols* or *words*, and that *activities* are prior to *meanings*. Nor is the priority merely chron-

---

[2] T. H. Green, *Prolegomena to Ethics*, Fifth Edition (Oxford, England, Oxford University Press, 1907), pp. 77-78.

ological in nature, behavioral adjustments to surroundings not only come earlier than language and thought, they also constitute the matrix from within which all conceptions of relationships, or meanings, are developed. Conscious or cognitive experience is a derived mode of experiencing; it is sourced in the doings, the undergoings, the sufferings and the enjoyments of primary experience, and its ultimate controls and tests are also provided by the events of primary experience. No matter how deep our respect for the life of reason, we do not serve the ends of reason when we attempt to make it a thing in and of itself. The life of reason has its vital continuities with the life of action and feeling, and although there is a sound basis for our high regard for the transformations wrought in experience by the development in man of the capacity for reflective thought, we should never assume that reason can become the source of its own subject-matter. The process of human thought is indeed a distinctive kind of functioning, but it is nevertheless a form of human functioning, and like all other functionings of the living creature it is carried on by means of an environment. Apart from some context of ordinary human experience, the activity we designate as mind or reason does not occur.

This non-dualistic, functional theory of mind has important consequences for the work of education. Indeed, the evolutionary interpretation cuts the ground from beneath all of those educational practices that assume mind is an inborn essence that unfolds according to its own pre-formed and rational principles. The empirical evidence has never corroborated this doctrine of a universal, inborn mind; it has always supported the view that minds are the kind of affairs that are conditioned by particular cultures, and that they reflect the actual life experiences of the individuals who live in these different cultures. And with the development of an evolutionary, functional view of mind we are rapidly growing in the ability to provide an empirical explanation for those mental phenomena which were long supposed to demand a dualistic theory to account for them. Educators concerned to develop a program of education in harmony with modern thought and knowledge, will not continue to ground their activity in a view which assumes that mind is an inborn latency that unfolds in its own predetermined way irrespective of the life history of the individual human being. Fortunately, there is a growing tendency in education to recognize that we can understand the life and the mind of a child only as we understand the character of the surroundings in which he lives.

Nor does the faculty theory of mind with its reliance on formal discipline as the preferred mode of educational preparation rest on more defensible foundations. The experimental data do not justify the educational claims made for this theory, and its basic assumption that mind is a substance is obviously an inheritance from the transcendental, dualistic conception of an earlier philosophical outlook. Neither the findings of science nor everyday human experience support these preconceptions. Our modes of thinking and intellectual mastery are conditioned by our modes of experiencing:—the sailor is at home on the sea, the farmer on his land, the artisan with his tools and materials, the research scientist with his techniques and his special subject-matter of inquiry, the statesman with the affairs of the world of politics, and the artist with his paints and brushes. There is no universal subject-matter and no single form of training that can develop competency in all of these different fields apart from actual experience in them. What we know about the conditions for the "transfer" or "spread" of training, would seem to indicate that a process of exclusive concentration on the manipulation of symbols, would be one of the least promising of all possible educational practices for the development of the intellectually mature and resourceful human being.

§ 4. *Experiment and Meaning*

These evolutionary interpretations of the nature of experience and of the significance and patterns of intellectual activity are confirmed and enriched by an analysis of the procedures of experimental science. We owe much to the pioneer studies of Charles Sanders Peirce in the nature of the pattern of thought implicit in the procedures of modern science. In his discussion of the characteristics of the mind that has been molded by scientific practice, Peirce declares that whenever you have discourse with a typical experimentalist, "you will find that whatever assertion you make to him, he will understand as meaning that if a given prescription for an experiment ever can be and ever is carried out in an act, an experience of a given description will result, or else he will see no sense at all in what you say."[3]

In this statement, Peirce contends that a significant idea is always an "assertion" or a "proposition" about some determinate situation or subject-matter. He holds that an assertion, an hypothesis, a proposition, or an idea, has a dual function. On the one hand, it *prescribes* an experiment or an act to be tried out; on the other, it *describes* an experience or a condition that will follow when the idea—the meaning—is put to the test of action. Thus an idea or a meaning is at one and the same time a plan for an action to be performed, and a prediction of a result.

An idea is therefore intrinsically prospective in character: it asserts that if these definite things are done, these definite results will follow. The having of an idea, or the making of an assertion also involves the making of inferences—that is, present and given things are taken as the signs of future and absent things. In other words, thinking is a process in which given things are taken as the ground, the evidence, or the sign, of future things, or occurrences. Without the use of things as signs, no mind, for mind denotes the ability to use present and given things as reliable indicators of future and possible things.

But these conceived or projected possibilities can be tested and turned into actualities only by the means of action. An idea is therefore not only an expectation of a result; it is also a defined

---

[3] Charles Hartshorne and Paul Weiss, *Collected Papers of Charles Sanders Peirce*, Vol. V, (Cambridge, Mass., Harvard University Press, 1934), pp. 272-73.

plan of treating or acting on certain materials or conditions in order to bring an anticipated result, or consequence, into existence. Hence our statements make sense—they are possessed of significant meaning—only as we are aware of what they signify for action. Without this reference to behavior, or experience, a statement is a verbalism; it is void of genuine intellectual significance.

In his article, Peirce generalizes this insight into what has come to be known as the *operational* theory of concepts. He contends that for a mind disciplined in the practices of experimental inquiry, the meaning of a concept—the rational purport of any term or proposition, lies exactly in its "bearing upon the conduct of life." He states:

> Endeavoring, as a man of that type naturally would, to formulate what he so approved, he framed the theory that a *conception,* that is, the rational purport of a word or other expression, lies exclusively in its conceivable bearing upon the conduct of life; so that, since obviously nothing that might not result from experiment can have any direct bearing upon conduct, if one can define accurately all the conceivable experimental phenomena which the denial or the affirmation of a concept could imply, one would have therein a complete definition of the concept, and *there is absolutely nothing more in it.*[4]

The great merit of this operational theory of the nature of a concept is that it brings together into a coöperative partnership two factors—"sensory experience" and "reason"—that our rival traditions of empiricism and a priori rationalism have tended to separate and to oppose to each other. In the operations of experimental inquiry the subject-matters of ordinary experience and the world of meaning, made possible by the development of concepts, are shown to have dynamic continuity. Experiment is action within the context of some empirical subject-matter, but it is also action that is guided by an idea. The idea, or hypothesis, is the product of both knowledge and observation. It originates as a possible response to the observed characteristics of the problematic or doubtful situation, it is elaborated

---

[4] *Ibid,* p. 273. Italics in the original.

and refined in imagination by the utilization of concepts and meanings developed in previous experience, and it is ultimately either rejected, or put to the test of overt behavior.

Experimental activity is thus not mere random physical manipulation of things; neither is it a self-enclosed process of ratiocination. It is reflective activity—a controlled procedure in which inferences are made by the disciplined use of observation and reason—by use of the companion processes of induction and deduction. We think, only as we think experimentally, that is, in terms of actions to be performed. Meanings or concepts are functional in nature. They are primarily properties of behavior, and, by extension, they become properties of things that have become known through having been subjected to experimental treatment. We may be said to know things when we can predict the manner in which they will behave—that is, the effects or consequences they will produce when brought into specified connections with other things. All meanings are meanings of— we have the meaning of a thing or a situation, not when we have simply memorized the name by which it is designated, but when we know what to expect of it, how to behave with reference to it, and what can be done with it.

The educational implications of this functional, or operational, interpretation of meaning are fundamental. In order to communicate a meaning to a child, it is necessary to do more than to put a sound into his ear, or to get him to learn how to spell or pronounce a word, or to read a sentence. Words are not ideas, or meanings. These verbal forms or terms have their referents in the behaviors of things and persons; we grasp their intellectual significance only as we acquire an appreciation of the concrete conditions and behaviors for which they stand.

Unless we are to burden the young with meaningless catchphrases—sheer verbalisms—that may deaden their intellectual perceptions and weaken their capacity for thought, we must provide them with the experiences that will communicate the life significance of that which they are expected to learn from oral and printed sources. As the modes of living and making a living in our present-day industrial civilization tend to lessen the opportunity of the young for direct participation in the life activities of their society, the obligation of the school to provide a program of rich and varied primary experience becomes ever more urgent.

These primary activities of observing, manipulating, doing, exploring, and making, as well as the opportunity for pupils to coöperate in significant life projects, are not made a part of the work of the school because educators want to relieve children of the rigorous demands and disciplines of the life of intelligence. On the contrary, these experiences are now provided in the curriculum of the school, because in contemporary industrial society they have been so largely subtracted from the life the young now lead outside the school. The crucial point is that without this body of primary experiences, we simply do not have the conditions essential to the growth of meanings—of mind. Nothing is deeper in the life of the person than his characteristic ways of responding to conditions and people, and no education meets the moral test which fails to provide for this medium of primary experience in and through which immature human beings achieve the modes of their personhood. Experience is the ultimate source of human competence and intellectual authority; a school that fails to provide these primary conditions for the growth of mind is immoral—it fails to treat children as ends in themselves.

§ 5. Dewey's View of Activity and The Nurture of Mind

Respect for the child and concern for his present happiness and welfare were undoubtedly important considerations in the minds of those who led in the development of the experience, or activity, curriculum. Scientific study of child behavior had demonstrated that children, with their restless and abundant energy, have a more satisfying experience when they are engaged in purposeful, group activities, than when they are isolated, confined to fixed seats, and subjected to endless routines of drill and memorization in a formal school situation in which study and learning are measured by the ability of the child to re-cite assigned lessons in prescribed textbooks, and the good pupil is defined as the docile child who adjusts to the fixed regimen of the classroom without making trouble for the teacher. But deep as was their concern for the present happiness and welfare of the child, the pioneers in the activity curriculum were fully aware that these more immediately satisfying experiences would be gained at too dear a cost if they were attained by the sacrifice of his deeper intellectual needs and potentialities. Nor did the emphasis on the all-round growth of the child—emotional, social, and moral, as well as intellectual—imply that the development of the intellectual powers were not primary in the new educa-tion. This emphasis on the primacy of thought in the nurture of the young has been expressed by Dr. Dewey.

> The sole direct path to enduring improvement in the methods of instruction and learning consists in centering upon the conditions which exact, promote, and test thinking. Thinking *is* the method of intelligent learning, of learning that employs and rewards mind. . . . Processes of instruction are unified in the degree in which they center in the production of good habits of thinking. While we may speak, without error, of the method of thought, the important thing is that thinking is the method of an educative experience. The essentials of method are therefore iden-tical with the essentials of reflection.[5]

The moral insistence of the new education that we cease viewing childhood as a mere preparation for a remote future and seek instead a school that would increase the meaning of present experience, was not the product of indifference to the demands of adult life; it was rather a product of the insight that the best possible preparation for the future is found in the most significant living in the present. This conviction, of course, is the correlative of the faith that a satisfying and rich experience in the present necessarily involves growth in meaning—in mind.

---

[5] John Dewey, *Democracy and Education* (New York, The Macmillan Co., 1916), pp. 179-80.

Nor were the educational views of the founders of the activity curriculum the result of a lack of appreciation of the intellectual and moral worth of the social heritage. Their conception of the social genesis of human personality necessarily points in another direction. The pioneers in the philosophy and psychology of the new education believe that the child literally learns his distinctively human attributes by virtue of his membership in a human society. It was Dewey, not a traditionalist in education, who wrote:

> It is of grace not of ourselves that we lead civilized lives. There is sound sense in the old pagan notion that gratitude is the root of all virtue. Loyalty to whatever in the established environment makes a life of excellence possible is the beginning of all progress. The best we can accomplish for posterity is to transmit unimpaired and with some increment of meaning the environment that makes it possible to maintain the habits of decent and refined life.[6]

No one with this regard for the rôle of culture in the nurture of human beings, could have been uncertain about the importance of providing opportunity in the life of the school for the young to learn that which man has achieved through all that he has undergone, suffered and enjoyed. As a matter of fact, it was concern for cultural and intellectual values, not indifference to them, that led Dewey to experiment with an activity, or experience, curriculum. He was searching for a theory and practice of education that would take account of revolutionary developments in the intellectual and moral outlook of modern man.

He perceived, first, that any thorough-going adoption of the evolutionary point of view involved a reconstruction of the classical view of the nature of human experience and the nature of man. When human experience is viewed as "certain modes of interaction, of correlation, of natural objects among which the organism happens, so to say, to be one," it has no place for

[6] John Dewey, *Human Nature and Conduct* (New York, Henry Holt and Co., 1922), p. 21.

the earlier dualistic assumption "that experience centers in, or gathers about, or proceeds from a center or subject which is outside the course of natural existence, and set over against it: it being of no importance, for present purposes, whether this antithetical subject is termed soul, or spirit, or mind, or ego, or consciousness, or just knower or knowing subject." [7]

Once this dualistic view of human experience and mind is abandoned, the conception of knowledge as the view of a "spectator" must also be discarded. We gain knowledge not by making a photograph, or a copy, of an external object. If meanings, as Peirce had affirmed, are intrinsically operational in nature, Dewey perceived the assumption that there can be knowledge by immediate acquaintance, by a mere process of beholding, or by sheer intuition, was untenable. We gain knowledge not by gazing at things, but by having interactions with them, and by discovering the connections they sustain to other things. Knowledge is acquired through experience, and experience is not a process in which a subjective mind beholds or intuits an external world; it is, as Dewey has emphasized, an active process of doing and undergoing—a process in which we do things to the environment and the environment reacts on us, and we make connections between that which we do and that which we undergo. In other words, we get knowledge in and through activity, and without activity there is no acquisition of knowledge.

Dewey also recognized that a dynamic conception of learning was involved in this functional view of experience and meaning. We learn as we experience—as we have interactions or transactions with our environment. Habits and attitudes are inevitably developed as we experience and adjust to the qualities of the diversified affairs that constitute the environment. But although learning is involved in all experiencing, not all learning is of the kind that results in the apprehension of meaning,

---

[7] John Dewey, *Creative Intelligence* (New York, Henry Holt and Co., 1917), pp. 30, 37.

and in the growth of mind. Activity becomes meaningful—intellectually significant—only as we consciously apprehend and retain the connections between that which we do and that which happens as a result of what we do.

If it be true that the self or subject of experience is part and parcel of the course of events, it follows that the self *becomes* a knower. It becomes a mind in virtue of the distinctive way of partaking in the course of events. The significant distinction is no longer between the knower *and* the world; it is between different ways of being in and of the movement of things, between a brute physical way and a purposive, intelligent way.[8]

The meaning of freedom resides in this distinction between experience as brute, physical involvement in "the movement of things," and experience as a purposive, intelligent way of interacting with the course of events. Obviously this distinction is foundational in Dewey's conception of the relation of thought to activity. Our acts are *free*, not simply because they are not under constraint from others, but because they are becoming *intelligent*. They become intelligent as they grow in their grasp of meanings. We become free as we *learn* to *think*. And the heart of thinking is the capacity to make inferences that enlarge our ability to control events in the interests of human well-being. There can be no growth of freedom without activity, because there can be no growth of mind without activity. But there can be a type of activity that does not result in the significant enrichment of meaning. We grow in the knowledge that means power to do—freedom—only as we use our experiences, our activities, to form reasonable expectations. We grow in our capacity to form reasonable expectations as we grow in our ability to use given conditions as signs of future consequences and to control our behavior in accordance with these forecasts of future occurrences.

Utilizing these conceptions of the nature of experience and of the relation of knowing—cognitive experience—to the

---

[8] *Ibid*, p. 59.

doings and the undergoings, the sufferings and the enjoyments, the attractions and the aversions, the loves and the hates of primary experience, Dewey undertook the development of a theory of the nature and pattern of reflective thinking. For Dewey, the long search of man for a dependable method to control the course of his own intellectual activity has culminated in the logic of discovery and testing inherent in experimental inquiry. In his logical studies he has distinguished the five phases or aspects of this process of experimental inquiry, and in his theory of education he has sought to develop an educational practice that is grounded in this analysis of the pattern of reflective thinking. He describes the essentials of this educational practice as follows:

First, that the pupil have a genuine situation of experience—that there be a continuous activity in which he is interested for its own sake;

Secondly, that a genuine problem develop within this situation as a stimulus to thought;

Third, that he possess the information and make the observations needed to deal with it;

Fourth, that suggested solutions occur to him which he shall be responsible for developing in an orderly way;

Fifth, that he have opportunity and occasion to test his ideas by application to make their meaning clear and to discover for himself their validity.[*]

Thus for Dewey, the cultivation of thinking is central in his view of both the ends and the means of education. His demand for an activity curriculum was a demand for a school program better designed to foster the intellectual powers of the young. He perceived that thought was inquiry, and that inquiry could be real for the child only as it was grounded in problems of felt significance, and that the school therefore should provide the conditions for the purposeful pursuit of ends as well as the opportunity for the exploration, the utilization, and the ordering of means for the attainment of these ends.

---

[*] John Dewey, *Democracy and Education* (New York, The Macmillan Co., 1916), p. 192.

Nor was this emphasis on *inquiring,* something that was hostile to *acquiring.* On the contrary, *inquiring* was approved because it was believed to be the essential method of *acquiring,* particularly of the acquiring of the kind of knowledge that means power. Meanings that signify increased power to function—to predict and to control—cannot be poured into children as water is poured into empty containers; neither are meanings acquired by a process of mechanical addition, they are, rather, developed in the process by which present experience is purposefully reconstructed. It was the insight of the founders of the activity curriculum that this kind of reconstruction cannot be carried on by adults for the young; without the purposeful participation of the young in the program of the school this meaningful reconstruction of experience does not take place. The problem and the art of education therefore is to provide the conditions in which the young will be encouraged to engage in those complete acts of inquiry—of reflection—by which new meanings and new powers of control are developed.

It is this form of purposeful reconstruction of experience that signifies the growth of mind. And this kind of reconstruction finds both its stimulus and its test in the varied affairs of primary experience. An educational program therefore that is concerned to treat individuals as ends, will also be a program that is concerned to provide all of those conditions which are essential to the nurture of their minds, that is, the conditions through which individuals develop the capacity to learn from their own first-hand experiences. A primary moral responsibility of the school is to provide opportunity for those complete acts of thought in which knowledge is gained as a result of that which the children do and undergo. The deepest discipline of mind results when the young *acquire* because they are encouraged to *inquire.* To be most fully educative the realms open to inquiry should be co-extensive with the life affairs of a human group. Whenever we block inquiry, we block the means through which minds are developed in the young.

It may be that to carry through this kind of reconstruction of the school will involve a parallel reconstruction in our society, for at present there are important groups in American life that resist inquiry into the spheres of their special interest. But a democratic society ought not to shrink from undertaking any reconstructions in its group affairs that are required to enrich the quality of the experience of its individual members. Since a democratic society has no good other than the good of individual human beings, the ultimate test of all of its institutions should be the definite consequences they produce in the lives of its members. To preserve a democratic society grounded in respect for all men, involves us in the unending effort to provide those conditions both in our social arrangements and in our schools, through which human beings can achieve that liberation of mind which is freedom.

CHAPTER VIII

The Morality of Inquiry

IN THE previous chapter, we have stated that the deepest moral issue in education is whether we shall treat each child as an end in himself, or whether his growth is to be subordinated to the maintenance of some pre-established system. We have also emphasized that the characteristic of a democratic program of education which distinguishes it from all authoritarian programs, is the fact that it seeks to make the growth of each child the supreme objective. In the morality of democracy growth is the ultimate criterion because a democracy recognizes no good other than the good of individual human beings. It is this opposition to the sacrifice of the potentialities of the child to the requirements of any absolute system that gives significant moral meaning to the maxim that "growth is its own end."

§ 1. *Group Nurture and Individual Growth*

But to say that "growth is its own end" is not to say that "growth" defines itself, or that the child should be left to develop in his own way. Nor is this *moral* individualism to be confused with the individualism of an atomistic social system in which each individual is a law unto himself. The good life is a community affair and its ways are learned, not inborn. As we have emphasized throughout this book, adults organize and maintain schools because they are convinced that the immature human being needs help in his efforts to attain the means of his own development. The most basic of all these adult contributions to the growth of the child is the provision of the conditions that will help him achieve a mind of his own. By growth of mind is meant growth of the capacity of the individual to have ideas, to form reasonable expectations, to make good judgments, and to take responsibility for the consequences of his deeds. Without this capacity for reflective behavior, a human being is less than a complete person. All authoritarian systems of education at some point or in some manner seek to curb this full intellectual development of the young. Insofar as a program of education molds the child so that he is deprived of his ability to inquire into a particular sphere of human experience, it confiscates some of the potentialities of his personhood.

We have also emphasized that the capacity to make good judgments—the capacity for reflection—is not an original endowment. Apart from the nurture of culture, human creatures do not acquire the meanings that enable them to share in the life of reason. Any program of education, therefore, that is committed to the development of the intellectual potentialities of the young must provide for the transmission of race experience. Democratic societies should, of course, strive to transmit their values in such a manner as to provide for their further development, but this does not make the rôle of transmission in a program of democratic education any the less important. Without the transmission of meaning there can be no significant nurture of mind, and we misconstrue the whole nature of the process of human development when we assume that freedom and individuality can be intelligibly opposed to social nurture and the communication of that which the group has achieved.

Experience also clearly shows that the immature acquire meanings—scientific, aesthetic and moral—as a result of their participation in group activities as well as by their study of printed materials. Indeed, learning from books attains its maximum possibilities only when it is associated with opportunity for direct experience in human affairs. We educate for intelligence—the capacity to make valid judgments—not by insistence on the mechanical rote learning of that which others have discovered and organized into systems of life and thought, but by providing varied means for the child to grow as a result of his own first-hand experience with the affairs of his physical and social surroundings. It is by virtue of this direct participation in the world of persons and things that each human being achieves the structure of habits, meanings, and appreciations that is required to provide him with a basis for his own individualized reponses to the practices of his society.

A mature mind cannot be developed by a program devoted solely to the instruction of the child in meanings derived from the experiences of others—a program that excludes all opportunity for criticism and for learning from direct observation and experience. Books can do much to broaden and deepen the perspective from which we interpret our own life circumstances, but they do not constitute a substitute for direct experience. Knowledge of what the intellectual and moral leaders of mankind have thought can nourish imagination and help free us from provincialism and parochialism, but it cannot in and of itself provide the core of personhood. Background is background, and to become a mature mind one must have done more than accumulate a stock of verbal generalizations; he must also have had experience with those primary events from which all generalizations or principles have been developed, and within whose context all principles must be applied, tested, revised and expanded. Apart from perception of their connection with conditions of primary experience, scientific principles and moral generalizations are not apt to function as tools of understanding; they are likely to become a non-functional, verbal possession or burden.

In brief, to become persons, we must own our ideas and not be enslaved by them. We grasp the significance of meanings that others have discovered and formulated only as we master their functional value in our own experience. Hence, education for the growth of persons must be a process in which acquiring and inquiring—the study of human records and participation in life affairs—are so interrelated in the experience of the developing child that the knowledge he acquires about the world becomes a real part of his ability to function in that world.

To hold that primary experience is essential to the development of mind is also to hold that empirical or experimental procedures should constitute the basic method of the school in a democratic society. Now the selection of the method by which the young are to be educated is one of the most crucial decisions in the organization of a school. No single factor has greater influence on the development of the basic intellectual and emotional dispositions of the young than the pattern of the method which permeates and regulates their mode of experiencing and interpreting their surroundings. In the course of their experience, human groups have developed rival and conflicting methods of responding to life conditions and of interpreting the significance of human events. Each of these modes of behavior, analysis, and interpretation has its basic intellectual and moral presuppositions; each inescapably has its definite consequences in the life practices, attitudes, and allegiances of those who are nurtured under it. The choice of an educational method therefore involves more than a choice among rival pedagogical devices; it is literally a choice among basic life alternatives and it is attended by far-reaching moral consequences. If educators are concerned to keep faith with parents, they will not try to conceal the intellectual and moral consequences of the method, or methods, that the school uses in the nurture of their children. In this chapter, we shall seek to make explicit some of the moral factors involved in the consistent reliance upon empirical procedures in the education of the young.

§ 2. Empirical Method and The Nurture of The Young

Man lives in a world in which he has to act. And the aim of any program of education governed by respect for human personality is to help each child make his own actions more meaningful and more effective. All parents want their children to grow in their ability to form "reasonable expectations," to behave responsibly, and to take a creative rôle in the activities of their society. They also want them to develop competency in some particular sphere of human activity. They recognize that direct participation in life activities is required if their children are to achieve these abilities and attitudes. To this extent, at least, the choice of an empirical method for the education of the young is not an arbitrary choice; it is in line with that which experience shows is essential to the welfare of man.

As a matter of fact, all schools, regardless of their formal theories about educational method, necessarily give considerable place to empirical and experimental procedures. Experimental attitudes and methods have become so dominant in certain areas of human experience that reliance on alternative modes of gaining knowledge and control has all but disappeared. This shift in life outlook and method in so many different fields is now exerting profound influence on our view of the way in which children should be educated in these fields.

For example, if a school is to teach the children to garden, it will make every effort—irrespective of whether the school is private or public, religious or secular—to provide for an actual experience in gardening. The young will be given experience in marking the field into garden plots, in the preparation of the soil for planting, in the selection of seeds and plants, in the cultivation of the soil to keep it soft and to prevent the growth of weeds, in the use of fertilizers, in the control of the various means of irrigation, in the use of sprays and powders to destroy parasites and insects, in the protection of the plants against animals, in the pruning and the staking of plants, as well as in the gathering and caring for the fruits and vegetables as they mature. Manuals that outline the general principles of gardening, along with special tracts that give details about the cultivation of particular plants will be used, and these may well lead eventually into more systematic studies and lectures on plant life, the chemistry of the soil, and similar technical or scientific topics. Training may also be given in the use and the care of the different materials and tools that are involved. These special instructions—printed and oral—are indispensable for the nurture of the young in the knowledge and techniques of gardening, but their use in the introduction of the young to the art of gardening does not signify a blind reliance on tradition or external authority. All of this information has been accumulated from experience and experiment, and it has functional bearing and sensed significance for the children because it is taught in connection with an activity in which they are directly engaged. The young, moreover, have opportunity to put the directions they receive from lectures and printed materials to the test of action. In connection with their own gardening activities, they are encouraged to observe and to evaluate what happens, when under specified conditions, certain definite operations are performed.

In sum, in the sphere of gardening it is universally recognized that all controlling principles are developed from within the matrix of the activity itself, and that the young can achieve the ability to care for growing things only as they have first-hand experience with them. The children learn to garden with skill, understanding, and responsibility by direct sharing in the process; they grow in their capacity to form "reasonable expectations" by participating in the how and the what of the art of gardening. Through this participation—informed and broadened by what others have previously discovered—the children develop their own ability to order concrete means to accomplish significant outcomes.

This growth through experimental inquiry may be contrasted with learning from sheer trial and error, with slavish adherence to tradition and precedent, with reliance on external authority, with random activity, with all forms of wishful thinking, as well as with memoriter processes in which learning is construed as a passive acquiring for the purpose of the mere re-citing of prescribed lessons. The empirical principles and

methods that are utilized in teaching the young the art of gardening are now recognized by most schools to hold for learning in
many other fields. Few schools, for instance, would seek to nurture the young in the various sciences without opportunity for
observation and first-hand experience through field trips and experimental work in the laboratory. The laboratory is now considered an essential part of the equipment of the ordinary high
school, just as workrooms and playgrounds are also coming to
be considered indispensable in providing opportunity for primary experience during the earlier years.

No school would attempt to teach children to play basket-
ball, tennis, or any other game, by simply having them read
books or listen to lectures by experts. Nor would we expect
children to learn how to behave in their relations with other
human beings apart from immediate experience with them.
Knowledge of people may be greatly enriched by the study of
anthropology, history, biography, novels, and dramas, but all
that is acquired from these literary sources is necessarily sifted,
interpreted, and evaluated by the young in terms of that which
they have experienced and learned as a result of their own intercourse with their fellow human beings. The principles that hold
for learning how to garden, to play games, to develop understanding in the various natural sciences, and to coöperate in
group affairs, are now also accepted without question by both
religious and secular schools in the education of the young in
domestic science, in the various skilled crafts, in the operation
of tools and machines in industry, in the interrelated fields of
nursing, dentistry, and medicine, in various community undertakings, and in the different fine arts. In all of these areas we
recognize that creative acts require acquaintance with conditions,
materials, and tools, and that knowledge, standards, and regulative principles must be evolved from the actual field of practice. As one field of human experience after another thus
becomes autonomous, it inevitably becomes permeated by experimental practices and outlooks, and the manner in which the

subject-matters of these different fields are conceived and communicated to the young are modified accordingly.

§ 3. *Experimental Inquiry and Patterns of Thought*

Parents and teachers miss the deeper significance of this empirical trend both in life and in education, if they do not perceive that it involves more than the mere increase of bodies of knowledge to be transmitted to the young and the development of new techniques in which the young must be trained if they are to be at home in the affairs of their society. Actually, this shift to experimental procedure and authority denotes a transformation in human experience that is breeding a new human mentality. It is because these new life attitudes are becoming established in the practices of the community that they are beginning to pervade the deliberate education of the young. The child who is learning by his own participation in experimental practices is not only acquiring new techniques, skills, and items of information, he is also acquiring an altered view of man and of the relation of man to his world. In fine, he is acquiring a new human outlook, for the outlook that is molded by a life practice that has become experimental in nature has its very definite characteristics.

It has in the first place a more vivid recognition of both the necessity and the possibility of human control. It is time that all who desire the young to grow in this capacity to understand and to control, came to realize that the experimental practices which the schools must use in order to nurture these abilities have deeper implications. The child, for example, who is learning to grow plants in order to help assure a human food supply is also learning that nature is so constituted that it will not take care of him apart from intelligent effort. In other words, he is learning, contrary to certain traditional views, that nature is not one, it is many; and that evil is not an illusion or a mere appearance, but a real trait of existence. So far as gardening is concerned, nature is a collective name for a variety of conditions, some favorable and some unfavorable to human interests. From the standpoint of the child's purpose to have a productive garden, these natural conditions have to be discriminated and dealt with, not in a wholesale, but in a piecemeal fashion. Seeds, soil, water, sunlight, and fertilizers are all natural things and they can be used as means to help further the life purposes of the gardener, but weeds, parasites, pests, killing frosts, droughts, and cyclones are equally natural, and they are the kind of natural forces that can destroy crops and frustrate human purposes. Through his daily experiences the child is learning that control is a function of an intelligent, discriminatory response to this plurality of conditions—friendly and hostile—we call "nature." Nor do the facts of man's experience show that this struggle for control is unreal, because affairs are so arranged that essential outcomes are assured regardless of the effort human beings put forth. Apparently the processes of nature that operated to bring human life into existence, also operated to produce many conditions antithetical to human existence. Man can survive and attain a satisfactory experience only as he learns to master these conditions. Implicit in the effort to achieve control through empirical means is the recognition that man lives not by passive trust in nature, but by the creative use of the conditions of nature for his own purposes.

Few teachers nowadays in either religious or secular schools will permit a child to substitute magical practices for the use of natural cause and effect relationships in the care of his garden plot. Few will permit him to rely on supernatural powers to water his garden; they expect him to get this result through empirical or natural means. Nor will the manifestation of a humble and contrite spirit in the life of the child be accepted as an adequate substitute for the exercise of intelligence and industry on his part. In the project of gardening teachers will not accept as satisfactory any alternatives of this type. The child is required to work and to try to get desired outcomes by the intelligent control of concrete, objective conditions. Society, having reached the conclusion that gardening involves mastery over definite empirical conditions and procedures, demands that its teachers nurture the young in the knowledge and the practices that are essential to this mastery.

But parents should recognize that as the school daily relies on procedures of this sort, it necessarily breeds in the minds of the young the experimental outlook inherent in these practices. This experimental outlook rejects the wholesale optimism that assumes nature is so biased in favor of human interests, that intelligent effort on man's part is not continuously required. It also rejects the wholesale pessimism or fatalism that assumes natural conditions are so stacked against human interests, that man is doomed to fail in spite of all his efforts to achieve a control that makes a humane existence possible. The experimental practice leads instead to the recognition that we live in the kind of world in which success is contingent. From the standpoint of human interests our world is a mixture of resources and obstacles; it must be accepted for what it is, an affair of affairs. In this plural world existence is precarious, and human well-being depends upon our ability to comprehend these diverse affairs and to learn how to use them on behalf of human interests. This recognition of the necessity of control is an attribute of the mind nurtured in experimental practices.

§ 4. The Seat of Intellectual Authority

The mind that has been molded by experimental inquiry has, in the second place, a definite conception of the meaning of truth. Truth denotes truths, and truths are not properties of existences, they are rather properties of human ideas about the nature of existences. As we emphasized in the previous chapter, an idea or a meaning is operational in character. An idea is significant if it defines (1) an action definite enough to be performed, and (2) an occurrence or an experience that will take place when the idea is put to the test of action, or experiment. It is by these operational criteria that the truth of an idea is tested. For an idea to be true, it must be valid in both of these aspects; it must define an act that can be carried out, and it must also define a condition that actually will come into existence when the prescribed action is carried out. In brief, ideas, or assertions, are warranted—they have the property of truth—if they verify when they are tested by experiment. Truth denotes accurate prediction. We have knowledge in any given field when we can predict how things in that field will behave under certain specified conditions.

This means that the mind nurtured by experimental procedures places the seat of intellectual authority within, not outside, the empirical procedures by which ideas are developed and tested. To return to the situation of the child learning to garden; a valid idea about gardening is not measured by the aesthetic appeal the idea makes to the mind of the child; nor is it measured by how fast his heart pounds and how hot his blood becomes when he contemplates the majesty of his vision, or intuition— the validity of the idea is not measured by any of these subjective feelings, but rather by what the idea actually leads to in the world of objective action. Unless an idea is responsibly defined as an operation to be performed—as a means adapted to some specified end—it will be dismissed as of no intellectual worth by those who are concerned with the practice that is gardening. Daily in our schools children are being taught in many different areas to think in terms of action, and to test their ideas by their consequences in action.

Similarly, no matter how exalted the person, the institution, the tradition, or the book from which an idea is derived, if the idea when put to the test of actual practice in the garden —to the crucial test of experiment—fails to produce the conditions or the consequences that it as idea predicts, it will be held invalid. On the other hand, no matter how lowly the source from which an idea comes, if the idea can make good in actual practice, it has worth and validity. For the mind habituated to empirical procedures both the meaning and the truth of an idea are internal, not external, they are internal to the operations by which they are subjected to the test of existence.

Experimentally established principles, to be sure, may be revised or even discarded by subsequent inquiries. All "truths" are subject to this correction by later developments and investigations, but this does not lead the experimental mind to retreat to external authority, or to seek refuge in the attitude of wholesale skepticism. The primary faith and security of the experimental inquirer is not lodged in this or that particular scientific finding or principle, but rather in the empirical method by which all beliefs are developed and tested. When the views of Newton are amended by the verified insights of an Einstein, the new situation in physics is readily accepted; it is viewed as a further triumph, not a defeat, for the procedures of experimental inquiry. In a world in which change is real, it marks a great human advance to have achieved a method of confirming beliefs that escapes alike the dogmatism of absolute, fixed truth, and the paralyzing skepticism that holds all views are equally worthy, or unworthy, because all alike are mere human opinions and all may be modified by the findings of later investigators. The experimental mind is the mature mind in the sense that it can operate on the basis of probability; it retains its confidence in the worth of intelligence in a world that makes knowledge a human necessity, and yet denies absolute finality to any particular human conclusion. For the empirical thinker many ideas and ideals have earned the right to our firm adherence, as they have been confirmed by a long experience, but none can be exempt from further scrutiny if developments call them into question.

§ 5. Experience and Moral Standards

The experimental mind, in the third place, believes that values evolve within the course of ordinary experience. They have a natural basis and origin because man is a creature of interests, and he has to react selectively to his surroundings in order to maintain these life interests. Men become intelligent

about values as they become intelligent about their actions—
about the conditions upon which they depend, about the consequences to which they lead. As Dewey has emphasized, not all
of the things that are immediately liked are likeable, nor are all
of the things that men desire really desirable.[1] The difference
between the merely "desired" and that which is counted "desirable" is the difference between organic impulsive acts, and
those acts whose conditions and consequences have been in-
spected, evaluated, and judged to be good. The latter activities
are considered desirable or valuable not simply because of their
immediately prized qualities, but because they are judged to
harmonize with other valued interests and to "lead-on" in such
a way as to expand, not contract, the totality of significant
experience, meaning and activity.

For the mind nurtured in experimental practices, morals
and values do not constitute a separate realm and subject-
matter. Since consequences cannot be separated from conditions,
judgments about values cannot be divorced from judgments
about facts. A human being can make an intelligent manifestation of preference only as he has knowledge of the concrete
conditions that are involved in his various activities. The child
who is learning through empirical procedures to discriminate
the better from the worse in the different mundane spheres of
human activity is, at the same time, growing in capacity for
moral judgment. It is in and through these varied and interrelated life activities that the real occasions for moral decision
arise, and the child grows in his capacity to function as a responsible moral agent as he grows in his ability to make judgments of the good and the bad in terms of concrete consequences.
Moral behavior is thus a function of the entire experience of the
child, and all education is inescapably a form of character
education.

This capacity to judge life practices by their concrete conse-

---

[1] John Dewey, *Quest for Certainty* (New York, Minton, Balch & Company, 1929), pp. 260-261.

quences is what is meant by a reflective or experimental morality. It may be distinguished, on the one side, from a customary morality which automatically accepts the standards that happen to be current in the practices of a society as the norms for human conduct, and, on the other, from an authoritarian system of morality which holds that ordinary human beings are not qualified to develop their own governing principles, and therefore must rely on a supernatural source or other external authority to provide these controlling standards. An experimental morality is also to be distinguished from the formal and myopic morality that bids men to cling to such abstract and absolute principles as "right for right's sake," and "duty for duty's sake," without regard for actual consequences. The difficulty with an abstract morality of this sort is that it ignores the fact that men never act in a vacuum, but always in a definite life context, and that he who follows "right" and "duty" without empirical analysis and evaluation of consequences is most likely permitting others who know what their concrete interests are to determine the actual meaning of "duty" and the specific content of the "right." Finally, a reflective morality is to be distinguished from that of the cult of spontaneous self-expression—that is, from the practices of the group which identifies self-expression with impulsive activity that is not regulated by a regard for conditions and consequences. A reflective morality recognizes that the good life is a life within a human community, and that the desires of the individual must not only be reconciled with one another, but also with those of his fellows who share a common experience.

The young, nurtured today in empirical, experimental procedures that foster the disposition to judge all actions by their consequences, naturally find it difficult to turn to mystical and authoritarian modes of making value judgments. Intuitive and authoritarian modes of behavior simply do not harmonize with the life habits and attitudes of those who have been led by their own primary experiences to the conviction that in order to be moral you have to be intelligent, and that in order to be intelligent you have to take critical account of actual life alternatives.

§ 6. *Empirical Method and the Search for Causes*

Finally, and possibly most fundamental of all, the mind nurtured by experimental procedures develops a mode of response that has no place for unconditioned events. The experimental theory of knowledge is grounded in the empirical, operational test of meaning. It assumes that ordinary events are so involved in one another that certain conditions or phenomena may be reliably taken as the evidence of other conditions and developments. It also assumes that even the most *extraordinary* events are *ordinary* events, in the sense that we must seek to explain and understand them in terms of their operations—that is, in terms of the empirical conditions from which they arise, and of the empirical consequences to which they lead. In other words, the basic postulate of experimental method is that we get meanings—knowledge—by the process of referring consequences to conditions and conditions to consequences, and by no other method whatsoever. Without this resolute determination to seek for causes, meanings, and means of control within, and not outside, the course of observable occurrences, the expanding body of organized knowledge by which we increasingly regulate our activities would be deprived of its methodological foundation. It is this emphasis on unity of procedure in all realms of experience that is the distinctive mark of the experimental method. Its successes have been won by its steadfast refusal to turn the search for causes and explanations into a mystery by the introduction of non-identifiable and non-describable, and hence non-controllable, agencies.

Consider, for instance, the effort to discover the nature and the cure of cancer. It would be simple of course to declare that cancer is an evil that is due to the invasion of the body by an army of "demons," but science refuses to resort to this kind of explanation. Its interest is in knowledge that gives power to control, and that kind of knowledge about cancer comes only as we succeed in locating and describing the actual empirical conditions and processes that result in the definite developments in the human organism that we call cancer. No matter how difficult and costly the search, science continues to seek for causes that can be subjected to this sort of experimental description and prescription. Should it abandon its effort to refer "effects" back to determinate conditions and operations, it would abandon the process by which "reasonable expectations" are developed and powers of control are extended. Such an abandonment of empirical method would signify a retreat from the ways of reason, it would mean the betrayal of the procedures that are mind. This faith in methodological continuity—in a method that can operate in all realms of human experience—is implicit in all educational efforts to get the young to become responsible, mature minds through reliance on empirical, experimental procedures. The commitment to the methods of experimental inquiry involves commitment to this empirical outlook. As one of our foremost students of the logic of scientific method states:

It is frequently asserted that the principle of scientific method cannot rule out in advance the possibility of any fact, no matter how strange or miraculous. This is true to the extent that science as a method of extending our knowledge must not let accepted views prevent us from discovering new facts that may seem to contradict our previous views. Actually, however, certain types of explanation cannot be admitted within the body of scientific knowledge. Any attempt, for instance, to explain physical phenomenon as directly due to providence or disembodied spirits, is incompatible with the principle of rational determinism. For the nature of these entities is not sufficiently determinate to enable us to deduce definite experimental consequences from them. The Will of Providence, for instance, will explain everything whether it happens one way or another. Hence, no experiment can possibly overthrow it. An hypothesis, however, which we cannot possible refute cannot possibly be experimentally verified.

In thus ruling out ghostly, magical, and other supernatural influences, it would seem that scientific method impoverishes our view of the world. It is well, however, to remember that a world where no possibility is excluded is a world of chaos, about which no definite assertion can be made. Any world containing some order necessarily involves the elimination of certain abstract or ungrounded possibilities such as fill the minds of the insane.[2]

Thus experimental method not only postulates universal causation, it also has definite criteria by which it defines the characteristics that a thing must possess if it is to be accepted as a causal factor or agency. The compulsions, the efficacies, the correlations, and the sequential bonds that we associate with the principle of causality are held to be within, not outside, the course of natural events. The determination not to try to explain either physical or human phenomena by resort to extra-empirical agencies such as demons, angels, fairies, witches, and ghosts marks not merely a great change in our methods of seeking "practical" control; it also is associated with the dawn of a new human mentality. Not all areas of human experience have been penetrated by this empirical outlook, and there are groups who still contend that the moral and spiritual interests of the human race depend upon our refusing to permit the experimental method and outlook to achieve universal dominion. Before teachers and parents will be equipped to evaluate these so-called "moral" and "spiritual" claims, it will be necessary for them to perceive that experimental inquiry is not only a method of "practical" control, it is also a pattern of moral behavior. The morality of experimental practice marks a new approach to the problem of discovering, testing and reconstructing the principles by which men live.

§ 7. *Morality and The Socialization of Inquiry*

Undoubtedly much of the prestige of scientific inquiry derives from the success it has achieved in expanding the power of human control in so many different areas of human interest and need. But the claims of the method of experimental inquiry rest on *moral* as well as on *practical* grounds. Man is a creature of belief, and his operating beliefs about existences and values

---

[2] Morris R. Cohen, *Reason and Nature* (New York, Harcourt, Brace and Co., 1931), pp. 158-59.

constitute the very core of his personhood. Human beings have often shown by their deeds that they are the kind of creatures who are willing to sacrifice life itself for that which they believe and value. As current conditions tragically demonstrate, differences of belief and value both within the same nation and between different nations frequently result in antagonisms that make coöperation for common ends difficult, if not impossible.

To the extent that beliefs are acquired automatically and are held dogmatically, they tend to foster stubborn, aggressive, and even fanatical behavior. Scientific inquiry signifies an effort to reduce the rôle of fanaticism in human affairs by removing arbitrariness and dogmatism from the processes by which beliefs are acquired, tested, revised, held, and communicated. Experimental procedures tend to result in this more rational behavior because of the extent to which they have socialized the process by which beliefs about questions of fact and value are developed. These socialized procedures of experimental science contain significant moral implications. They are frequently subjected to attack by moralists whose own methods are actually morally inferior to the very experimental procedures they attack—inferior because they are less socialized and hence more subjective, intuitive, and arbitrary. One of the most impressive tendencies of our period, has been the growing readiness of peoples in all parts of the world to adopt the empirical methods and the socialized attitudes of experimental inquiry. The moral characteristics of a method that has been able to evoke this universal human response in a period marked by intensified national rivalry, and by a growing conflict of cultural values, are worthy of serious consideration. Experimental procedure is grounded in the perception that the attainment of knowledge is a process from which the human factor cannot be eliminated. Recognizing the inescapable rôle of fallible human agents in all efforts to get knowledge, experimental inquiry seeks to get rid of an arbitrary individualism by the deliberate and the coöperative control of the process by which men reach conclusions and establish beliefs. One of the ways by which it gets this result is to open the process of inquiry to all who have competence in the field, irrespective of nationality, cultural tradition, race, sex, class status, religious affiliation, or geographical location. In other words, experimental inquiry seeks objectivity through universality, and it seeks universality through reliance on procedures which are equally available to all who are concerned to conduct investigations in a given area. It is opposed to all attempts to make a private monopoly out of the procedures by which knowledge is gained.

In a world marked by rival and infallible systems of supernatural revelation, by conflicting group folkways and mores, by alternative sets of "first principles," by competing institutional authorities, by divergent intellectual and moral intuitions, as well as by rival deliverances from what is known as "common sense," experimental method undertakes a new approach to the problem of developing and testing beliefs. It recognizes at the outset that the fallibility of human experience cannot be overcome by refusing to admit its existence through the assumption that we have privileged, transcendental roads to knowledge, or by any kind of procedure that makes the source or the parentage of an idea or a belief the test of its validity or authority. It lodges the authority of a principle, a value, or a belief not in the nature of its originating source—be it supernatural revelation, hallowed institution, mystical experience, the so-called laws of the mind, the intuitions of the heart, necessary axioms, or "common sense" —but rather in its actual working, that is, in its observable outcome or consequence.

When the priests of a fanatical order, during the Boxer trouble, told the Chinese leader, General Yuan Shih-kai, that his men need have no fear of foreign guns and bullets, because their magical rites had taken all potency from these foreign weapons, Yuan ruthlessly disposed of the dispute by lining the priests against a wall and subjecting their claims of magical control to the actual trial of bullets fired at them from the alleged impotent foreign guns. Most operational tests are not so cruel, simple and final as this, but they, nevertheless, have an authority against which the dogmas and the intuitions rooted in the mere superiority of origin or source are not able to stand. The fact that everybody knew by "common sense" that the earth was flat, was not sufficient to make that belief prevail when men demonstrated the world was round by sailing around it. The public deed settled the private and subjective doubts.

It should be noted that this shift from first principles and sources to ultimate consequences does not eliminate the human factor from the process by which we discover and test beliefs. Experimental method gains its control over the personal human factor by socializing and in a sense democratizing the manner in which that factor plays its rôle in the process of inquiry. Human beings have no part in determining the cultural groups and traditions into which they are born, but irrespective of these factors of group birth and membership, scientific inquiry invites all to join the community of those who verify beliefs by the observation of their workings and the evaluation of their consequences. Beliefs from any source are welcome, provided their sponsors are willing to have their credentials put to the test of operational procedure. On the other hand, no belief is its own warrant, no matter how exalted its source. In this crucial respect all beliefs stand on the same footing—all must be subjected to the test of an experience that is experimentally directed.

This is not to say that those untrained in particular fields can directly check the diagnosis, the operations, and the results of the experimental work of experts in those fields. But the growing tendency of the lay public to commit itself to the procedures of the expert is not a blind faith in authority. A farmer may not know how the hybrid seed corn is produced, but he can nevertheless judge of the results when it is substituted for the earlier seed corn. A patient is frequently unable to observe and interpret the data on which the surgeon relies in his diagnosis, but he trusts the surgeon with his life because he has come to trust the empirical and public methods and controls under which the surgeon serves. The increasing demand among medical leaders for universal autopsy is further evidence of this tendency to bring the work of specialists under the control of competent observers. The authority of the expert is an authority that rests, in the last analysis, on the empirical and public character of the methods by which he works and produces his results.

Experimental method also seeks to promote the ends of objectivity by the exclusive reliance on data and procedures that can be identified and observed by all concerned to work in a particular field. Thus the opposition of empirical method to private, esoteric data and processes is not an arbitrary thing. It is a function of the demand for a public procedure that seeks to eliminate the subjective and the arbitrary by opening the avenues of inquiry to all interested investigators. The same concern for objectivity lies back of the demand for a full and accurate public record of each experiment. This record with its description of the factors involved in the problem, of the definite actions undertaken, and of the concrete results attained by the experiment, supplies an account of the undertaking that makes it possible for others to check on both the procedures and the findings. The unwillingness of the experimental worker to "cook" his data, or to over-extend the generalizations he draws from the data of his experiment are also aspects of the morality implicit in a public, coöperative method of conducting inquiries. The fact that all scientific findings are regarded as tentative because they may be corrected by the work of later investigators is further recognition that the principle of socialization should be extended to include not only the inquiries of our time but those of generations yet unborn.

At no point does the morality of experimental inquiry make more exacting demands than in its mode of treating doubt. It seeks security of belief not by suppressing doubt, but by making a constructive use of it. Minds habituated to the principles of experimental activity do not seek to minimize or to override the objecting case, or factor. On the contrary, they cherish those ele-

ments that resist the existing explanatory principle or law, because these objecting factors can be made into *objects* for further
observation and inquiry and may become the means of new
knowledge.

Thus experimental method demands of its adherents the
intellectual and emotional maturity to recognize that our most
cherished beliefs are not absolute—they may be revised, reconstructed, or even discarded, by the results of further study. For
the experimental mind security of belief is not sought by cling-
ing tenaciously to tradition and precedent, by asserting that
whatever is in line with our preferences must be true, nor by
holding to dogmas in spite of evidence; it is rather gained by
eliminating doubt through the resolute pursuit of inquiry until
that inquiry culminates in conclusions that are indubitable—
indubitable because they cannot be doubted significantly by any
responsible inquirer. In a world in which change is real, intellectual and moral security is attained, in the first instance, by
putting our confidence in public experimental methods of testing
existing beliefs, and, secondly, by giving our allegiance to those
beliefs that demonstrate they are trustworthy because they have
gained a real consensus in and through the process of open and
untrammeled inquiry.

But the tentative attitude of experimental inquiry is not to
be confused with an attitude of indifference or of wholesale
skepticism. Faith in the process of "winnowing and sifting" is
actually faith in the possibility of attaining knowledge. The open
mind of experimental inquiry does not denote the empty mind.
As the history of modern research science indicates, the self-
correcting procedures of experimental inquiry are the best means
known to man of furnishing the mind with beliefs worthy to
organize and direct human experience.

Experimental inquiry reaches unity of belief, not by reliance on external authority and suppression of difference, not
by persuasion through propaganda, not by the individualistic
process of inner intuition, but by universalizing the community

of inquirers, by confronting and utilizing doubt to test and expand beliefs, and by employing empirical and public data and methods that foster uncoerced coöperation in the search for knowledge and standards. Through the use of these procedures, experimental inquiry has socialized the process by which man comes to know. The morality implicit in this socialized method of attaining belief defines a primary objective in any program of education concerned to treat human beings not as mere means, but as ends in themselves.

CHAPTER IX

The Morality of An Open Society

DEMOCRACY is a movement of plural moral meanings. We believe that the deepest of these is its regard for the worth of human personality. According to the democratic conception, individual human beings constitute the realm of ends, and all social and political institutions, including the state, pertain to the realm of means. One of the distinguishing characteristics of a democratic society is that it recognizes flesh and blood human creatures as the only centers of value, and it therefore knows no good, and it has no moral purpose, other than the enrichment of the lives of individual human beings.

We have emphasized that a democracy interprets respect for human personality to involve, as its most significant meaning, respect for the mind of the individual. It expects each person to play a responsible part in the determining of the system of laws and institutions under which he lives. Thus in its regard for the ordinary citizen the most benevolent system of paternalism falls far short of the ethical standard implicit in the democratic principle that government be of, by, and for the people. Government through the participation and the consent of the governed is prized not simply because it secures, in the long run, the most just and progressive laws and institutions, but also because it provides the conditions necessary for the growth of mature human beings.

§ 1. *The Meaning of Education for Human Freedom*

These basic democratic principles carry significant implications for the education of the young. They mean, as we have indicated, that the growth of the child constitutes the controlling moral aim of a democratic program of education, and this process of growth is so conceived that primary emphasis is given to the cultivation of the intellectual capacities of the individual. In a democratic society, neither concern for the perpetuation of an established set of institutions, nor concern for the achievement of a projected program of social reconstruction, can justify a scheme of training or indoctrination which curbs the opportunity of the child to learn to think for himself—to develop a mind of his own.

But this emphasis on the growth of the child through the nurture and the liberation of his intellectual powers does not imply, as some have asserted, that educators in a democracy are morally precluded from any and all efforts to commit the child to a definite pattern of social living. A free society in which the individual members are expected to share in the basic procedures by which the group ways of living are determined is not a form of anarchic individualism, nor is it an atomistic system in which individuals live as hermits isolated from one another. On the contrary, a democratic society is an organized form of human association, and this coöperative mode of human living has its distinctive characteristics and its necessary moral foundations. Experience clearly shows that a society in which men strive to live together in peace and coöperative activity under their own laws and institutions, as well as under their own freely chosen governmental leaders, is a society that makes exacting moral demands on all of its members. The citizens of this kind of a society have their responsibilities as well as their rights; their common and controlling loyalties as well as their personal freedoms and opportunities.

Moreover, these principles of democratic life and thought are not inborn. They are acquired, as we have repeatedly emphasized, only as the child learns them through a directed course of experiencing. Any educational program that is genuinely committed to the life of freedom and intelligence, must in moral consistency be prepared to nurture the young in those group behaviors and life attitudes that make this life of freedom and intelligence possible. Educators do not manifest real loyalty to the democratic way of life whenever they pretend to be morally neutral about the means required for the perpetuation of that way of life.

But we err greatly if we assume that education in and for democracy can be reduced to a simple program of authoritarian imposition. A democracy is not only an *organized* society, it is also an *open* society. By an open society is meant a society that deliberately seeks its own improvement, not the mere perpetuation of the *status quo*. A democratic society is organized to take account of the fact of change in human affairs; it accepts change not as a sign of inevitable decay, but as a natural condition that intelligent, coöperative effort on the part of all its members may be able to turn into an occasion of growth and human progress. A society which thus deliberately strives to improve its own ways of living through the free use of knowledge and invention is necessarily a pluralistic and a dynamic society. It not only accepts and tolerates minorities, it is grounded in the realization that minorities have an indispensable and creative rôle to play in the evolution of the common ways of living.

It is at this point that a democratic society differs fundamentally from all authoritarian or totalitarian systems. It does not seek to suppress inquiry and criticism; on the contrary, it legalizes these social practices. It recognizes that these processes of inquiry, of proposal, of discussion and criticism are indispensable factors in any society that aims not at the preservation of inherited arrangements, but at their peaceful reconstruction in the interest of the good life for all of its members. But a society that gives legal protection to the processes of inquiry, criticism, and institutional reconstruction, can maintain its unity and its stability only as its members have certain common loyalties, and certain universally accepted means of defining their governing purposes and of conducting their public affairs. In brief, an "open" democratic society has its own distinctive group procedures and morality.

In this chapter we shall be concerned with an analysis of the characteristics of an "open" or democratic society with particular reference to the implications of its patterns of life and allegiance for the education of the young.

§ 2. Democratic Education and Established Institutional Forms

In a democratic society, as in all others, adults organize and maintain a system of schools in order to guide the development of their young. Through their duly chosen representatives on the community school board, they employ teachers to take charge of this educational work. Since these teachers are the paid agents of their society, and hold positions of public trust, it is obvious that something other than private interest and preference should govern their educational activity. But to say that teachers have a public function in a democratic society does not automatically define the standards by which that function shall be discriminated and judged. Nor is the problem of the rôle of the teacher adequately clarified when we adopt the social interpretation of education, and say that the primary responsibility of the teacher is to introduce the child to the ways of life and thought of his society. We still have to define what the distinctive patterns of a democratic society are, and we also have to determine the definite means by which the young are to be equipped to take part in the ways of this society.

The record of education in America makes it quite clear that different groups have had somewhat different conceptions of the nature of the public responsibilities of the teacher in our democracy. Some hold that the answer is simple. Teachers are, according to their view, the hired agents of the public, and hence it is their duty to nurture the young in whatever beliefs and institutions are established in their society. Indeed, a number of very powerful groups in our country tend to take this view of the matter when the fundamentals of their own particular system of beliefs and practices are involved. It is not difficult for the leaders of certain groups to identify the welfare of the whole community with the perpetuation of their own favored institution, and to assume that if the attitudes, the beliefs, and the loyalties involved in the established practices of this system or institution are bred into the emotional and the intellectual dispositions of the young, the good of our democratic way of life will necessarily be served.

Thus certain leaders of American business have urged that the teachers have a high responsibility to nurture the young in the faiths, the principles, and the conceptions of social welfare inherent in the capitalistic, or private enterprise system. In the opinion of these business leaders, this is an eminently reasonable demand. They hold that the competitive, open-market system is a basic feature of American life; that its primary incentives are in harmony with the acquisitive instincts of human beings and thus automatically inspire each individual to the maximum of socially useful labor; that history shows most of our economic and social progress is due to the virtues of this competitive system; and that morally this enterprise system is the ultimate foundation of our whole system of democratic liberties, because all of our other freedoms—political and cultural—have no secure foundation apart from its economic rights and freedoms. Acting on these convictions, certain groups have succeeded in getting laws enacted in a number of states that require all teachers to take oaths of loyalty to the American system with the clear implication that the heart of the American system is the historic pattern of private ownership and enterprise. Special committees of business organizations have examined and condemned certain textbooks in the social studies of the schools on the ground that these texts do not provide a sufficiently positive view of the private enterprise system.

Nor is this tendency to identify the values of democracy with the values of a particular institution confined to business leaders. Members of church groups have from time to time taken a somewhat similar view of the public function of the school in American democracy. In their case the concern has been of course with the traditions and the outlooks of religion, not with those of the capitalist system. The leaders of certain fundamentalist sects have been particularly aroused by college and high school courses in biology which present evolutionary views of the origin of man that are not in harmony with the doctrines of special creation as given in the Bible. In support of their opposition to courses that include this evolutionary account of the genesis of man, these religious spokesmen have declared that the "rock of ages" constitutes a more authoritative and beneficent source of information than the "record of the rocks." They have affirmed that our country is a religious country; that its faith in the equality and dignity of all men is grounded in the recognition that all alike are children of the same Spiritual Being; that our democratic regard for the worth of personality and human brotherhood is dependent upon our continuing faith in this spiritual interpretation of the universe; and that without the moral basis provided by their system of revealed religion our democratic way of life possesses no secure foundation. In a number of states these church leaders have even succeeded in getting legislatures to enact laws prohibiting the teaching of any views in the school that are in conflict with the central doctrines of their tradition of supernatural religion.

Leaders of various patriotic groups have also shared this conception of the responsibility of the school and the function of the teacher in a democratic society. They have put on militant campaigns to get laws enacted that would both define essential meanings of democracy and prescribe certain subject-matters for the curriculum. Some of these laws have made "flag drills" and other patriotic exercises compulsory, others have required definite kinds and amounts of instruction in American history, in the Constitution of the United States, in the special responsibilities of the citizen, and the like. In certain states laws have been passed that require all discussion of alternative systems of government be excluded from the teaching of the school, particularly discussion of the Communist system of the Soviet Union. The Daughters of the American Revolution have had a leading part in this drive for American patriotism in the schools, and their view has been well summarized in an address of a former President General of that organization:

> We want no teachers who say there are two sides to every question, including even our system of government; who care more for their "academic freedom of speech" and opinion (so-called) than for their country. Academic freedom of speech has no place in school, where the youth of our country are taught and their unformed minds developed. There are no two sides to loyalty to this country and its flag. There is nothing debatable about allegiance to that flag and the Republic for which it stands.[1]

Simple and straightforward as is this demand that the young be inducted into the cherished beliefs and practices of the various pressure groups, it involves a view of the function of education that is open to grave objection when examined from the standpoint of the values of the whole democratic community. In the first place, a democratic society is a plural society, composed of many interest groups. These sub-groups are not of one persuasion touching many of these so-called "fundamentals." When teachers function as the servants of the interests of the most articulate of these groups, they may not be communicating to the young the values that are cherished by other and more numerous groups who are less skilled in the arts of propaganda. Thus, to make the schools docile spokesmen for business interests may make them hostile to the interests of industrial workers and farmers, or to make them the mere instruments of the supernaturalists may involve them in deep conflict with scientists and humanists, and to turn them into propaganda agencies for the narrow nationalism of chauvinistic patriotic groups, may make the schools quite unacceptable to those who

---

[1] Address by the President General in the *Magazine of the Daughters of the American Revolution*, 57 (May, 1923), p. 270.

believe that human survival now depends upon the development of a system of international coöperation and world organization.

But considerations of expediency are not the chief reason for rejecting this conception of the social function of the school. Plausible as the plan of having the teachers serve as the agents of established institutions and beliefs may seem to some of its advocates, it actually involves a negation of fundamental democratic principles. It violates the conception that each person shall be treated as an end in himself; it also violates the principle that a democratic society is a free society, open to continuous change from within, not a finished, closed, authoritarian system, determined to maintain the *status quo* regardless of changes in life conditions. Each of these objections is fundamental and merits more detailed consideration.

As we have seen, the essence of the effort to treat a child as an end in himself means that we strive so to direct his education that he will grow in his ability to think—to have a mind of his own. To be possessed of mind involves the ability to form reasonable expectations, and the ability to form reasonable expectations necessarily involves opportunity to learn to evaluate existing group beliefs and practices in terms of developments in life conditions. Each of the foregoing pressure groups wants to use the school to breed a mind in the child that is regimented to the pattern of interests that it considers fundamenal, and it also demands that its respective system of belief and practice be communicated in such a way that the child will not have a chance to get the knowledge that is required to judge of its present worth and validity. In other words, each of these groups in its own special sphere wants the mind of the child molded in its own pattern, but it does not want a mind developed that is qualified to judge of the worth of that pattern.

Although each of these pressure groups professes to be committed to the democratic life of freedom, it shows by its actual practice that it fears the most basic of all freedoms—freedom of thought. The reason that groups of this sort ask for laws to control teachers is because they have a system of special interest and behavior that they want protected against the processes of free inquiry. They appeal to the power of the state to prescribe the patterns of the curriculum because they want to prevent the young from having access to certain bodies of knowledge. Each pretends to have respect for human personality, but each advocates an educational practice that is incompatible with the full growth of the mature and independent mind. Actually there is no more potent way to confiscate the potentialities of personhood of the immature human being than to habituate him to a pattern of belief and conduct through a process of sloganizing his mind that keeps him from becoming acquainted with significant life alternatives in any given sphere.

The leaders of these pressure groups—economic, ecclesiastical, and patriotic—are apparently indifferent to the fact that children have real freedom to learn to think for themselves only in a school in which both pupils and teachers are free to inquire. They move to deprive the children and the teachers of this basic freedom of inquiry by bringing pressure to bear upon them, as well as by direct appeal to the authority of the state. In the realms where their special interests and values are involved they demand a loaded educational process—a process of nurture in which *acquiring* is shielded from *inquiring*. Whoever seeks to have the young acquire beliefs without at the same time providing suitable opportunity for them to inquire into the grounds of those beliefs, is negating the process by which the young mature into morally responsible—reflective—human beings. Although the outcomes sought may be sincerely believed to be good, the concrete educational means by which they are sought are authoritarian—they are not in harmony with the morality of an open society that makes the growth of its children the supreme educational objective.

These authoritarian educational practices constitute an offense not only against the individual child; they weaken the foundations of the whole democratic community. To the extent that they close the avenues of inquiry and discussion, they tend to undermine the confidence of a people that it can attain necessary reconstructions in its established modes of life and thought by rational and peaceful—non-violent—means. It is this faith in the possibility of maintaining social and political procedures that can make even revolutionary adjustments by peaceful means which is one of the most distinctive moral features of a democratic society. It is this sincere attempt "to institutionalize the process of revolution" that makes a democratic society a society that must forever be open to the processes of inquiry. Obviously a society that is open, not closed, has its distinctive moral patterns, and these patterns have definite and far-reaching implications for the education of the young. We turn now to a more detailed examination of the educational consequences of our effort to make and keep America an open, democratic society.

§ 3. *Democracy and the Legalization of Revolution*

The conception of democracy as an attempt to institutionalize revolution is not a recent idea. It is as old as our country for the fundamentals of this democratic conception are implicit in the instrumental view of the forms of government set forth in The Declaration of Independence. The authors of the Declaration clearly refused to merge society and government as is done in the totalitarian state. They believed that a people should be recognized as having certain rights which the government should not seek to abolish. They also refused to identify the great human ends of "life, liberty, and the pursuit of happiness" with any particular institutional form. So far as the institution of government is concerned, the Declaration holds "that whenever any form of government becomes destructive of these ends, it is the right of a people to alter or to abolish it, and to institute a new government, laying its foundation on such principles and organizing its powers in such form as to them shall seem most likely to effect their safety and happiness." According to the democratic morality defined in the Declaration of Independence, the supreme allegiance of the citizen is not to any specific pattern of social organization, economy, or government, it is rather to the principle of the general welfare and to the right of the people "to alter or to abolish" traditional arrangements whenever they judge them to be unsuited to the maintenance of their liberty, safety, and well-being. That Jefferson had in mind the social as well as the political implications of this assertion of the primacy of human welfare over particular institutional forms is evidenced by his substitution of the term "the pursuit of happiness" for the traditional emphasis of Locke and other political theorists on "security of property" as a basic end of government. Jefferson was not opposed to the system of private property, but he was concerned to distinguish the basic moral objectives of our nation from all such specific economic forms or means.

The Bill of Rights upholds this principle of the Declaration on the primacy of persons over institutional forms, but it goes farther and seeks to establish certain definite means by which the American people can within the framework of ordered government make real its sovereignty over its ways of life and thought. It seeks on the one hand to give security of the person against "lawless violence, arbitrary arrest and punishment." Later, as a result of the Civil War, this security of the person was held to be a universal human right and, in the Thirteenth Amendment to the Constitution, "slavery and involuntary servitude" were abolished, "except as a punishment for crime whereof the party shall have been duly convicted." The Bill of Rights also recognizes such basic freedoms as freedom of conscience and religious belief, freedom of speech, freedom to publish, and freedom to meet and to discuss. Obviously freedom of belief, of speech, of assembly, and of press were meant to imply the freedom to inquire and the freedom to associate, for without these two freedoms, the ones listed in the Bill of Rights would lack substance.

Now it is these civil and political liberties that provide the basic means for the maintenance of our American way of life. Loyalty to our democracy involves loyalty to these liberties, and loyalty to the social and political procedures they entail. Loyalty to these liberties and procedures necessarily involves opposition to any and all groups who would curtail the public processes of inquiry, discussion, criticism, and proposal in order to perpetuate an established doctrine or institution. The American people in the Declaration of Independence and the Bill of Rights gave classic expression to the faith that a democratic society is an open society, and that an open society can preserve itself only as it refuses to close the avenues of inquiry and criticism. This faith in the morality of "free trade in ideas" has been given memorable formulation in an opinion by former Justice Holmes of the U. S. Supreme Court.

When men have realized that time has upset many fighting faiths, they may come to believe even more than they believe the very foundations of their own conduct that the ultimate good desired is better reached by free trade in ideas—that the best test of truth is the power of thought to get itself accepted in the competition of the market, and that truth is the only ground upon which their wishes safely can be carried out. That, at any rate, is the theory of our Constitution. It is an experiment, as all life is an experiment.[2]

In other words, American democracy is committed to the experiment of maintaining a society in which the policies that are to govern will be determined by the voluntary response of the people to them, and this response of the people can be a genuine public verdict only as the processes of inquiry, proposal and discussion are open to all. Thus faith in democracy involves faith in the ability of the people to make their own determinations of the good. Anything that curbs the process of inquiry and communication distorts and obstructs the free de-

---

[2] Justice Holmes, *Abrams v. United States*, 250 U. S. 616, 624 (1919).

velopment of that public opinion by which the good is defined in public policy and enacted into law.

Nor is this means of determining the desirable and the valid, restricted to beliefs about so-called "practical affairs." According to the Bill of Rights the same freedom is to be exercised in the sphere of morals and religion. Thus freedom of conscience in ultimate objects of allegiance and belief is expressly affirmed in the First Amendment which declares that "Congress shall make no law respecting an establishment of religion, or prohibiting the free exercise thereof." As a national community we have no established religious institution, and we have no official religious creed. Freedom of religion has been repeatedly interpreted to mean the right to believe and the right not to believe. Our governing religious principle is unity amid diversity. Nor does the Constitution qualify either the right of citizenship or the right to hold public office by any religious tests whatsoever. Article VI explicitly states that "no religious Test shall ever be required as a Qualification to any office or public Trust under the United States." So far as citizenship and participation or leadership in the public affairs of our country are concerned, religion is held to be a private, not a public affair. It would therefore involve a change in the foundations of our society to make teachers in the public schools subject to religious tests of any kind.

The American public has a right to expect and demand that those who are to introduce the young to its ways of living shall be loyal to the foundations of our democracy. But these foundations have been defined in our democratic tradition in such a manner as to demand loyalty not to this or that particular institutional form, but rather loyalty to those more basic liberties and procedures by which the adequacy of all inherited institutions and beliefs are tested. In his personal beliefs a teacher may be a capitalist or a socialist, an individualist or a collectivist, a Jew or a Christian, a supernaturalist or a humanist, a nationalist or an internationalist, so long as he is considered qualified by those competent to judge of his scholarship and his educational methods to lead the young in those processes of discovery and test which are alike foundational in the life of scholarship and the life of a free society. This is not to say that what a teacher believes about these social and economic matters is unimportant, nor that his outlook on them will not influence his educational activity. Neither is it implied that the teacher is not responsible to achieve the most adequate view possible concerning these issues, nor that he can be indifferent to community attitudes on these questions. Our concern here is with another and different point, namely, that loyalty to certain definite intellectual and social procedures, not to particular institutional forms, or doctrines, is the criterion by which a democratic society should judge of the qualifications of the teacher.

This basic educational criterion of a democratic society has been affirmed from time to time by many educational authorities. One of the best of these formulations was given in 1894 by the lay members of the Board of Regents of the University of Wisconsin when they were being urged by certain pressure groups to dismiss an able economist, Professor Richard T. Ely, for his first-hand investigation into a management-labor dispute. After a thorough review of the case, the Board confirmed Professor Ely in his position and declared in its report that "whatever may be the limitations which trammel inquiry elsewhere, we believe the great State University of Wisconsin should ever encourage that continual and fearless sifting and winnowing by which alone the truth can be found." [3]

Freedom of inquiry is a valued human right. It is much older than Western democracy for many of the Greeks recognized with Plato that "an unexamined life is not one fit to be led by man." But in a democratic society this right to inquire is more than a private right; it is also a public necessity. As we have emphasized, a democratic society is an open society—it

---

[3] Quoted in Edward N. Doan, *The La Follettes and The Wisconsin Idea* (New York, Rinehart and Company, 1947), pp. 14-15.

seeks to deal with differences among its members not by suppression, not by resort to brute physical force, but by the rational adjustment of old views to make them conform to new knowledge, and by the peaceful reconstruction of inherited institutions through the coöperative action of those who live under them. Freedom to inquire, to discuss, to organize, and to advocate are necessary freedoms in a society that seeks to make its adjustments through peaceful means; that is, through the bold moral effort to institutionalize the process of revolution. The schools of a democracy should not only illustrate these practices in their modes of instruction; they should also seek to nurture the young in the disciplines, the attitudes, and the loyalties essential to the maintenance of this kind of an open society.

§ 4. The Morality of Due Process

The foregoing conception of a democracy as a society that seeks to determine the common good through the processes of public inquiry, group proposal, free discussion and a system of free elections has been dismissed by some as utopian. The argument on which their objection is based runs somewhat as follows. The disinterested search for truth may be a value for the favored few, but it is not the basic human value. All men, including scientific research workers, have interests more imperative and immediate than their interest in the search for truth. They are concerned, for example, about bread and security for themselves and their families. They are therefore primarily concerned about the means of their livelihood—about their businesses, their jobs, their professions, their farms, and their savings and investments.

In our interdependent society, moreover, the interests of the members of these different economic groups are often in conflict. There are serious conflicts of interest, for example, between owners and workers, between management and investors, between farmers and the people of the cities, between those engaged in competing industries in such fields as transportation, fuel, food, and the like, between factory and white-collar workers, between various regional and sectional groups with their specialized economic interests, between those who work in the public services and the taxpayers, as well as the ceaseless conflicts between groups of producers and groups of consumers. All men, it is asserted, are inescapably motivated by these concrete material interests, and a society therefore is not primarily a group of individuals bound together in a coöperative search for truth and the common good, it is an affair of conflict and struggle between these major functional groups each seeking its own advantage. Human intelligence is not an abstract principle of reason; it is a tool of these mundane interests, and it operates as a weapon in the endless struggle of groups to defend and extend their economic interests.

We also are told that we deceive ourselves if we assume that the democratic state is a neutral agency which can operate as an umpire above and outside of these conflicts, and which is able to pass impartially on the rival claims of these conflicting interests. The men and women in the legislatures, in the executive posts of the government, as well as the judges who serve in our courts, all come from these conflicting economic groups, and their conceptions of welfare—of the public good—are necessarily conditioned by the mentalities that their participation in these groups has bred in them. Indeed, they owe their very positions in the government to the activities and the votes of the members of these interest groups. It is therefore fanciful to suppose that a society dominated by these economic pressure groups can ever subordinate them sufficiently to make the maintenance of a system of free inquiry, free discussion, free education, and free elections an object of common concern.

Clearly there is much of substance in this criticism, and any theory which seeks to interpret democracy as the deliberate effort to institutionalize revolution must take account of the stubborn facts in which this criticism is grounded. It must be recognized at the outset that if free education is to rest on a solid foundation, it will not ground its enterprise in a conception that presupposes man is a creature of pure reason, devoted to the pursuit of the true and the good independent of the imperatives of human existence. Human beings are creatures of interest, not disembodied spirits, and the pursuit of truth in and of itself can never be made a substitute for the processes by which men get their bread, their security, and their opportunity for a share of the good things of life.

But the real issue is not whether man is a creature of interests, nor whether society is marked by conflicts not only between economic groups, but between racial, religious, nationality and cultural groups as well. These things are obviously a basic part of the picture, and any social or political theory that denies or ignores their reality has no claim on the attention of serious men.

The crucial issue, however, is whether the presence of conflicting interest groups in a society really cuts the ground from beneath the democratic faith in a free society that maintains itself through the continuous and peaceful reconstruction of its ways of living. Much depends, of course, on our preconceptions about democracy. If we assume that the democratic conception presupposes a society in which all conflicts between interest groups have evaporated, because the members of all these groups have abandoned their special interests and perspectives in a common devotion to something called the "public good," it is apparent that democracy is a fanciful theory not in harmony with the realities of human existence. On the other hand, if we recall that democracy did not emerge as the result of wishful thinking, but is rather the product of an actual historical movement that developed within the context of bitter struggles between human groups, we may reach a very different conclusion about its present prospects. We shall then view democracy not as an alternative or substitute for social struggle, but rather as the best means men have devised for the conduct and the control of the human struggle. Viewed in historical perspective democracy appears as a form of government that does not ignore the struggle between interest groups, but seeks to order that struggle within a basic political and legal framework. It tries to introduce intelligence into the struggle by getting the various groups to take a broader view of their interests. It also sets up a common authority that establishes rules that define and punish unfair practices in the pursuit of the struggle, and it seeks to nurture those common interests and loyalties that confine the struggle to peaceful and lawful—non-violent—procedures. Democracy, thus interpreted, is still in the nature of an experiment—not an assured thing—but it denotes an experiment of the greatest moral and practical significance.

It is important for educators to recognize that democracy is an actual historical movement and that it was evolved from within the clash of human interests. A democratic society is not a society of self-less men and women; it knows no "public good" that is anything other than the good of the members of its various component groups. These members have interests that bring them into severe conflicts with one another, and they often have divergent conceptions of the general welfare and the means by which it is to be promoted. But the distinctive thing about a democracy is that it seeks to adjust these differences, not by suppressing them by the police power of the state, but by providing opportunity for the conflicting groups to present their respective claims to the public as a whole. The policy that finally achieves the support of the majority of the elected representatives of the people becomes the public policy. This policy gains its ascendance by convincing members of the various sub-groups that under the existing circumstances it is superior to all alternative proposals in its provision for their interests. Devotion to the public good is thus not a devotion to an abstract principle of reason and morality; it is devotion to "the greatest good of the greatest number." But this is a real devotion and it makes its exacting moral demands on the members of all sub-groups, for the greatest good is determined not by a privileged, "elite" group acting for the people, but by the people themselves. The people determine the "common will" of their society not by automatic reliance on tradition, not by resort to force and the "smashing of heads," but by inquiry, criticism, discussion and resort to the ballot and the "counting of heads." The guiding principle in a democratic society is that all shall have opportunity to present their needs and their views to their fellows, but that any group which seeks to get its views adopted by suppressing the views of others is breaking with the morality of the democratic process and is therefore to be condemned and its views held suspect. Only those views—whether supported by ecclesiastical, military, business, labor, farm, lay, or professional groups—which are willing to meet competition in the open field of public discussion are considered to be worthy of the confidence of the public.

The procedures that govern the development of policy, also apply in principle to the selection of officials—to the making and the remaking of the group that constitutes the government. We primarily determine the general pattern of our public policies by the people we select to enact and administer our laws. In a democracy, at stated times, the leaders of the governing administration must go to the people, stand on their record in office, and compete with the candidates of rival parties in a free election for the right to continue to govern. If a rival group polls a majority of the votes, the authority and the leadership of the government is transferred into its hands. Even during their period in office, the leaders of the administration must submit their policies and proposals to the criticism of opposition groups. These opposition groups are an inherent part of the democratic system of government. They have their legally recognized status and functions. They cannot be suppressed without the destruction of the very foundations of the democratic state, for the legalization of an opposition is one of the elemental marks of a democratic society.

It is asserted, by some, that this democratic system can work only so long as it confines itself to the detailed reform of existing institutions—that it could not survive were it to attempt basic reconstruction of the major institutions of a society. In our period, this has generally meant that a democracy would destroy itself should it seek to change or supplant the capitalist system of private ownership. According to these critics, the ultimate loyalties of a people are not to the processes of an open, democratic society, but to their property interests, and a democracy survives simply because it evades this economic conflict—the deepest conflict of interests of our time. Certain groups on the "left" have a dual reason for rejecting the idea that any democratic society can reconstruct the basis of its economy by peaceful and legal means. They assert that in view of the present concentration of wealth, and the great power the owners of this wealth exercise over all means of communication—press, radio, moving-pictures, theater—it is utopian to suppose that a majority could ever become sufficiently informed and unified by democratic educational and political procedures to support a program for the socialization of the basic means of production. These spokesmen of the "left" also assert that even assuming such a majority could develop and were finally to succeed in electing an administration pledged to a program of drastic reconstruction of the economy, the transformation could not be achieved because the owners of productive property would in that event use their vast economic power to protect their interests against the acts of the duly constituted political government. In other words, these "left" groups dogmatically assert that the conception of the "institutionalization of revolution" is unreal, because no entrenched economic class would ever consent "to its own erosion" by legal, peaceful means. It would resort instead to some type of direct counter-revolutionary action.

In this connection, recent developments in the social and political life of Great Britain are worthy of careful study. With the organization of the Labor Party during the first decade of this century, the people of Great Britain have had a political party frankly committed to the principle of the socialization of the major means of production. In spite of gloomy predictions this Labor Party was not suppressed. On the contrary, it gradually grew to become the official opposition of His British Majesty's Government, and its parliamentary head was voted a salary for his services as leader of the official opposition. As a result of its economic program and its long campaign of adult education, the Labor Party increased its supporters and finally won a decisive victory in the general election at the close of the Second World War. The overriding issue in that crucial election campaign was precisely that of the socialization of major means of production. The victory was the more remarkable because it was won over the Conservative Party, a Party whose standard-bearer was Winston Churchill, the man whose courageous, able and resolute leadership had played such a crucial part in the struggle to save Britain and the civilization of Western Europe from the brutal forces of Hitler.

Once the results of the general election were known, Prime Minister Churchill sought an audience with the British King and turned in the seals of his office. He did this with full knowledge that the Labor Party which would succeed him in office was prepared to undertake a vast program of socialization. By conforming to the established legal procedure, Winston Churchill and his associates of the Conservative Party demonstrated their loyalty to the morality of democracy. Deep as was their allegiance to the capitalist system, the conservatives disclosed by their actual deeds that their ultimate loyalty was not to a particular institutionalized form—the system of private ownership of productive property—but rather to those democratic procedures by which the will of a people is defined, and its representatives are duly elected and clothed with the authority of government. Obviously, high political and moral maturity is required of any people thus to make the principles of democracy sovereign in their life practices, but without this devotion to democratic procedures, the values of a free society cannot be preserved.

One of the first responsibilities of the schools in a democratic society is to nurture the young in the historical perspectives, the loyalties, the techniques and the attitudes that blossom into this kind of political maturity and social morality.

§ 5. *Teachers and The Morality of Due Process*

It is apparent that the schools can nurture the young in the ways of life and thought of a democracy only as the teachers who direct their modes of experiencing and learning are devoted to those ways. Inasmuch as a democratic society is an open society committed to the processes of free inquiry, it is natural that teachers should be numbered among its sturdy supporters for in addition to their general interest in the democratic way of life, their own professional interests and activities lead them to cherish the values of freedom of thought and expression. We have already emphasized that lay educational authorities have a responsibility to support their teachers against those pressure groups who permit their interest in some existing system of belief and practice to lead them to demand that the freedom of teachers be curtailed. An open society has a dual reason for keeping its schools open to all of the processes that make for human enlightenment. There can be no adequate exercise of that "continual and fearless sifting and winnowing by which alone the truth can be found" in a society in which research and teaching are subordinated to forces external to them. Nor do the young have a real opportunity to learn the ways of freedom in an educational system that denies its teachers freedom to teach.

But the teacher in the educational institutions of a democracy has his responsibilities as well as his rights. Freedom of the teacher in research and publication as well as freedom to discuss his subject in the classroom, carries with it the responsibility for the teacher to be accurate and forthright in his statements, to have regard for the views of those who differ with him, and to take due account of the degree of maturity of his students. The teacher is also under the continuing obligation to give his pupils knowledge of the considerations of fact and value upon which his conclusions are based. In brief, the teacher is responsible to observe all those standards which competent scholars have discovered are essential to the maintenance of objectivity in both inquiry and teaching. The first concern of the teacher in a democracy is not to win disciples to his ways of thinking, but to nurture the resourceful and independent mind that can progressively accept responsibility for its own judgments.

During this period of social change and transition a further question has been raised about the freedom of the teacher. Suppose as a result of his studies a teacher becomes convinced that a socialist economy is required to secure that equality of condition essential to a democracy, and that he also believes this socialist economy is opposed by such powerful interests it can never be achieved by peaceful, constitutional means, but only through resort to direct, revolutionary action,—should this teacher be maintained in his educational position? The instance cited raises two questions: the nature of the right of revolution, and what, if any, limits should be put on tolerance in a democratic society.

Many eminent Americans have agreed with the view expressed in Lincoln's first inaugural address that whenever the people "grow weary of the existing Government, they can exercise their *constitutional* right of amending it, or their *revolutionary* right to dismember or overthrow it." It should be noted, however, that although Lincoln clearly affirms the right of revolution, he is careful to distinguish it from a constitutional right. Indeed in a subsequent message to the Congress, Lincoln declared:

Our popular government has often been called an experiment. Two points in it our people have already settled—the successful establishment and the successful administering of it. One still remains—its successful maintenance against a formidable internal attempt to overthrow it. It is now for them to demonstrate to the world that those who can fairly carry an election can also suppress a rebellion; that ballots are the rightful and peaceful successors of bullets; and that when ballots have fairly and constitutionally decided, there can be no successful appeal back to bullets; that there can be no successful appeal, except to ballots themselves, at succeeding elections. Such will be a great lesson of peace: teaching men that what they cannot take by an election, neither can they take by war; teaching all the folly of being the beginners of a war.[4]

The net conclusion would seem to be, as Madison stated, that the right to revolution is a moral, not a legal, right, and whoever plans to exercise it should be ready to take the consequences in case his revolutionary effort fails. The appeal to bullets in place of ballots may be morally justified under certain conditions, but no constituted democratic authority can or should be expected to recognize itself as a tyranny and to give its protection to those who conspire to destroy its established ways. In brief, tolerance is not an absolute in a democratic society— a democracy recognizes and legalizes the position of minority and opposition groups in its total procedures, but it demands that these minority groups rely upon persuasion and various forms of peaceful action to attain their ends.

But does the principle that thus defines and limits the right of political action groups also apply to the rights of belief? If so, what becomes of freedom of inquiry, and the freedom of the educator in a democratic society? Freedom of inquiry is necessarily suspect in any regime that prescribes in advance the conclusions that must be reached by those who inquire. Nor can the effort of teachers to nurture the young in the moral worth of peaceful, democratic procedures be morally effective if both parents and pupils are aware that any teacher is subject to immediate discharge once he entertains doubts about the adequacy of these procedures. If the young are to have confidence

---

[4] Abraham Lincoln, The Message to Congress in Special Session, 1861. Cited in Bernard Smith, *The Democratic Spirit* (New York, Alfred A. Knopf, Inc., 1941), p. 416.

in the integrity of those who guide their learning, they must not be encouraged to develop the cynical impression that their teachers are under coercion in the beliefs that they seek to communicate to them. As our Courts have on occasion recognized, there are important reasons for distinguishing between ideas and overt political deeds, and a democracy would do well to keep those teachers in their positions who sincerely believe that direct action may be required to achieve the life conditions essential to economic democracy. These teachers, however, have their responsibilities: they must be prepared to make their views public, to define the considerations of fact and of value on which they are based and to join in discussions with their students and their fellow teachers concerning these issues. In the last analysis, the freedom of the teacher is grounded in the faith of the public in the worth of the processes of inquiry, public discussion and criticism, and therefore no teacher can be exempt from the moral requirements of these public or socialized methods that are also the essence not only of democracy but of science and scholarship.

The foregoing has its implications for teachers who are connected with totalitarian political groups. At the present time, most people recognize that a Fascist teacher, that is, a teacher who is a member of a secret conspiratorial group operating as the agent of the leaders of a Fascist state, has no right to a position in the schools of our country. More uncertainty exists, however, about the status of the rights of a teacher who is a Communist, for the Communist Party is now recognized as a legal party in many of the states. Some educational authorities take the position that a teacher should not be discriminated against because of his membership in any political party of legal standing. But this is to hold that the standards governing those who are to introduce the young to our democratic way of life should not be other than those obtaining in the general political life of the country. This view may be the correct one, but it is certainly not self-evident.[5] A growing number in the educational profession are convinced that Communists do not now meet the essential educational standards of a democratic society.

Unfortunately, the issue is beclouded because of the loose way in which the term "Communism" is frequently used. There are those who are ready to label any person as a "Communist" who desires to bring about any change in the existing institutions of our society. It is clear from the foregoing analysis that those who condemn all efforts at reconstruction as subversive are themselves guilty of subverting some of the most fundamental of our democratic procedures and values. Democracy commits suicide whenever it lets those who favor established arrangements organize pressures that suppress and terrorize those who work in good faith to adjust our institutions to changing life conditions in order that they may better serve the life interests of the people. Indeed it is fair to say that the deepest threat to our democracy at the present time comes from those reactionary forces who in order to protect their privileges would turn our country into a closed authoritarian system. Parents and teachers must organize to protect the schools from attacks by these repressive groups. But educators also would do well at the same time not to underestimate the threat to democracy that is involved in totalitarian political practices on the so-called "left." If teachers are to enjoy the confidence of the public, they must convince the public that they are for democracy, and that they are prepared to defend the cause of democratic education against all who would subvert it, whether they be Fascist or Communist.

As here used, the term "Communist" is restricted to those who are adherents of the world Communist movement. There is such a world Communist movement and this movement has

---

[5] This is the position of the American Association of University Professors: Its Committee "A" states, "so long as the Communist Party in the U. S. is a legal political party, affiliation with that party in and of itself should not be regarded as a justifiable reason for exclusion from the academic profession."

clearly shown that it has certain incontrovertible features. For the adherents of this world movement, the first value is the Communist fatherland, and their controlling purpose is the achievement of world Communism through the protection and the extension of the interests of the Soviet Union and the countries now associated with her.

In the second place, there is much evidence to show that the governing policies of this movement are made and controlled by the leaders of Soviet Russia, not by the leaders of the various national Communist parties in the non-Communist countries. Consider, for example, the shift in position of the American Communists. During the past ten years they have been for the popular front in support of collective security against the aggressions of the Fascist nations; following the Soviet-Nazi Pact in 1939, they were opposed to all efforts such as lend-lease and universal military training that would help America get ready for her part in the world struggle; when Hitler invaded Russia two years later, the American Communists reversed their position, ceased fomenting strikes and stopped chanting the "Yanks are not coming"; they became instead super-patriots in the effort to mobilize America for full industrial and military participation in the war against the Fascist powers. Once Russia came under attack, the war against Hitler and Mussolini was no longer an imperialist war. When the war was over and America and Russia began to have differences about the patterns of the peace, the American Communists again attacked our foreign policy as imperialist war-mongering, and created an independent political movement to punish Truman for his support of the Marshall Plan for aid to Western Europe.

In the third place, the world Communist movement believes that it is in a holy war with the rest of the world. Its revolutionary end is held to justify any means required to win this war for what it considers the exploited people, and these means include concentration camps, slave labor for political dissenters and prisoners, the practice of wholesale deception, persistent conspiracy under the protection of civil liberties, savage attacks on social-democratic political movements and non-Communist labor leaders, character assassination, and whatever else will help in the struggle to confuse and divide the forces that do not unite with them.

Finally, the world Communist movement is a disciplined movement ruled with an iron hand by those who hold the official positions. No member can remain in good standing who refuses on the demand of the leaders of the Party to subordinate his mind and conscience to the line imposed from above. Loyalty to science and scholarship, to his colleagues in trade union, political party, school or college, as well as devotion to the interests of his own nation must all be made to conform to the world revolutionary cause as defined and redefined by the men in the Kremlin, and obediently accepted by the American Communist leaders. The wholesale repudiation by the American Communists of their former cherished leader, Earl Browder, is but one illustration of the power of this dictatorial control from abroad.

It is highly doubtful if the reasons of expediency that prompt certain of our leaders to call this movement an authentic American political party have been adequately considered. The desire to keep the movement above ground can be understood, but certainly great moral confusion is brought into the life of the American people, particularly its youth, when we accept the practices of the Communist Party as in harmony with the morality or the freedoms of the democratic way of life.

In any case, it is difficult to see how the educational system of our country can accept adherents of this world Communist movement as qualified to teach in our schools and to share in the introduction of the young to the American way of life. They are compelled by their allegiance as Communists to abandon the principles of science and scholarship whenever the Party line defines the "truth" in any given sphere; they must also change their views on social, political, and cultural matters whenever the line of their Party changes. They are forced by their membership in a conspiratorial group to conceal their real views and thus to deprive their pupils and their fellow teachers of the opportunity to share in honest discussion with them about subjects that are of the most basic concern. Nor is this all. Communists are actually possessed of a dual citizenship but, unfortunately, their citizenship in the land in which they live is subordinated in all crucial matters to their citizenship in the world Communist movement dominated by Soviet Russia.

Whatever may have been the case earlier, no teacher at the present time, intellectually competent to guide the young of our country, can be ignorant or innocent of the essential characteristics of this world Communist movement. He, therefore, can no longer be excused on the ground that his devotion to social justice and the welfare of the underprivileged led him innocently to become party to its activities. It is also clear that the morality of world Communism is in deep conflict with the morality of an open democratic society and those who are the adherents of the Communist morality are not qualified to nurture the immature in the practices essential to the American democratic way of life. Particular care must be exercised in the procedures by which a teacher is judged to be a Communist, but if it becomes clear beyond all doubt that he is a member of this movement, the educational profession should not seek to protect him in his effort to remain a teacher in the American school.[6]

As we shall indicate in a later chapter, coöperation between the United States and the Soviet Union is essential to world organization and peace, but this coöperation will have no stable foundation so long as the Soviet Union maintains and utilizes this world conspiratorial movement. The sooner the democra-

---

[6] Since the above was written, both the Commission on Educational Reconstruction of the American Federation of Teachers, and the Educational Policies Commission of the National Education Association, by unanimous vote have declared that membership in the Communist Party involves a surrender of intellectual integrity that unfits a person to discharge the duties of a teacher in American democracy.

cies of the world demonstrate that the attempt to divide and disrupt them by the use of these totalitarian political practices is not to succeed, the better the chance for genuine world organization.

CHAPTER X

The Morality of Function

WE HAVE emphasized that deliberate education is best understood when it is viewed as a social undertaking. It is social not simply in the sense that a school system is always maintained and controlled by a human group living at a definite time and place, but also in the deeper sense that the modes of life and thought of this cultural group inescapably condition both the purposes and the content of its program for the nurture of the young. The more therefore we know about the structure of a society and the process by which it changes, the better we shall be able to understand the nature and rôle of organized education.

§ 1. The Organic Nature of Culture

A society is neither an organism nor is it a mere aggregation of discrete interests and practices. Its various activities— technological, economic, social, political, scientific, artistic, religious and educational—have mutually conditioned one another in a common process of social development, and as a result they now function as an interrelated whole. In the totality of the ways of any human group no factor plays a greater rôle in shaping the pattern of the whole than its ways of *making a living*. As new inventions and techniques modify the ways by which a people makes its living, correlative adjustments have to be made in its system of social and political institutions. These changes in economic, social, political, and legal arrangements call, in turn, for changes in the group's conception of the rights and responsibilities of individuals and thus involve its basic moral code. Eventually, the program and emphases of the school are modified so as to take account of these transformations in the ways of living and in the moral outlooks of a society.

Although the above account of the general pattern of social change is in the main accurate, it tends to minimize the positive rôle of the non-material aspects of a culture. The knowledge and the moral attitudes of a people as well as their social and political institutions are not the mere passive "effects" of a self-regulating and predetermined process of technological and economic development; they also play a real part in shaping the course of cultural evolution. Thus a democratic social system committed to the worth of all men will adjust to the life conditions of industrialism in a pattern quite different from that of an autocratic system ruled by a class who considers "the masses" to be mere instruments of its interests and purposes. Both of these social systems will have to be modified in order to take account of the factor of economic interdependence that necessarily results from power production, but their respective social philosophies will profoundly influence the pattern of their response to this change in the ways of making a living.

Nor is it necessary that each cycle of significant change in a society begin with new inventions in the technological and economic realm. As the recent experience of the Soviet Union shows, it is possible for a group equipped with an understanding of the developments in modern science and technology in other lands to use its own agencies of government and education in order to bring about revolutionary changes in its inherited modes of production. In our interdependent world we may expect that this tendency of cultural groups to borrow from the discoveries and practices of other societies will increase. It is also possible that the rôle of technological and economic factors may become less decisive in social affairs as man's control over nature expands, and the problem of production becomes less coercive. Up to the present there has been a strong tendency for a more efficient system to supplant a less efficient system of production. This may not forever continue to be the case. If the social costs of "efficiency" become too great, other considerations may play a more important rôle. A democratic planning society conceivably could decide that sheer technical efficiency in production is only one of a number of factors that should be taken into account in the determination of the further evolution of its affairs. Present tendencies in city and rural redevelopment programs indicate that considerations of human decency and comfort are already playing a larger rôle in the total process of social development. As men become more aware of all the forces that influence their lives social evolution may become more consciously purposeful. Indeed, the moral implications of the concept of social planning may be fully as important as the economic.

The crucial point for the educator to grasp is that in any culture, the geographical, technological, scientific, economic, social, political, and moral factors are so interrelated that important developments in any one of these factors tend to spread to involve the others. The recognition that these departments are interrelated and mutually condition each other in the evolution of the life of a people does not, however, involve a denial of the central rôle of the ways of making a living in the affairs of a society. Man does not live by bread alone, but he cannot live without bread. And every department of human activity has its economic foundation. A human society is indeed much more than a group of people coöperating in a common effort to make a living, but the beginning of realism and wisdom in our thought about the human enterprise is to perceive that if a society is to survive, it can never be less than a shared way of making a living.

The problem of the good life remains what it always has been, the problem of achieving and organizing a common way of making a living which at the same time provides a basis for making a life worth the living. As we have seen, human beings achieve their development through the modes of their functioning, and their modes of functioning carry the greatest potentialities for personal growth and satisfaction when they are socially useful or productive. Today, our conception of productive work needs to be broadened, but we are convinced that it is in some form of socially useful activity, not in a mere passive enjoyment or a private use of leisure, that men will experience the richest opportunity for growth. The good life for the individual still remains a function of a community so organized that all of its members are sustained and sustaining partners in a diversified program of productive activity. Living as members of an interdependent human group, one of our deepest personal needs is to have the sense that we belong to the group and are needed in the activities by which the group maintains itself. Hence, the most searching test to be applied to any society is the functional test—that is, the measure of its success in providing opportunity for its members to engage in some recognized form of socially productive activity.

§ 2. The Need for a More Functional America

The discussion thus far has been couched in general terms, but it has its important implications for life and education in contemporary America. Our lives are disordered and uncertain, because our ways of making a living are disordered and unstable. Today many are insecure because they are not confident our country has a place for them in its productive activities. Many also are not sure that much which they now are asked to do in order to make a living is really necessary or desirable from the social point of view. Undoubtedly one of our deepest moral problems is to restore life significance and stability to our basic means of livelihood. This problem has both its international and its domestic aspects.

In this new atomic age, our major forms of production do not nurture an adequate sense of security and meaning in those who participate in them, because these activities are believed to be geared to a war economy. The average worker fails to find genuine life significance in a program of national production that is organized for the purpose of waging another world war, not even if the war be one of national defense. Many are therefore uniting in the demand that the vital interests of our own country be coördinated with those of humanity as a whole. This demand is involving us as a nation in a search for an alternative to war through a workable system of world organization. The bearing of this effort to develop a genuine system of collective security on the present task of American education will be explored in a later chapter. So long as we are haunted by the fear of an atomic war it will be difficult for the people of our country to clothe their life activities with full human meaning.

Our concern in this chapter, however, is with the domestic phase of the problem of production and employment. As a people we have much to do if we are to restore order and moral meaning to our own American ways of making a living. This problem of domestic reconstruction, moreover, is organically related to the larger problem of world security and peace. The record shows that industrial nations which fail to organize their increased productive powers so as to provide all of their own people with opportunity for steady work and an adequate income, have a strong tendency to try to resolve their domestic social and economic difficulties by a program of imperialistic and militaristic adventures. The outlook for the human race would be dark should America with its vast economic potential resort to this alternative in order to conceal its failure to solve its own internal problem. Many now believe that one of the most important contributions our country can make to world order and peace would be to resolve its problem of developing an economy that can sustain production and employment.

This task of economic reconstruction has its important educational aspects. We have already indicated that the problem of providing jobs and security for workers in their jobs is at heart a moral problem. But by designating the problem as a problem in morals, we do not intend to imply that it is one which can be resolved by simply working on the hearts and minds of individuals taken apart from the institutions in and through which they live. The school program for the nurture of individuals becomes formal and sterile whenever its guiding purposes are not wrought out in terms of actual life circumstances.

The re-ordering of our ways of educating the young therefore must be associated with the efforts of the American people to re-order their ways of making a living. No program of democratic education is worthy of the name which refuses at this time to accept responsibility for discovering the implications for individual human beings of the vast changes which the rise of industrialism has brought into our means of livelihood. Responsible nurture of the young must now take account of the new framework of life conditions that has been in process of development for many decades. The plain fact is that in the life arrangements of interdependent, industrial America, the morality of our historic system of economic individualism and the morality of our democratic system of respect for the individual human being have come into deep conflict. Unfortunately, the American people—businessmen, laborers, farmers, and members of professional groups—have not as yet achieved a common theory of welfare to serve in the place of the pioneer, individualistic philosophy which has become an irrelevance and an encumbrance.

A past that has largely disappeared from our ways of making a living, still lingers on as the operating pattern of morality in the life of the American people. Education can do its part to nurture the necessary new morality only as it grasps the nature of this split between the ways in which we live, and the social philosophy by which we seek to order our collective affairs. To overcome this split, a reformulation of the meanings of democracy must be achieved. This effort at reformulation will be less arbitrary and dogmatic if it takes account of certain factors in the historic experience of the American people—factors which have led us to associate the principles of economic individualism with the moral meanings of American democracy.

§ 3. *A Nation of Freehold Farmers*

One of the most powerful influences that has operated to determine the life attitudes of the American people is the fact that we began our experiment in democracy as members of a relatively small human group in a continent of rich and undeveloped natural resources. Indeed, it was this vast domain of uncultivated land, together with the physical isolation from Europe, that largely accounts for the failure of European feudalism to reproduce its hierarchical patterns in the new world. For more than 300 years of its history, America has been a country marked by an open frontier. During this long period, free land on the frontier meant that opportunity for a new start in the struggle for a life of economic independence and freedom remained literally open to the rank and file of the American people. Thus the older and more developed regions were kept in a state of continuous competition with the harsh but "free" conditions of life in the frontier West.

Life in a country with an open frontier left its imprint on the psychology of the American people. As Turner has emphasized, it accustomed us to look upon change as a normal phase of human affairs. For many generations Americans lived as members of a society that was constantly renewing its social arrangements as the zone of habitation steadily moved across the continent. The view that all social and governmental institutions are human instruments came more readily to those accustomed to the formation and the reorganization of their social and governmental agencies in order to meet the needs of their changing life situations.

The vast reaches of the virgin territory, the relatively large holding of the individual farmer, along with the fact that roads were few and poor, tended to encourage each farmer to live on his own farm, and thus in America the farmstead also became the homestead. For most of its history, America has been a society composed of these rugged, independent families, each living a sovereign life on its own piece of land. Gouverneur Morris is reported to have said in the Constitutional Convention of 1787 that "nine-tenths of the people are at present free-holders."

American democracy in both its social and political aspects was a product of these favoring economic conditions. These free-hold farmers of the new Republic were not governed by an out-side bureaucracy. Such governmental officials as they had were selected from their own ranks and most of these officials continued to cultivate and to live off their farms during their term in office. Custom provided for the regular rotation of many of these offices among the different farmers of the district. What held for those in political office was also true of many in the professional services—even clergymen and judges were expected to provide most of their livelihood from their work on their own farms. Alexis de Tocqueville who visited the young Republic in 1831-32 begins his classic work on *Democracy in America* with a statement about the remarkable equality of condition prevailing among the people, and the influence of that fact of equality upon their life attitudes and institutions. He reports:

Among the novel objects that attracted my attention during my stay in the United States, nothing struck me more forcibly than the general equality of condition among the people. I readily discovered the prodigious influence that this primary fact exercises in the whole course of society; it gives a peculiar direction to public opinion and a peculiar tenor to laws; it imparts new maxims to the governing authorities and peculiar habits to the governed.

I soon perceived that the influence of this fact extends far beyond the political character and the laws of the country, and that it has no less effect on civil society than on the government; it creates opinions, gives birth to new sentiments, founds novel customs, and modifies whatever it does not produce. The more I advanced in the study of American society, the more I perceived that this equality of condition is the fundamental fact from which all others seem to be derived, and the central point at which all my observations constantly terminated.[1]

---

[1] Alexis de Tocqueville, *Democracy in America*, American Edition, Vol. I, edited by Phillips Bradley (New York, Alfred A. Knopf, Inc., 1945), p. 3.

The America of the freehold farmer was not only a functional society marked by an unprecedented equality of condition, it was also well suited for the growth of faith in certain of the central doctrines of economic individualism. Although the principles of the laissez-faire system were not first developed in the United States, it is doubtful if any other people has given them such sincere and whole-hearted acceptance. As a result of their own life experiences, Americans were inclined to interpret democracy as a way of life that was grounded, on its economic side, in the practices of individualist enterprise. Indeed, many Americans have been disposed to regard the principles of economic individualism as the definition of the essential moral foundation of a free society. We shall examine, in the next section, major elements in this individualistic theory of economy and government along with factors in the experience of the freehold farmer which made it easy for him to view this system as nature's own system for the organization of human affairs.

§ 4. Private Enterprise in the Economy of Self-Sufficient Farms

One of the primary principles of economic individualism holds that each man naturally seeks the improvement of his own condition, and, since each person is the best judge of his own interests, he should be left free to work out his own means for taking care of himself and his family.

This principle was certainly foundational in the faith by which men lived and managed their affairs in pioneer and agrarian America. Each family had its own plot of land, and it determined what should be done for the development and the use of this holding. It decided, for example, where the house, barn and other buildings should be located. It determined their number and style as well as the kind of materials from which they should be constructed. Each family also worked out its own plans for clearing the land of forests, for the drainage of low-lying places, for the maintenance of a water supply, and for the cropping of its fields and the pasturing of its livestock. It decided the number of horses, cows, sheep, and pigs that should be raised, as well as the size of its various poultry breeds. Appropriate places were also reserved and prepared for the family orchard, the various patches of berry bushes, and the vegetable and flower gardens.

The farm was also a manufacturing establishment. The men made and repaired most of their own tools and furniture in the farm workshop, while the women made the clothing, the bedding, the rugs, the curtains, and similar household articles from cloth processed by their own hands from raw materials produced on the farm. In sum, the family-farm was, in the main, a self-sufficient economic unit—its food, clothing, fuel, shelter, furniture, tools, utensils, and adornments were largely supplied through the industry of parents and children in the fields and in the home. As one writer has remarked of this pioneer farmer "how little he bought, and how much he continued to supply his wants by home manufacture would astonish this generation."

Nor was this economic individualism and independence of the farmer an expression of a mean and selfish life attitude. These self-sufficient farmers were rugged individualists, both in activity and in thought, but they were good neighbors possessed of generous sympathy for their fellow pioneers. They were ever ready to help a fellow farmer in time of illness or other emergency, and they coöperated in many tasks, such as the raising of the frame of a building, which were more than the members of an individual family could easily manage by themselves. They worked together in providing some form of common defense against all who sought to prey upon them; they coöperated in the construction and maintenance of a common system of roads; they had their district school, their common religious meeting house, and their simple forms of government. But all of these coöperative activities of the community were incidental—each family was expected to stand on its own feet and to assume primary responsibility for its own livelihood and for its own advancement. In this important respect, the pattern of pioneer and agrarian America was in accord with that of the system of economic individualism.

Another basic faith of economic individualism is that through the automatic operation of natural economic laws, each individual is necessarily rewarded in proportion to his industry, his foresight, his managerial ability, his endurance, and his willingness to deny himself immediate pleasures and results for long-run improvements and satisfactions.

In the society of freehold farmers this conception of a self-regulating system of economic and social justice seemed to be abundantly confirmed by experience. The farmer who had a long-run plan for the clearing of his land, and who worked year after year to extend the fields available for cultivation, was almost sure to be rewarded for his foresight and his industry. So also were there material rewards for the farmer who built up his land by the efficient manner in which he plowed, cultivated, and fertilized it. Better returns were secured by the thrifty farmer who kept his granary, hay-shed, machine shed, and his barns for the livestock in a state of good repair. Hunting, fishing, and trapping were approved as an auxiliary source of food and clothing material, but the average farmer held in frank contempt the shiftless fellow who permitted the pleasures associated with these activities to usurp the time that was needed for the steady improvement and cultivation of his farm.

Charity was available for the neighbor who suffered illness or accident, or who had his buildings destroyed by natural calamities over which he had no control such as fire, flood, and windstorm but the hard-working, thrifty pioneer had little respect for the man who was in need because he had a tendency to loaf instead of giving attention to his business. The puritan maxim that "God helps those who help themselves" was deeply woven into the moral consciousness of those who were engaged in the unremitting struggle to make a living in the primitive and harsh conditions of the frontier. Gradually as the battle with nature was won, and the farmer was able to look out on his fertile fields of growing grain, on his green pastures in which ample herds of horses, cattle, and flocks of sheep were grazing, and on his barns and other buildings freshly painted and securely equipped to care for the harvest and the livestock during the cold winter months, it was natural for him as owner and operator to associate this prosperity with his own individual ability, thrift and enterprise. The condition of a man's farm was accepted as a genuine index of his worth—a man was worth that which he had accumulated.

A third major principle of economic individualism is that property is the fruit of the toil and sacrifice of the individual, that the right to hold property is a natural and inalienable right, and that this right of property is foundational to all other human rights.

This tendency to identify property with human personality came easy for the American pioneer. In his world there was an abundance of free land, and a homestead was available for the person who was prepared to qualify for a claim. But a "claim" on the raw frontier became a home and a piece of productive property only through the labor, sweat, hardship, and sacrifice of the pioneer. In the free competition of frontier and agrarian America, property was literally the fruit of the toil of the individual human being. As a result of his own care, labor, planning, and self-denial a piece of virgin land had been taken from the state of nature and turned into a human habitation and a means of human livelihood. Thus it was widely believed that a man owned that which he had earned.

Nor was this struggle for property in any important sense a sordid scramble for material gain at the expense of one's fellows. For the most part, the pioneers were struggling to subdue nature, not one another. They made common cause against those who sought to exploit them. Nor was the struggle for the homestead a petty struggle, devoid of larger social significance. As the farmer beat back the forests, or turned the wild lands of the prairies into fields suitable for cultivation, he was doing his part

to lay a foundation for a more secure and abundant life for the
generations that were to come after him. He worked and sacri-
ficed in the thought that he was making a home and providing
a means of livelihood for his children, and for his children's
children. For many a pioneer, his farm was more than a physical
thing, it was a symbol of the future—of the good life that was to
come. In brief, his farm was the concrete evidence of the value
of his career—the visible expression of his own achievement. It
was not only the source of his own security, it was also the assurance of a livelihood for those who were to follow him. Anything that would take his farm from him would also take the
security as well as much of the meaning from his existence.

Another basic principle of economic individualism is that
the social good is the sum of the goods of all the individual members of society, and that this social good requires no government
to promote it; it is the inevitable by-product of an economy in
which each individual concentrates and consecrates his energies
to the single-minded pursuit of his own material gain.

A government of minimum functions was the natural correlative of a social order composed of relatively equal and self-
sufficient farmers. The freehold farmer wanted no government
agency to plan, regulate, and supervise his activities. He preferred to be on his own. He knew the conditions upon which his
welfare depended, and he and the members of his family had
direct control over most of these conditions. Since he bought and
sold very little, his security and welfare were not subject to the
vicissitudes of uncertain national and world markets. Much of
the little trading he engaged in was on a person-to-person basis
and, for the most part, he had opportunity for first-hand inspection of the animal, the tool, the piece of dry goods or the building
material he got in exchange for his own produce.

The members of the farm family were both producers and
consumers, and they deliberately planned their production to
serve their needs as consumers. Differences of opinion might
develop, of course, between husband and wife, and between

children and parents about how they should administer their affairs, as well as about the specific life-ends for which any surpluses should be devoted, but they neither wanted, nor required, any help from the agents of government in the adjudication of these domestic disputes. Each family stood on its own feet, and it gladly accepted responsibility for the conduct of its life affairs. It was able to do this because the main factors that conditioned its livelihood were under its immediate control, and if it failed to take advantage of its opportunities, its own members were the ones who suffered the consequences.

On the whole the system worked well. Life opportunities were restricted, but there was a basic security. Farmers knew want when seasons were unfavorable, but they knew nothing of want in the midst of plenty. Nor did they suffer the physical and spiritual consequences of unemployment, for there was always work of one sort or another for everybody on the homestead farm. Children were economic assets in this agrarian society, and they were early assigned their own responsible tasks in the productive work of household and farm. In a self-contained farm-unit in which whatever was grown or made was for use, there was no need for government inspectors to protect against adulterated foods, or to make sure that the family got articles of good quality. The longer manufactured articles lasted, the better, for no one was interested in a rapid turn-over of goods. Pride of craftsmanship was a constant in the productive work of this functional, family economy.

Government, to be sure, did have its necessary functions. It was important that there be a public agency to keep original land titles clear, and to keep accurate records of the various transfers of titles through sale and inheritance. As regions developed, it became necessary to provide for protection through duly constituted public officers, although these officers often required the coöperation of volunteer deputies to establish the authority of the law. Highways were built by coöperation of the farmers interested, but some authority was required to define just where these highways were to run, and to make sure that all did their full part to maintain them. Much of the education of the young was achieved through responsible participation in the life activities of the farm and neighborhood, but there were certain skills such as reading, writing, and arithmetic which could be better taught in a common school, and this school was generally a public institution, maintained by a tax levied on all. But on the whole these rugged farmers were not for strong government, they desired to see its functions kept to a minimum.

In sum, in a society of self-contained freehold farms there was much of truth in the view that the public welfare would be essentially cared for if each individual devoted himself to the single-minded pursuit of his own material gain. He could get ahead economically only as he improved his farm, and as he improved his farm he advanced not only the well-being of his own family, but the wealth of society as well. But the autonomous unit of this freehold economy was the family on its own holding, and this family lived not in and by the operations of a complex price and market system, but through the deliberate planning of its productive activities to satisfy life needs. In agrarian America, the interests of owner, manager, laborer, and consumer were unified because these interests were the interests of one and the same human group. The members of the productive family group all lived in and by their functions. These functions involved the ownership of productive property, but the property was operated by its owners as a means for making a living and a life, not primarily as a means of profit through the exercise of control over the life activities of others. These families living in and by means of their relatively autonomous productive functions were in most matters clearly the best judge of their own interests. They needed no governmental authority to direct, inspect and coördinate their processes of life and labor.

It is not surprising that the American interpretation of democracy should have been deeply influenced by these life experiences of a pioneer people. It was natural for a society of freehold farmers to develop the sturdy conviction that a democracy denotes a society in which individuals accept full responsibility for their own welfare, that the public good is the necessary by-product of an economy in which each family concentrates on the pursuit of its own private affairs, that a system of private ownership and enterprise is a just system that automatically rewards each family in proportion to its industry, foresight, endurance, and thrift, and that the best government is a government of minimum powers which exercises its police functions to maintain an environment of security and peace within which individuals can work out their own destinies and be protected in their property and the fruits of their labor.

But the America of the freehold, self-sufficient farmer has gone. Long before the frontier disappeared from American life at the close of the last century, much of America had become industrial, commercial, and urban in character. Today only about one-fifth of our people are directly engaged in agriculture, and many farms are now operated by workers who do not own them. During the past century as a result of mechanical inventions and industrial organization the amount of energy available per person in the United States has been multiplied more than forty fold, and this in spite of a vast increase in the population. This shift from the agrarian, handicraft culture based on the energy of human beings, work animals, windmills and waterwheels to the culture of the power machine factory production is now underway in all parts of the world. It is one of the most momentous changes in the history of mankind and it is making necessary a re-assessment of many things long considered axiomatic in the life of man.

This transformation in the modes of living has its peculiar significance for the United States because it has destroyed the essential features of those pioneer conditions of life in which our individualistic conception of democracy was developed and bred into the life outlook of the American people. Our actual practices have already departed radically from these historic

forms, but our new and interdependent ways of living will remain discordant, uncertain and insecure until they are given
moral reënforcement through the acceptance of a more socialized
conception of the pattern of our democratic way of life. Education has its important part in the development of this new moral
orientation.

§ 5. Old Faiths and New Conditions of Life

The economy of the self-sufficient farm was marked by a
basic security, because each family produced most of that which
it consumed. Standards of living were not high, but people felt
secure because they had direct control over the essential means
of their livelihood. Jobs were available for old and young if they
were willing to work, and if a person was unemployed there
were sound reasons for assuming that the responsibility was
primarily his. Hard times undoubtedly occurred in the periods
of panic and depression of the nineteenth century, but it was
easier for individuals to adjust to them by leaving the town and
factory for work on the farm, or for a homestead on the frontier.
In other words, in agrarian America there was considerable economic and social justification for the doctrine that each person
is the best judge of his own interests and should be left free to
work out his own means for taking care of himself and, his
family. The individual could assume this economic responsibility
because he was so largely economically independent.

Today our standards of living are higher in many respects
and the productive capacity of the nation has been greatly expanded. We have achieved this high productive level by the use
of power machinery, and the power machine has resulted in a
mode of specialized mass production that has eliminated the
economy of the self-sufficient farm. Today, even the one-fifth
of our population who are farmers operate in a commercial and
industrial environment. Agriculture itself is specialized by regions and we have wheat farms, cotton farms, corn and hog
farms, as well as a wide variety of fruit and garden truck farms.

Most of the products of these specialized farms are sold on the market, and even the farm family now buys much of its food, most of its clothing, and practically all of its tools and machinery, household furnishings, building materials and the like. With growing mechanization the tendency for farms to increase in size still persists, although with rural electrification and improved all-service tractors the possibility of maintaining the family farm is good, if we are ready to plan for its welfare.

Farming in many parts of the country still remains a way of life, and the farmer is a productive craftsman primarily interested in his life function. But that way of life is no longer economically self-sufficient, for agriculture is now an inherent part of a national and world system of finance and trade over which the single farmer has no real control. An abundant crop today does not necessarily mean prosperity for the farmer's family, and no group of the population suffered more severely during the prolonged depression of the 'thirties than did the farmers. Many of them even lost their farms, a further evidence of the extent to which they have lost direct control over the means of their livelihood.

But, as we have indicated, whereas at the time of the founding of the Republic nine-tenths of our people were freehold farmers, four-fifths of them are now involved in ways of making a living that are non-agricultural. They work in factories, mills, and offices, they live in great cities, and they are utterly dependent on the steady functioning of a vast network of interdependent activities for the means of their existence. Most of them work for large impersonal corporations and some of these continental and world enterprises own more productive property than is found within the borders of many of our states. A number of these corporations also employ more workers and have more people dependent on the wages they supply than were found in the realms of many of the former monarchs. In spite of these momentous changes in our economy, we still cling to the official theory that production is primarily a private affair. If the direc-

tors of a corporation do not consider market conditions favorable
to their interests, they are under no obligation to operate at a
loss in order to maintain production and employment.

As a result our society is haunted by a chronic sense of insecurity. These millions of urban and industrial workers are
conscious that the historic economic and social theories do not
correspond to the facts of their present existence. They realize
that operating as single individuals, or families, they literally
have no sure means of providing for their livelihood. Indeed,
they are not even confident that they shall have a job of any
sort. To assume that in this interdependent, industrial America,
the individual functioning singly and alone can carry the responsibility for his own welfare is to make an assumption that is
without foundation. The right to a job when there is no job, the
right to start in a business of your own when the concrete means
of launching the business are not available, the right to buy in
a free market when one has no effectual purchasing power, and
the right to live in a great urban center when its essential service
can be disrupted by the arbitrary decisions of private groups—
rights such as these have been shown to be empty affairs. The
lack of alternatives and real opportunities in their environment
can put human beings under a coercion fully as cruel as that
exercised by the tyranny of an autocratic ruler.

The basic point is that human responsibility and human
freedom cannot be dissociated from power to control. In order to
recover some measure of control over their means of existence,
these factory and office workers are abandoning a fictitious personal independence, and they are uniting in labor organizations
so that they can bargain collectively with the heads of these giant
corporations. This right to associate has at last been given legal
sanction by our legislatures and courts, but the belief that organized labor should be condemned as a form of conspiracy is
still retained by certain rugged enterprisers who pretend to be
concerned for the freedom that membership in trade unions has
taken from the individual worker. Significant and important

from the standpoint of democratic values as is this movement for the organization of labor, it is evident that in and of itself it is no complete answer to the problem of security in affairs of livelihood. The future rôle of functional pressure groups in our society will be examined in the concluding section of this chapter. At this point we desire to emphasize that the American people need a new interpretation of the freedoms and responsibilities of individuals which will take adequate account of the interdependent character of the conditions under which all now live. Security and freedom for individuals can be achieved in industrial America only by the creation and utilization of positive economic and social means. Without the development of forms of deliberate and coöperative control, the economic security that is basic to human freedom cannot be had. In brief, if we are to make our democratic respect for the individual human being a living thing, we must supplant our historic system of economic individualism with some form of socialized planning and control. We dare not accept the defeatism of those who assert that the road to planning is the "road to serfdom"; individual initiative and freedom are quite compatible with a system of coöperative planning carried on within a framework of policies established by the government acting as the representative agency of the whole public.

Industrialism has other tendencies which also must be controlled if we are to preserve the values of our democratic way of life. Power production under a system of unregulated private accumulation has resulted in a concentration of wealth and power that has seriously undermined equality of opportunity in our country. American democracy, as we have seen, was born in a freehold agricultural economy marked by an unprecedented economic and social equality. The assumption has been that this condition of equality would be maintained if men were left free to manage and to develop their own property holdings. In a society of freehold farms in which the individual owner managed and cultivated his own piece of land this expectation had reasonable social roots. But in present-day industrial society operating through the instrumentality of the corporation the nature of private property has been transformed. About 90 per cent of our manufacturing is no longer carried on by individuals or by partnerships of individuals; it is provided by corporations. In fact, without the corporation form of management the huge sums of money needed for many of our continental transportation and industrial undertakings simply could not have been attained.

But as students of the problem have emphasized, under the corporation the functions of ownership and management have tended to become separate. As a result of this fundamental "split in the atom of property," it is now possible for a person to own extensive properties that he has never even seen, and to share in the profits of enterprises to which he contributes nothing whatsoever in the way of direction and management. Conversely, as the records of many corporations demonstrate, it is possible for *management* through a system of non-voting stock, and proxy control, to enhance its own power and returns even at the expense of the owners. In brief, in our corporate age, the historic assumption that property is the product of the toil and the thrift of the owner, that the owner is best qualified to conserve and manage his own property, and that in a free system of competition rewards would be distributed in terms of the productive and social contribution of each individual, has little of substance to support it. In an economy of giant corporations, exercising virtual monopoly control in their fields, and managed by directors and executive staffs who own but a small fraction of the stock, there is no longer any significant correlation between the income an individual owner or investor receives and the contribution that he makes to production. Indeed, in many of our industries the workers who operate the machines and tools know much more about the enterprise on which their livelihood depends than do the people in whom legal ownership reposes.

A century after Alexis de Tocqueville made his classic comment on the remarkable equality of condition prevailing among the American people, the Brookings Institution brought out a report on family incomes in the United States. Their figures have never been seriously challenged, and they show how radical is the inequality which has developed under the corporate form of property ownership in our mass production industrial economy.

The 11,650,000 families with incomes of less than $1,500 received a total of about 10 billion dollars. At the other extreme, the 36,000 families having incomes in excess of $75,000 possessed an aggregate income of 9.8 billion dollars. Thus it appears that 0.1 percent of the families at the top received practically as much as 42 per cent of the families at the bottom of the scale.[2]

We are frequently told by the spokesmen of the private enterprise system that the right to own productive property is fundamental to all of our other rights, both political and civil. If there be truth in this assertion, then it is clear that something must be done to restore an economic foundation for the liberties of the American people. Today most American citizens directly own and manage little or no productive property. The above figures clearly indicate that a system of unregulated private ownership and enterprise can no longer be relied upon to maintain the condition of equality which was the original economic basis of our democracy.

Nor should we follow those who attribute our economic troubles and insecurities to the machine, and who ask us to turn our backs on science and invention in order to return to the simplicities of the freehold farm economy. That primitive and simple mode of living has gone beyond recall, and for better or worse we must now work out our destinies within the framework of the complex conditions of industrial society. The power age, moreover, has its positive side; it has its resources as well as its problems, its possibilities as well as its coercions. It has made

---

[2] Report of the Brookings Institution on America's Capacity to Consume, (Washington, D. C., 1934).

available the material means for overcoming the age old economic problem of producing sufficient food, clothing, and shelter. Indeed, the power age has given us more than this, for the science and technology that give the promise of abundance have also contributed the means of providing richer cultural opportunities than even the most utopian dreamers ever believed were to be enjoyed by human beings. As yet few grasp the vast possibilities in the use of atomic energy for peaceful purposes of production.

To make actual these new possibilities, however, we must accept the fact that we have entered a new age. In this new age, new conceptions of human welfare, of human and property rights, and of the means of human security and freedom must be formed to replace those which were developed in pioneer America. Great tasks for the pioneer remain, but today these tasks lie primarily on the social, not the physical, frontier. We need to discover and create the means by which a life of equality, peace and freedom can be made secure in the interdependent world of power production. One of the primary tasks of democratic education in our generation is to help the young achieve a mind that is consonant with the life imperatives and possibilities of this new age.

§ 6. *Democratic Values and a Functional Society*

Men have learned to be suspicious of those whose general professions of faith are negated by the actual tendencies in their daily practices. We therefore would do well to be on our guard against the advocates of economic individualism, for all of its major organized groups of supporters—business, labor and agriculture—now reject in their own actions some of its most basic principles. For example, economic individualism assumes that the individual is the ultimate unit in economic affairs, and should be left alone to promote his own interests. Businessmen, laborers, and farmers, all show by their faith in group action that they have lost their earlier confidence in the capacity of the single individual to care for his interests. The members of each of these major functional groups now seek to attain many of their most important ends through large-scale organizations, and they also are increasingly demanding that affairs in their particular sphere of the economy receive the aid of government.

Economic individualism also affirms that the best means of promoting production and of securing justice for all of the various types of producers is to rely on the unregulated exchange of goods and services in the open-market. Indeed, the theorists of the private profit system have long asserted that competition is nature's own law, and any attempt to regulate the operation of supply and demand is to abort benevolent natural processes. Despite this alleged deep faith in competition as the law of life each of these major functional groups now does its best in its own sphere to supplant competition with monopoly control, and to substitute an administered price and wage system for the unregulated adjustments of the competitive market.

Business is the most vocal of the different propagandists for "free" enterprise and this may be partly due to the fact that it was the first of all the functional groups to desert in its concrete demands the principles of the free-market system. Much of American industry developed under the protection of favoring tariff laws, and our railroads, mines, lumber, and oil industries were made possible through generous allotments from the national domain to private interests. Banking has had the friendly help of the government all through its history, and bankers have done much to control currency and governmental means of credit to their own advantage. The business of shipping has all along sought cash subsidies and other substantial aids from the government. During the long depression of the 'thirties many of our greatest corporations were kept solvent through government aid administered through the Reconstruction Finance Corporation and a vast program of public work projects. Through relief doles, loans to private agencies, and these public work programs the government functioned to maintain a demand for goods which individuals by themselves could no longer supply. Through the U. S. Chamber of Commerce, the National Association of Manufacturers, the American Bar Association, and the American Bankers Association, as well as through the public relations agents of the various individual industries, the interests of business have been consistently represented in all of the state capitals and at Washington. Through unremitting pressure business has fought to get the particular laws enacted that it desired, and it has also fought to keep off the statute books the various legislative proposals that it considered unfavorable to its interests.

After years of bitter struggle, labor has also won the right to organize. Today it has achieved a power that puts it in a position to bargain on more nearly equal terms with business interests. Organized labor has also long been active at the state and national level on behalf of legislation to protect the interests of workers. Through its initiative and support we now have laws that put a floor under wages and a ceiling over hours, that give special protections to women and children in industry, that provide insurance and compensation for accidents, that require protection against dangerous machinery, and which provide for government inspectors in factories, mines, meat-packing plants, food processing industries and the like. Labor has united with other groups in the struggle for old-age benefits, for a comprehensive social security system, for public housing, for welfare and unemployment benefits, for public education, public health programs, public parks, playgrounds, libraries, and similar social welfare agencies. Although labor leaders join with business men to proclaim the virtues of free, private enterprise, they nevertheless struggle to get that control over the market for workers that gives power to determine the conditions of labor for the individual members of their trade unions. One may perceive that without this development of labor through organization and the power of collective bargaining we should have sunk to serfdom in industrial America, and still recognize that the welfare of labor in the long run rests with the maintenance, not the restriction, of production, and that labor's historic weapon of the strike is becoming a very costly and unpredictable method of procedure in our interdependent and tenuous industrial civilization.

Farmers are also losing their confidence in the ability of the individual to care for himself and they likewise show an increasing tendency to function in national organizations. Through their expanding producers and consumers coöperatives they seek to exercise some measure of direct control over the system of manufacture and distribution upon which so much of their livelihood now depends. Farmers have long benefited in the care of their land, livestock, and crops, from the magnificent experimental work of the Department of Agriculture of the Federal Government, as well as from the important services carried on by the experimental stations in the various states. As farmers have observed the aggressive measures taken by both business and labor to get the agencies of government to provide for their special interests, they also have moved to strengthen their own state and national political pressure groups. As a result the agricultural lobby is today quite strong, and farmers will never again sit idly by while their farms are taken from them by an impersonal but ruthless deflationary process that drastically cuts the prices of the agricultural products they have to sell, but which fails to bring commensurate reductions in the prices of those industrial products they have to buy. Unfortunately, in the case of the farmer, as with the other powerful pressure groups, economic interests and political measures are often narrowly conceived, and they also tend to seek security through the restriction rather than the maximization of production.

In fine, in contemporary industrial America we now function economically not primarily as individuals, but rather through huge corporations, through business and banking associations, through powerful labor organizations, through various farm organizations including a farmers' union, through various professional associations, as well as through coöperatives and other consumer organizations. The principle of a state of minimum, police-power functions has given way in actual practice to the social-service state, and the government also operates a vast system of administrative and regulatory bodies. Our life is in fact associational in character, but we lack a guiding social and political philosophy that takes open account of the corporate nature of our present ways of making a living.

In spite of these various practical adjustments we still adhere in theory to many of the old dogmas of economic individualism, and we seek to justify the new forms of economic practice by explaining that they are all undertaken in the interests of the historic system of private enterprise.

As a result of our failure to develop a more adequate social philosophy, we are intellectually and morally on the defensive. Our generation appears to be unable to deal with its problems in the bold spirit of our forefathers who proclaimed that institutions should be "altered or abolished" when they failed to meet the needs of living men. We tend to fear the instrumentality of government—we pass laws under the coercion of new life conditions that authorize public agencies and corporations such as the Tennessee Valley Authority, the Public Housing Authority and the Rural Electrification Authority, and then we condemn as bureaucrats and ridiculous "brain-trusters," the individuals appointed to administer these agencies. Our legislatures often refuse to appropriate the funds required to carry on the very functions they have sanctioned by their own acts. We still assume that production and employment are essentially private affairs; we tend to regard social and economic planning as an evil, and many oppose as regimentation and enslavement all efforts to coördinate and direct the various parts of our economy. In spite of the many bitter things we have suffered we officially hold to the view that the public welfare is best advanced by an unregulated process of competition and conflict between the major economic interests. As a consequence, the leaders of these groups are frequently forced against their better judgment to fight for narrow, sectarian interests without regard for the effects of their factional and partial proposals on the health and stability of the economy as a whole.

We have, as yet, provided no solid means by which the basic functional groups—business, labor, agriculture, and the various professions—can openly and systematically coöperate in planning for the growth of our nation, for the steady maintenance of production and employment, and for the efficient mobilization of our resources to meet great public needs such as housing, health, education, as well as the re-development of our cities and the great farming regions of the different river valleys. Everybody knows that the boom-bust pattern of an unregulated market system has become a menace in our highly integrated national economy, and we also know that our economy cannot continue forever to be disrupted by the suspension of basic services while management and labor settle their so-called "private" disputes.

These things we know, but we hesitate to move to meet these problems. Controls, however, of one sort or another we must have. Either these controls will be exercised by private groups serving narrow and class ends, or they will be exercised coöperatively, through some form of representative national economic council operating under policies and laws formulated and periodically reviewed by the government acting as the agent of all.

As we have emphasized the problem is economic, and it is therefore also moral in nature. Indeed, the moral elements in it are as fundamental as the economic. What is really at issue is whether our ways of making a living can be turned once again into ways of making a life. The means of livelihood in an industrial society can become a way of life clothed with significant social meaning only as these means are coöperatively planned and conducted in order to serve the needs of men, and are not permitted to continue as exploitive and speculative activities controlled by private groups for essentially private ends.

The foregoing has its implications for education. Our schools have long been torn between two moralities—the morality of individual success as measured by pecuniary gain in the private competitive system, and the morality of individual success as measured by socially useful work consciously directed to the welfare of the whole community. It is time education made up its mind as to the kind of America it wants, and sought to educate the young on the basis of that integrated morality. American democracy was a product of a society in which the great mass of the people lived in and through their productive functions; it will recover meaning and vitality as it succeeds in reorganizing an economy in which all find security and opportunity in coöperatively planned functions that are recognized to be socially useful.

CHAPTER XI

The Morality of Community

THE young are educated not simply by the instruction given in the classrooms of the school but also by the manner in which the school itself is organized and its various activities are conducted. Nothing more clearly demonstrates that a program of deliberate education can never be a morally neutral undertaking, than the fact that each school is necessarily organized and administered according to some definite pattern. The maxim that actions speak louder than words holds with special force for all agencies concerned with the deliberate nurture of the young. All that we have learned about human development and the process by which life attitudes are formed, supports the view that concrete ways of living are more potent than moral preachments in the shaping of the character and the conduct of the young.

We tend to learn that which we experience and it is important for those who are committed to education *in* and *for* democracy to recognize that a school is inescapably a mode of experiencing. All of the ways of the school, moreover, enter into the experience of the young and they have their educative effect. A school, for example, may drill its children in the classroom to recite the creed that "all men are created free and equal," but if the school is racially segregated, or on a "quota" system, or if it excludes from its social gatherings pupils of minority racial or religious groups, the children will learn that in actual life situations people are to be treated not as equals, but as "first" and "second" class citizens. A school may also constantly empha-

size in its curriculum and in its general assemblies that all who
engage in socially useful work merit the full respect of a democratic community, but if the members of the schoolboard as well
as the community leaders who are invited to speak at special
school functions always come from white-collar groups, the
school will tend to breed in the young the impression that those
who work with their hands are socially less significant than
members of other functional groups. Or, again, a school may
stress in its courses the moral superiority of a democratic system
of self-government over all forms of dictatorship, but if its daily
affairs are so conducted that its administrative officers deny both
teachers and pupils any real share in shaping the life of the
school, the children will be getting habituated to authoritarian,
not democratic, patterns of living. In brief, a school can be a
consistent and effective moral agency of democracy only to the
extent that its ways of organizing and conducting its own affairs
are in harmony with the democratic ideals it seeks to foster
through its modes of instruction.

§ 1. *The Democratic Community and The Common School*

There should be no uncertainty about the moral right of a
democratic society to use its schools to cultivate its characteristic
patterns of conduct and thought in the lives of the young. A
democratic society prizes individuality and human liberty, and it
fosters diversity, not authoritarian uniformity, but we misconstrue the nature of a free society, if we do not perceive that it
could not exist unless its members were loyal to a common way
of life. Individual freedom is real and significant, but it is a
function of a democratic community, and that community is an
organized form of group life with its definite and distinctive
characteristics. We have already emphasized that the personal
attitudes and behaviors that sustain this democratic community
are not given in the native equipment of the young, they have
to be acquired by the members of each successive generation

through a process of directed experiencing and learning. The Harvard Report on *General Education in a Free Society* quite properly calls attention to the fact that a democracy is more, not less, dependent than authoritarian social systems on the processes of deliberate education.

> Democracy, however much by ensuring the right to differ it may foster difference—particularly in a technological age which further encourages division of function and hence difference of outlook—yet depends equally on the binding ties of common standards. It probably depends more heavily on these ties than does any other kind of society precisely because the divisive forces within it are so strong. But, from what has been said, it is clear that this task of implanting common ties is far from simple.[1]

The task of nurturing the young in the basic outlooks and allegiances of a democratic society is truly "far from simple," but it is as important as it is difficult. Indeed, the factors that conceivably could operate to divide the American people are more numerous than the above excerpt from the Harvard Report suggests. Our continental nation not only is marked by regional and occupational groups with different economic interests; it is also composed of peoples of different races and of widely different cultural, religious, and national backgrounds. We early resolved that the unity and the stability of our democratic community should rest, not upon a system of regimentation and indoctrination, but upon a social policy of equal treatment and common respect that would nourish in each person an uncoerced devotion to the ways of life that are foundational in our system of self-government.

The American people have long realized that we can enjoy unity without coercion only as we are prepared to struggle to establish and preserve the equal rights of all in the fundamental arrangements of our society. Loyalty to this conception of equal treatment for all prompted the founders of our Republic to incorporate in the Bill of Rights the principle of religious free-

---

[1] *General Education in a Free Society*, Report of the Harvard Committee, (Cambridge, Mass., Harvard University Press, 1945), p. 12.

dom and the basic policy of the separation of church and state. As we have already indicated, our country has never had an official religious creed; it has no established church; Congress can make no law respecting an establishment of religion; no tax can be levied for the support of a religious institution; and the Constitution of the United States explicitly declares that no religious qualifications of any kind are required to hold any office or position of leadership in the government. In fine, American democracy has been organized politically in the form of a secular state; our basic law makes religion a private, not a governmental, affair, and a person of any religious faith or no religious faith is recognized as having the full rights of citizenship.

During our colonial days we began to move from a theocracy to a democracy in the forms of our political life. We progressively extended the right of citizenship from the Puritan to the Protestant, from the Protestant to the Christian, from the Christian to Christian and Jew, from Christian and Jew to the adherents of all religions and from the adherents of all religions to all men. Many believe that this evolution in the direction of a secular state that accepts all of its members, irrespective of religious outlook and affiliation, as qualified citizens marks a growing embodiment in our social and political order of the principle of the equal worth of all human beings. Nor does this acceptance of the ideal of the secular state imply any derogation of religion. On the contrary, this policy has the support of many church leaders who perceive that freedom of conscience in matters of ultimate belief and allegiance is the only sound ground for the growth of spiritual religion. It should be remembered that in a society in which all religions are thus tolerated, all are also under the moral obligation to adjust their particular allegiance and practices to the principles of behavior that are required to preserve this community of freedom and tolerance. In this sphere, as in all others, rights carry their correlative obligations.

Loyalty to the principle of equality has led the American people to other equally important decisions about the fundamentals of our democracy. It early led the various states to remove property qualifications from the right of suffrage; it led us in time into a long and bloody war to abolish slavery and the subordination of the colored people to the white; still later it led us to extend the right of suffrage so as to make it include women as well as men, and we are now taking positive steps to eliminate discrimination in matters of employment, education, housing and similar cultural affairs. We are aware that the morality of a free community is negated whenever we permit factors such as religion, race, property, sex, or national origin to introduce discriminations into matters of citizenship and qualifications for leadership in public affairs. American democracy is in a real sense an experiment in human brotherhood, and we realize that this experiment can be one of substance only as we succeed in maintaining a functioning equality of conditions.

In the effort to make our experiment in social and political democracy succeed we have founded a public school to nurture this sense of community in the children of our country. The public school was established not only to equalize educational opportunity, but also to breed in the young the basic moral attitude which recognizes that human beings are human beings, and that the things they have in common are not less fundamental than those things which differentiate and articulate them into a variety of functional and cultural sub-groups. The public school has been expected to nurture this basic moral consciousness, not simply by its instruction of the young in the history, the laws, the political processes and the social ideals of our democratic way of life, but also by the provision of actual opportunity for the children of the various component groups—economic, religious, and racial—to grow to respect one another by living, studying, working, and playing together. In other words, the common tax-supported school was deliberately founded in order to give the young a living experience of community along with knowledge of the history, the principles, and the institutions of democracy.

Undoubtedly, the public schools of our country have many limitations, but the American people would do well to recognize the great resource for our democratic way of life that is inherent in this program of public education. It is no small achievement to have developed a universal tax-supported system of schools which from nursery school to university is open to all on equal terms. Although the democratic principle of equality involves much more than mere equality of educational opportunity, it is nevertheless fair to say that this program of free public education has kept alive in all the members of our society the sense that "equality" is more than a mere word in American life. Inadequate as has been the financial support given the public school, particularly in recent years, the fact remains that it has been the institution of the public school which has made it possible for most of our children to attain the equipment required to become competent members of our democratic community. Nor is this all. Through their first-hand experiences in the common public school our children have learned the meaning of community, and in spite of the many "divisive forces" in our continental, industrial America, the public school has helped to nourish the consciousness that we are one people, and that through the continuing use of our democratic institutions we can resolve whatever problems beset us.

Today, the American public school system encounters certain difficulties as it seeks to nurture the youth of our country in a common way of living by providing all of them with an experience of living together. One of these difficulties grows out of the fact that the members of a number of religious and economic groups are not willing to have their own children attend the community school, and they increasingly seek to provide for their education in private schools of one sort or another. Obviously, to the extent that these groups withdraw their children from the common school, that school is prevented from giving American children the richest possible experience of community. Moreover, once parents begin to provide for the education of their children in special private schools, it is inevitable that their interest in the welfare of the public schools begins to decline. Since the supporters of these private schools are becoming more militant and, in some cases, are demanding that these schools share in public educational funds, it is apparent that the American people will have to re-assess the importance of maintaining a system of common schools in our democratic way of life. In the development of a public policy on this basic educational issue, the value of freedom for private groups, and the needs of the whole democratic community will have to be weighed in relation to each other. The right to differ is a basic democratic right, but it cannot be turned into an exclusive and absolute right if we are to maintain the community which makes all of these particular freedoms possible.

The public school confronts another and very difficult problem as it tries to nurture American children in this basic sense of community. Although our country has paid a heavy price to establish the principle that all men are equal before the law, our schools are not as yet equally open to all. In many American communities white and colored children are educated in parallel systems of racial schools, and frequently the quality of these two school systems varies greatly. Stubborn historical factors underlie this policy of racial segregation in education, and any efforts to improve the situation must take due account of regional and community mores. On the other hand, it cannot be doubted that any community which educates its children in segregated schools will have difficulty in nurturing them in the consciousness that in our democracy all men are of equal worth. There is abundant evidence that a sense of human solidarity does not easily develop in a community marked by gross discrimination.

Each of the above tendencies raises problems that are highly controversial, but any serious discussion of education and morals cannot avoid the zone of controversy. In a democracy, education is expected to enlighten by dealing frankly and fairly with those spheres in which our ways of living are in process of re-evaluation and reconstruction. And these areas of life in which reconstruction is underway are necessarily controversial in nature.

§ 2. *The Private Religious School and The Morality of a Free Society*

The American principle of religious freedom has necessarily meant that the public school, open to all children, and taught by teachers drawn from the various component groups of our society, could not be turned into an agency for the propagation of the doctrine and practices of any particular religious group. Hence the leaders of certain church groups, on occasion, have had difficulty in accepting the pattern of a common public school. In addition to the religious instruction given their young by family and church, the leaders of these organizations have wanted their children educated in a school in which every subject would be permeated by their own religious point of view. In view of the variety of religious sects in our country, along with the fact that about one-half of our people are not affiliated with any church, it is not surprising that all attempts to satisfy this religious demand by having the public school teach a common core of religious beliefs have failed.

From time to time, Protestant groups have therefore sought to establish their own system of parochial schools, but most of these efforts have not met with solid response. Many of the most devout Protestant church members have all along preferred to have their children get their general education in the common public school. At the present time the Lutherans have the largest of these Protestant parochial school systems, but their church schools enroll but a fraction of their children, and many of the leaders of the church have openly opposed this effort to establish a special system of Lutheran schools.

On the whole, the Jewish groups have been strong supporters of the public school, and they have sought to provide supplementary programs for the religious nurture of their young. In many communities the Catholics, Protestants and Jews have recently united to support the movement for released, or dismissed, time. According to this plan, children are permitted to attend classes in religion conducted by their church leaders during a regular school hour. The program has met with criticism, and its ultimate standing has not as yet been decided, although the Supreme Court has already ruled that it is illegal to hold religious classes of this type in public school buildings.

Of all the religious groups in the United States, the Roman Catholic Church has experienced the most difficulty in accepting the American pattern of the common public school.[2] As early as 1864, Pope Pius IX included in his Syllabus of Errors, the error of approval by Catholics of the public school "freed from all ecclesiastical authority, government, and interference." Following this pronouncement by the Pope, the Third Plenary Council of the American hierarchy formulated in 1884 the following directives:

> Near each church, where it does not yet exist, a parochial school is to be erected within two years from the promulgation of this Council, and is to be maintained *in perpetuum,* unless the bishop, on account of grave difficulties, judge that a postponement be allowed. . . .
> All Catholic parents are bound to send their children to the parochial schools, unless either at home or in other Catholic schools they may sufficiently and evidently provide for the Christian education of their children, or unless it be lawful to send them to other schools on account of sufficient cause, approved by the bishop, and with opportune cautions and remedies.[3]

Although many of the clergy of the Roman Catholic Church are products of the American public school system, the Church has long been committed to the development of its own system of parochial schools to care for the education of its chil-

---

[2] A good brief discussion of this problem is contained in John S. Brubacher, *A History of the Problems of Education* (New York, McGraw-Hill Book Co., Inc., 1947), Chaps. XI and XVII.
[3] Quoted in *op. cit.,* p. 563.

dren. After many decades of ardent effort, backed by the full moral authority of the Church, the Roman Catholic school system now enrolls about three million children: of these 2,151,000 are in elementary schools, 475,000 in high schools and academies, about 240,000 in universities and colleges, and 25,000 in Church normal schools and seminaries. In other words, this Church has now about 60 per cent of its children enrolled in Catholic elementary schools, and about 35 per cent in its Catholic high schools.[4]

On occasion, this persistent effort of the Roman Catholic Church to provide for the entire education of all its own children in parochial schools has aroused opposition from other elements in the population. Undoubtedly some of this opposition is a product of religious bigotry, but much of it is an expression of sincere concern by those who fear that should this segregated educational program become all-comprehensive, it would tend to breed undesirable cleavages and conflicts in the body-politic. On November 7, 1922, the people of Oregon, acting under the initiative provision of their Constitution, voted an amendment to the school law of the State that, in effect, made attendance at public schools compulsory for all children of elementary school age. This law was challenged on constitutional grounds. It was finally declared unconstitutional by the United States Supreme Court on June 1, 1925. In its decision, the Court stated that "the fundamental theory of liberty upon which all governments in this Union repose excludes any general power of the State to standardize its children by forcing them to accept instruction from public teachers only. The child is not the mere creature of the state; those who nurture him and direct his destiny have the right, coupled with the high duty, to recognize and prepare him for additional obligations."

Encouraged by this decision, the leaders of the Roman

---

[4] Enrollment figures given by the General Secretary of the National Catholic Education Association and published in *The New York Times,* October 24, 1948.

Catholic Church have now begun to demand that their extensive and expanding parochial school system be recognized as an organic part of the total public educational system of the United States. The hope is that if the Catholic system of parochial schools can attain this official recognition, it will then be made eligible for its due share of tax funds. The Catholics are particularly concerned to get this recognition included in any bills providing federal aid to education. Thus the official representative of the National Catholic Welfare Conference stated at a Senate hearing on a federal aid bill that "several times the Department of Education of the National Catholic Welfare Conference has appeared before Congressional committees in opposition to measures providing federal aid to education." But it could at last appear in support of the federal aid program because "this Bill recognizes that public and non-public schools are equally important in the educational system of the United States" and, furthermore, "in making disbursements of funds the national board of apportionment is instructed to consider the extent to which the burden of the educational needs of the state is borne by the non-public schools."[5] As yet no federal aid bill has been passed and, now that the issues have been made clear, the opposition to the granting of public funds to private religious schools seems to be gaining in strength.

Obviously, spiritual issues of the most far-reaching importance are involved in this effort of our largest single religious group to provide for the education of all of its children in a separate system of Church schools, and to get the American government to vote funds for the support of these private religious schools. To the objection of many that this policy marks an abrogation of our principle of the separation of Church and State, the Roman Catholics maintain that this historic principle does not mean that the federal government cannot give aid to religious institutions, but simply that government aid must be

---

[5] *Hearings before the Committee on Education and Labor of the U. S. Senate*, Seventy-Ninth Congress on S717, pp. 591-92.

given in such a way that it does not discriminate among the various church bodies. In support of this interpretation of the relation of church and state in our country, they point to the fact that the government now exempts church property from taxation, and that it provides the various churches with fire and police protection and other general public services.

But the educational position of the Roman Catholics is also held to rest on deeper, moral grounds. The moral argument runs somewhat as follows. It is in accord with the Divine plan that the young be instructed in the truths of religion. The Church is the trustee of this body of revealed truth, and therefore the right of the parent to send his children to the schools of the Church is a *moral,* or *natural,* right. Indeed, this educational right is an organic part of the basic right of religious freedom, and this elemental *natural* right the government has neither the moral authority to grant nor to take away. The decision of the U. S. Supreme Court in the Oregon case is welcomed and approved, not because the government has the right either to grant or to prohibit religious schools, but because the decision is official recognition by the agency of final authority that the authority of the state is thus limited. It is argued by some Roman Catholics that the recognition of this right to establish private religious schools also puts the state under moral obligation to supply the financial means to make the right effectual. The injustice of the present situation is frequently denounced by those who feel it compels Catholic citizens to pay taxes to support public schools and also to provide the additional funds required to maintain their own parochial school system. Notwithstanding this burden of "double taxation," Catholic leaders point out that in many states their children are deprived of important social and educational services which are provided for all children enrolled in the public schools.

The feeling of the hierarchy of the Roman Catholic Church in the United States about this matter was well expressed in its recent frontal attack on the conception of the secular state as outlined in two recent decisions of the U. S. Supreme Court. These decisions deal with educational questions of "released time" and the right of the state to afford free transportation for children attending parochial schools. The statement of the Bishops of the Church was made public by the National Catholic Welfare Conference, November 20, 1948. It declares:

> The failure to center life in God is secularism—which, as we pointed out last year, is the most deadly menace to our Christian and American way of living. . . .
>
> We ask a deeper appreciation of the contribution our institutions of higher learning are making to a Christian reconstruction of society and we urge a more generous support of their work. For if we as Christians are to do our part in restoring order to a chaotic world, Christ must be the Master in our classrooms and lecture halls and the Director of our research projects. . . .
>
> Within the past two years secularism has scored unprecedented victories in its opposition to governmental encouragement of religious and moral training, even where no preferential treatment of one religion over another is involved. In two recent cases, the Supreme Court of the United States has adopted an entirely novel and ominously extensive interpretation of the "establishment of religion" clause of the First Amendment. This interpretation would bar any cooperation between government and organized religion which would aid religion, even where no discrimination between religious bodies is in question.[6]

As many have pointed out, this statement of the prelates of the Roman Catholic Church gives a strained interpretation of the historic American principle of the separation of church and state. Their attack on the secular state is clearly formulated, as their own pronouncement indicates, in order to provide a moral and legal ground for "coöperation between government and organized religion in the training of our future citizens." The concrete meaning of this pattern of coöperation between State and Church is frankly set forth in a resolution adopted at the 1949 annual convention of the National Catholic Education Association. This resolution recommends that

---

[6] Excerpts from *"The Christian in Action"* a statement by the Roman Catholic Bishops in the United States, published in *The New York Times*, November 21, 1948.

Federal aid should be granted equitably to all schools which serve the public good. Otherwise the very survival of private and church-related education will be imperiled by the favored position and virtual monopoly of public education. Such a development would tend to destroy that freedom of education which is fundamental to the individual's right to attend a school of his own or his parents' choice.[7]

This resolution, as is the case with all pronouncements of the Roman Catholics on this educational question, gives central emphasis to the right of the parents to decide the school in which their children shall be educated. But in actual practice this means that freedom of the parents to choose the school for their children is deeply influenced by the clergy of the Roman Catholic Church, for as the Statutes of the Diocese of Indianapolis state: "Where a Catholic parochial school exists, parents ordinarily violate the general Canon law of the Church if they send their children to public or non-Catholic schools. If they persist in this violation, they sin gravely and cannot be absolved until they make proper adjustment within the Ordinary through the Pastor." In this whole matter, the American Roman Catholics are acting in accord with a policy made in the first instance by the recognized world authority of their Church.[8]

Fortunately, not all American Catholics share these educational views of their own Church leaders. Many Catholic laymen believe that their Church has the right to maintain its own schools, but that its demand for public funds to support these private religious schools is not well grounded. They consider that this demand is contrary to the First Amendment of the Constitution which stipulates that "Congress shall make no

---

[7] Resolution adopted at the 46th Annual Convention of the National Catholic Education Conference, Philadelphia, Pa., April 22, 1949.

[8] Since the above was written, Cardinal Spellman of the Roman Catholic Church has made public a statement in which he declares that "under the Constitution we do not ask nor can we expect public funds to pay for the construction or repair of parochial school buildings or for the support of teachers, or for other maintenance costs." (*The New York Times*, Saturday, August 6, 1949.) Should this become the official and permanent policy of the Catholic Church it will of course greatly clarify and improve the educational situation in the United States.

law respecting an establishment of religion, or prohibiting the free exercise thereof." These Catholics are not at all confident that the long-run interests of spiritual religion will be promoted by government subsidy, for they are not encouraged by the state of religion in those countries where their Church is now officially established. In other words, they believe that the principle of separation of Church and State is good for the church as well as for the democratic community. Nor are these Catholics impressed with the reasoning which holds that because the government has recognized the right of religious denominations to establish their own schools, it is therefore responsible to provide the funds to make this right effectual—they realize that a democratic state necessarily permits groups and individuals to do many things that it does not positively support by the use of public funds. For example, the state gives individuals, under specified conditions, the right of divorce, but it does not promote the dissolution of family ties by providing government money to pay attorney fees and alimony for those who seek divorce.

These Catholics doubt the wisdom of the attempt to make the right to determine educational policies an intrinsic part of the principle of religious freedom. They recognize that in matters of education the interests of the whole community are involved along with those of parents and church, and that church educational policies should have due regard for their consequences in the community as a whole. They do not want a pattern of segregation to develop in the United States such as has been established in certain other countries, where Catholics are not only segregated in their own churches and schools, but also in their own trade unions, commercial associations, political parties, and the like. These American Catholics desire to conduct all public affairs, including the education of the young, so that Catholics will not be made into a group apart, but will rather be full and participating members in the general life of the community. They observe the present tendencies in the parochial school movement with alert interest, for they are deeply concerned to preserve the spiritual unity of the American people. It is important that these Catholic lay critics of the official educational policies of their Church make public their view of the values at stake in these developments. A number have already expressed their concern.

The problem of the position of the private religious school in American culture, however, is in no sense a problem for Catholics alone. It is obviously a problem of the whole community, for the future of American civilization is genuinely involved in these educational policies. Should the present drive to get public funds for non-public schools succeed, the educational situation would be profoundly changed. Should federal funds be authorized for the maintenance of the schools of our largest single Church, it is highly probable that many other religious bodies—both Protestant and Jewish—would feel obliged to establish their own parochial school systems. A competitive development of this kind among the churches might easily lead to the destruction of the common public school with all that school means in providing the basic sense of community which is so essential to our democratic way of life. Certainly the American people are under no moral or legal obligation to provide public funds to aid a tendency which in the long run might have such serious results for its own historic and distinctive educational program.

Nor is it necessary that the American people support certain deductions which are now drawn by certain religious groups from the Supreme Court decision which ruled against the Oregon law that made attendance at an elementary public school compulsory for all children. The Court was on sound ground in its argument that in a democratic community, families and churches as well as the state have a basic concern in the education of the young. It also enunciated a fundamental democratic doctrine when it said that "the child is not the mere creature of the state" and that the individual is more than a "citizen." But one may affirm all of these principles, and at the same time recognize that although the child is not "the mere creature" of the state, he is a member and charge of the state, and that the state has its due responsibility for him and should neither abandon its educational functions nor turn them over wholesale to any other agency. The state has the ultimate responsibility to see that each child is so educated that he will develop the attitudes and the allegiances that are necessary to the maintenance of our democratic society. It is too early to say that this basic sense of unity can be satisfactorily cultivated in all of the young, if any considerable number of them are segregated in a separate school system and thus largely deprived of the opportunity to live, work and play with those who are members of other church groups, or who are not affiliated with any church group. To say that the state should not have a monopoly of the education of its children, does not justify the conclusion that any particular church should exercise such a monopoly in the education of its children. American democracy might suffer great loss if different sects begin to segregate their young and breed in them the patterns of their own "in-group," to the exclusion of a full and free sharing of experience with the children of other groups.

Clearly in this sphere of education, the rights of the church and the rights of the whole democratic community must be viewed in relation to one another. Should experience show that the consequence of having children for their entire school period under the educational direction of the church was beginning to breed an undesirable sense of difference and was tending to foster cleavages which were a threat to the spiritual unity of the American people, the community would have every right and duty to reexamine the arrangement. In a democratic community, all policies are known by their fruits, and no doctrine of rights can be made so absolute as to preclude the right of the whole community to judge all policies, including educational policies, by their fruits in the life of the people. Certainly no doctrine of "natural rights" is to be trusted which seeks to restrict the right of the democratic community to pass on the validity of any of its existing practices.

§ 3. The Democratic Community and The Private Secular School

Not all private schools are religious schools, for two basic interests lead secular groups also to establish private schools. One of these interests is the desire to experiment with a new program of education which the public school is at present unwilling or unable to undertake. The other arises from the desire of parents in the more wealthy groups to provide a more elaborate and costly program of education than is to be had in the common public school. Judged from the standpoint of the democratic community these two reasons for organizing private schools are quite different and should be considered separately.

One of the distinctive characteristics of a democratic society is that it seeks to provide the widest possible freedom for its members to associate in voluntary groups for the promotion of cherished interests. A democracy believes that this right of individuals to associate in the pursuit of felt interests is a good in and of itself, and it also believes that through the initiative of such pioneering private groups much of good for the whole community may be developed. Indeed, the higher a society stands in the scale of civilized living, the more it tends to articulate into these voluntary interest groups—vocational, scientific, religious, social, recreational, and artistic—and the less it seeks to subordinate its individual members to the regimented control of the state. On the other hand, this free articulation of the life of a people into interest groups is achieved within the framework of an organized society, and all must share responsibility for the maintenance of this basic framework of conditions. A democratic society seeks to keep its government responsive to the life needs and interests of the people, and it therefore tries to provide genuine opportunity within all of its public agencies for individuals to exercise creative initiative. In brief, a democratic state desires to provide conditions favorable to creative activity and individual initiative within, as well as without, the agencies of the government.

It is a mistake therefore to assume that all pioneering in education must be a function of private, experimental schools. Already many of the most significant innovations in education come as a result of the initiative of those who work in the public schools, and we may expect more of these progressive contributions now that these schools are deliberately organizing to maintain departments of educational research and experiment. Nor is there anything to prevent a large metropolitan or state educational system from first trying out experiments in special classes, schools, or localities, before committing the system as a whole to the new plan.

On the other hand, there is every reason to give private groups of teachers and parents freedom to organize their own experimental schools, providing these private educational institutions are integrated into the general educational program of the community. It is easy, however, for a private group to launch an experimental program, and, after a few years, because of financial difficulties or other reasons, to lapse back into a routine, non-progressive program. There is no justification for the continued existence of routine private schools of this type, and much of the effort to advance education through private institutions might accomplish more if it were channeled through the public schools.

The democratic community, however, is deeply concerned with the existence of another form of private school that is organized, not primarily for the purposes of experimental educational activity, but simply to give the children of privileged economic groups a higher standard of education than is provided by the public schools of their community. Private schools of this type are essentially class schools and there is a double objection to them. In the first place, they tend to add a *social* inequality to the prevailing *economic* inequality. They prevent children of different economic backgrounds from having the opportunity to live, study, and play together and thus to develop something of that mutual understanding and respect which is required for the coöperative resolution of many of our deepest problems. One of the purposes of those who established our system of common schools was to bring the children of the rich and the poor into a common experience during their formative years. They believed this important in the preservation of our democratic way of life. It is, of course, easier for members of a favored group to treat other groups with calloused injustice when they have no direct knowledge of them, particularly if they are nurtured from childhood in a sheltered environment that disposes them to believe that the mass of people are of a lesser breed not qualified to benefit from that order of existence which they of the favored group were meant to enjoy.

In the second place, it is natural for parents to give their first interest and loyalty to the schools in which their own children are enrolled. Thus the existence of these secular private schools tends to subtract from the supporting constituency of the public schools, members of professional and other groups who have the highest educational equipment and who could do so much if they were interested in the public schools to raise their standards. Not only so, but frequently families who find their budgets strained to pay the high costs of these private schools, join forces with those reactionary tax-payers groups who fight to lower appropriations for the public schools. Thus a vicious cycle gets started. Parents originally withdraw their children from public schools because of their low standards and, as a result, have to bear the added financial burden of keeping their children in private schools. They then are inclined to demand the reduction of the budgets of the public schools, thus still further handicapping these schools in their effort to provide an equal and adequate educational opportunity for all children.

The plain fact is that the public school is a product of our democracy, and our democracy is a product of a general equality of living conditions, both economic and social. Neither our democracy nor the public school can retain their basic values in a civilization marked by gross economic inequality. It is not surprising that the common school has had its richest expression in those middle-class communities in which people have enjoyed an actual experience of having things in common—economic, cultural, and governmental. The public school can nurture the sense of community in all of our children only when it is maintained by a community that is willing to send its children to the common school—that is, by a community that demonstrates by its deeds as well as its words that it is devoted to a common way of life. Class schools are harmful and they negate the democratic ideal of community. But it will not be easy to get rid of them. They will probably continue to exist so long as our country is marked by the presence of sharply differentiated economic classes. The problem of community is an educational problem and our schools must do all that they can to cultivate a sense of the unity of our people, but the problem of community is also an economic, social and political problem. Democratic community and gross inequality in basic conditions of life have never got on well together. We shall either move to get rid of the latter or we shall not continue to enjoy the values of our democracy.

§ 4. Segregation and Community

The tendency of a school system to reflect the attitudes of its community is strikingly shown in the sphere of race relations in our country. As a people we are committed to the democratic way of life. We celebrate the Declaration of Independence as one of the supreme formulations of American social and political principles. This classic formulation contains the unqualified affirmation that "all men are created equal." The chief author of the Declaration was Thomas Jefferson, a Virginian. Jefferson and Lincoln are two of our most revered moral leaders—each is

cherished as a personal symbol of the American faith in democracy, and its ideal of human equality.

As a people we are also committed to the public school.
Many of our communities regard their system of public schools
as the best institutional expression of their moral ideals. We
expect the public school to nurture our children in the faiths
of our democratic way of life, and also to cultivate in them a
lasting sense of community based on a regard for the worth and
the dignity of each individual human being. And yet in many
localities, because of a legacy from the past, our children are
compelled to attend racially segregated schools, and thus are
deprived of the opportunity to live, study and play together.
This deep gap between our educational aims and our educational
practices helps to perpetuate a situation that is a growing threat
to the unity of the American people. The Report of the President's Committee on Civil Rights summarizes these educational
discriminations.

The United States has made remarkable progress toward the goal
of universal education for its people. . . . Student bodies have become
increasingly representative of all the different peoples who make up our
population. Yet we have not finally eliminated prejudice and discrimination from the operation of either our public or our private schools and
colleges. Two inadequacies are extremely serious. We have failed to
provide Negroes and to a lesser extent, other minority group members
with equality of educational opportunity in our public institutions, particularly at the elementary and secondary school levels. We have allowed
discrimination in the operation of many of our private institutions of
higher education, particularly in the North with respect to Jewish students. . . .

The South is one of the poorer sections of the country and has at
best only limited funds to spend on its schools. With 34.5 percent of the
country's population, 17 southern states and the District of Columbia
have 39.4 percent of our school children. Yet the South has only one-fifth
of the taxpaying wealth of the nation. . . . Negro and white school children
both suffer because of the South's basic inability to match the level of
educational opportunity provided in other sections of the nation. But it
is the South's segregated school system which most directly discriminates
against the Negro. This segregation is found today in 17 southern states
and the District of Columbia. . . .

In the North, segregation in education is not formal, and in some states is prohibited. Nevertheless, the existence of residential restrictions in many northern cities has had discriminatory effects on Negro education. In Chicago, for example, the schools which are most crowded and employ double shift schedules are practically all in Negro neighborhoods.

Other minorities encounter discrimination. Occasionally Indian children attending public schools in the western states are assigned to separate classrooms. Many Texas schools segregate Mexican American children in separate schools.

The second inadequacy in our present educational practices in America is the religious and racial discrimination that exists in the operation of some private educational institutions, both with respect to the admission of students and the treatment of them after admission. . . . It is clear that there is much discrimination, based on prejudice, in admission of students to private colleges, vocational schools, and graduate schools.[9]

The evil effects of this policy of segregation are widely recognized. Both parties suffer: those who discriminate and those who are discriminated against. To an appalling extent both are enslaved by the fears and antagonisms that these patterns of discrimination and segregation breed. Those who are officially rejected by their community have a deep struggle to keep from becoming embittered, and it is hard for them to maintain their faith in the sincerity of our democratic professions. They also suffer materially and culturally as well as spiritually. In spite of good intentions and much substantial progress, the existing program of separate educational treatment is still far short of equal educational treatment.

Members of the racial group responsible for this systematic negation of the democratic morality of community also suffer. So far as basic democratic values are concerned, they are obliged to be party to an ever-growing system of hypocrisies. The finer the spiritual perceptions of an individual the more is he torn today by this pattern of prejudice in the mores. The nation as a whole also suffers. Its inner unity is weakened, and its strength is sapped by the presence of millions of people in its popula-

---

[9] *To Secure These Rights,* The Report of the President's Committee on Civil Rights (New York, Simon and Schuster, Inc., 1947), pp. 62-66.

tion who realize that the basic arrangements of their society continuously operate to their personal and group disadvantage. The moral leadership of America in the world is also damaged, and this at a time when we greatly need the confidence of all peoples who are striving to achieve a life of freedom. About two-thirds of the people of the world are colored, and an America that discriminates at home against the colored groups in its citizenship will necessarily experience difficulty in gaining the confidence of the colored peoples of other countries.

When it comes to the problem of how to move to overcome these contradictions in our democratic affirmations and our actual educational practice, we encounter a number of difficulties. The deepest of these is a past that perpetuates itself by the action of the mores. Another lies in the fact that our educational system has been historically controlled not by the Federal Government, but by the different states and the local communities. We also believe that there are strong reasons for maintaining this principle of local control. In the main, the more that parents are responsible for the making of the specific policies for the education of their own children, the more democratic our educational controls are likely to be, and the less the danger that any national governmental administration will subordinate the schools to its own political purposes.

On the other hand, it is clear that if we are to have equality of opportunity in the education of the young of our country, the funds of the Federal Government will have to be used. As the President's Committee points out the seventeen southern states which have nearly 40 per cent of the school children of the nation, now command only 20 per cent of the taxable resources. It is only a matter of time until federal aid will be provided to meet this critical educational need. The aim of such legislation should be not simply to equalize educational opportunity between the different regions and states of the country, but also between the various racial, religious, and cultural groups within each region and state. The Congress, in seeking to provide federal funds for education, has the right and the obligation to stipulate that these funds shall be made available only to those states that are willing to provide genuine equality of educational opportunity. Arrangement should also be made for a system of reports and inspections which will insure that this principle of equality is observed in actual fact.

It is already clear that equality of opportunity cannot be economically provided at the higher educational level by a system of segregated colleges and professional schools. Hence the sphere of higher education would seem to be the most hopeful place to begin the disintegration of this historic pattern of segregation. There are various ways in which the strength of the Federal Government can be used to encourage the growth of non-segregated higher educational institutions in all parts of the country. Once the pattern of discrimination begins to disappear in the higher educational institutions, we can anticipate that, in time, it will also be removed from the elementary and secondary schools. Fortunately many educational, religious, and political leaders of the South—both white and colored—are eager to do their part to make their schools serve equally all the children of the community.

Nor should the Federal Government continue to support the existing system of segregated schools in the District of Columbia. The affairs of this District are under its direct jurisdiction, and it is crucial that our Government take early steps to make the Capitol of our democracy a community in which all men are in literal truth free and equal. The Capitol of the country which has been chosen to be the headquarters for the United Nations should not be a place where patterns of discrimination and segregation are tolerated.

In brief, American democracy has real "unfinished business" in this sphere of race relations. It is important that we begin at once to complete the job of developing a country that embodies in its everyday practices the morality of equality enunciated in its greatest state paper, The Declaration of Independence. The schools have a real responsibility to do their share in turning our country into a society in which *all men* have a living experience of equality.

CHAPTER XII

The Morality of Patriotism

WE HAVE sought in this book to consider the educational enterprise from the standpoint of morals. We have chosen to do this for a number of reasons. We have been concerned, in the first place, to counteract the notion that there is something unethical about the deliberate effort of adults to direct the development of the young. Our thought about education will be confused and our practice ineffectual, so long as we assume that we can direct the nurture of the young and not at the same time accept responsibility for the selection of the patterns for their development. Respect for the individuality of the child is an important principle, but it cannot be defensibly interpreted to mean that the immature human being should be left to develop in his own way. A child is never the sole architect of his own life. As we have seen, he becomes a human being by virtue of his participation in the ways of life and thought of his cultural group. Indeed, it is written into the very constitution of the process by which human beings experience and acquire the forms of their personhood that adults should play this formative rôle in the development of the immature members of their society. Man is a social animal, and it is in and through his association with others that each individual achieves his distinctively human attributes.

Schools are organized because adults desire to guide and weight the course of the experiencing and the learning of their young. Choices among real life alternatives are therefore inherent in the construction of all programs of organized education. These selected and weighted educational programs inevitably have consequences in the behaviors and the dispositions of the young. Hence the most basic problem of education is the moral problem of determining the patterns of life and thought in which the young are to be nurtured. Educational selections are grounded ultimately in value judgments; these value judgments become less arbitrary and more significant and responsible when we are aware of the moral preferences implicit in our educational activities.

We have chosen, in the second place, to discuss education from the standpoint of morals because of our interest in democracy. The democratic way of life in our own country and throughout the world is now undergoing a crucial test. We believe that education should do whatever it can to serve the ends of democratic civilization and, if it is to do this, it must understand the kind of thing a democratic society is. It is important for educators to recognize that the freedoms and opportunities of the democratic way of life depend upon the ability of human groups to organize and maintain a definite type of social and political life. Although a democratic society is grounded in respect for individual human beings and seeks their growth through the development of their ability to think, to choose, and to govern themselves, this does not mean that a democratic social system provides automatically for its own perpetuation. The values of a free society can be preserved only as its citizens recognize and accept the responsibilities that are the correlatives of their rights.

This basic social fact defines a major function of democratic education. The human dispositions—intellectual and emotional—that constitute the ultimate foundation of a democratic society are not inborn; they have to be nurtured in the children of each generation. The work of the school obviously becomes more important and more difficult whenever the citizens of a democratic country become uncertain and divided about the patterns for the further development of their institutions. Our own nation is now in the midst of such a period of social confusion and transformation. During the 'complexities and the conflicts of this transitional period, it is imperative that educators should not become cynical and defeatist about the prospects of our democracy, and that they should be alert and equipped to distinguish the essential from the non-essential in the heritage of the American people. As they continue to cultivate the primary faiths and allegiances of our democratic way of life in the young, they should also join with them in an honest search for the means of resolving our present problems. It is probable that this period of cultural mutation and world unsettlement will continue for decades, and it may well be that the course of human affairs for generations will be determined by the kind of education the children of America receive in our schools at this time.

We have viewed education as a moral enterprise, in the third place, because we have wanted to focus attention on the need for a reinterpretation of our view of morals. We have a tradition which tends to compartmentalize morals by restricting the domain of the moral to certain limited aspects of human experience. This tendency to regard morals as a thing apart, makes it easy for us to assume that moral standards are given and immutable, and that the essence of the moral problem is to get people to do the good they already know. This way of conceiving the moral task has a dual bad effect. On the one hand, it tends to make a formal thing out of morals, for whenever ideas or ideals are divorced from concrete social developments they tend to become abstract and mechanical. An abstract morality is a sterile morality; it is not qualified to sustain and direct human actions in a period of social transition and reconstruction. General principles such as human brotherhood and respect for personality have, to be sure, their enduring worth, but even primary moral conceptions of this kind are deprived of much of their significance when we restrict their application to the relationships of the family and of face-to-face neighborhood groups, and do not seek to discover their implications for wider social relationships. We need a morality today that is actively concerned with the organization and the control of our industrialized ways of making a living, with the development of more just conditions for minority racial and religious groups, and with the modification of the rôle of the nation-state in an interdependent world equipped with scientific means of massdestruction. The creative moments in the moral life of mankind have always been those occasions when old principles have acquired new meaning because they have been given a novel formulation and application in some developing sphere of human experience.

A compartmentalized morality, on the other hand, tends to mislead us. It misleads by nurturing us in the notion that we are beset by two kinds of problems—moral problems on the one side, and intellectual, economic, social, and international problems on the other. Actually the subject-matter of the moral situation is precisely the subject-matter of these practical life situations. The problem of the reorganization of our economy, for example, is not simply a problem of attaining maximum efficiency in the production and the distribution of goods and services, it is equally the problem of organizing our ways of making a living in such a manner that they will contribute to the enrichment of the lives of those engaged in them. What holds for the problem of our economy also holds for the other major problems of our civilization—all of these problems have their moral aspect and proposals for their resolution should be examined from the *human* as well as from the *technical* standpoint.

A compartmentalized morality further misleads because it tends to foster a spurious moral confidence. It prompts us to assume that we can have satisfactory moral ends or purposes without accepting responsibility for the development of the concrete means by which these general moral aims are to be attained. Americans have, at times, been disposed to this kind of moral sentimentalism, particularly in the sphere of international affairs. In view of the present great power and strategic position of our country, we must seek to become more responsible and consistent in our world policies. We can achieve this maturity only as we refuse to be satisfied with a generalized international good-will and undertake to define and organize our democratic aspirations into concrete and stable programs of international action. The moral purposes of America will be measured ultimately by the definite programs they lead us to adopt.

§ 1. *Education and the Re-ordering of the Patterns of American Life*

As the above indicates, our deepest reason for considering education from the standpoint of morals, stems from our conviction that we live in a period when great decisions and choices are required of the American people. We believe that organized education can have validity in our time only as it does its part to develop modes of human thought and relationship that are in harmony with the life imperatives of our scientific and industrial civilization. Although our democratic inheritance provides an indispensable orientation to this social and educational task, it is evident from the nature of existing conflicts about the basic meanings of American democracy that the answers to our present problems are not given ready-made in this heritage from our agrarian experience. Indeed, the clarification and the reformulation of these traditional democratic meanings is one of the most crucial parts of our present educational responsibility.

One of the most fruitful ways of making this moral audit of our civilization is to examine our institutions from the standpoint of their bearing on the welfare of our young. Many of our established practices can be viewed in more adequate perspective when they are removed from the context of the conflict of immediate interests and are explored from the standpoint of their consequences for the lives of our children. Education, concerned as it is with the long-run interests of the American people, has its distinctive approach to the problems that now press upon us. It may be that the road to stable consensus about the America of the future would more readily be found were we, as a people, prepared to evaluate all proposals for reconstruction from the perspective of the organization of a world in which we would like to have our children live.

Most Americans realize that modes of life and thought which have long been in process of formation are now in deep conflict with some of the oldest intellectual and moral perspectives of American and Western civilization. Adjustments are now required in both our intellectual outlooks and in our historic institutions. We have tried to uncover in earlier discussions some of the most basic of these conflicts. We believe that an integrated experience for the individual involves the achievement of a new integration in the governing beliefs and patterns of our civilization. As we have seen, the evolutionary account of the genesis of human beings and human culture is not in harmony with the static and dualistic presuppositions of our tradition of supernaturalism; the experimental method of developing and testing human beliefs cannot be reconciled with inherited authoritarian procedures which place the seat of intellectual authority outside of the ordinary and shareable experiences of mankind; the democratic faith in the ability of men to govern themselves and to develop all regulative principles and standards from within the context of their life affairs is not compatible with the conception that men must depend ultimately upon some elite class or institution—secular or ecclesiastical—to guide their destinies; the specialized and interdependent modes of making a living which are characteristic of industrial America cannot be administered by the social and economic doctrines of that system of laissez-faire individualism which developed during the pioneer and agrarian period of American life; the social conscience and the moral aspirations which have been bred in the American people by our commitment to the democratic principle of equality cannot dwell in peace alongside existing patterns of discrimination and segregation; nor can a dog-eat-dog system of competition that bids each person concentrate on his own private gain, be made into a tolerable morality for human beings who now live as members of an interdependent community whose actual life practices daily remind them that their bread, their security, and their very survival depend upon their learning how to coöperate and to use for peaceful ends the vast powers that science and technology have put into their hands.

An education which has faith in intelligence should not attempt to conceal or to minimize the fundamental nature of the adjustments in human thought and institutions that are made necessary by these modern developments; it should rather devote itself to the location and the analysis of those areas in which reconstruction in historic ways of life and thought must now be undertaken. We are confident our country will not achieve the conditions essential to bold democratic advance if it accepts the propaganda of those who continually remind us of the past achievements of the American people, but who refuse to come to grips with the roots of our present difficulties. It is true that the American people must have unity if they are to measure up to present demands, but the road to that unity lies through the resolution, not the evasion, of our problems.

In this concluding chapter we shall consider the most urgent of all these conflicts—the conflict that results from our tradition of national sovereignty and self-determination on the one hand, and the stubborn fact of a closely integrated, interdependent world on the other. It is apparent that developments in our atomic age are forcing basic readjustments in the traditional pattern of the relation of our country to the rest of the world. This change in the world position of the United States calls for modifications in the sentiments, the outlooks, and the objects of allegiance which our schools should now seek to nurture in the young of our country. In sum, American education must re-examine the meaning of citizenship and patriotism in a world in which human security is no longer to be provided by exclusive national means, but involves instead reliance on collective means that can be developed only through some form of world-organization.

§ 2. *Education for Citizenship and Freedom*

Our schools have always recognized that one of their fundamental tasks is the preparation of the young for their responsibilities as American citizens. Indeed, concern for the welfare of the nation was one of the primary factors which led to the founding of our tax-supported, public school system. In our country education for citizenship has been widely interpreted to imply education for enlightenment, because most Americans have believed that an informed citizenry is essential to the health of our Republic. But education for citizenship has also been interpreted to involve the cultivation in the young of a love for their country and a sincere regard for the history, the institutions, and the democratic aspirations of the American people. Our schools have assumed that in a nation in which the people create the government there is no intrinsic conflict between seeking to make a loyal citizen out of the child, and seeking to make him into a resourceful and independent person possessed of a mind of his own. In short, the American school has never believed that our democratic regard for the child as an end in himself should be taken to imply that we are morally obligated to develop him into a detached neutral, indifferent to the vital interests of his own land and people. For the most part, our schools have held that the real moral problem is not whether we have a right to make an American out of the child, but rather to determine the kind of person an American should be, and the educational means that should be used in the development of that kind of a person.

Much as we deplore some of the specific means which certain groups have used in their zeal to make patriots out of the children of our country, we are nevertheless in accord with the view that our schools should be deliberately used to prepare the young for their rôles as patriotic American citizens. We believe that full respect for the personality of the child is quite compatible with the effort to make him a devoted member of the American nation. This means that we reject the view of those universalists who contend that national interest and allegiance have no place in a genuine program of liberal education, whose true aim, in their opinion, should be the nurture of the child as a member of humanity, not as a member of any one historical society, and not as a person who is to live as a citizen of any particular nation. It also means that we reject the view of those extreme individualists who hold that the aim of education should be to develop the full individuality of each child, and that we arbitrarily impose upon his inborn uniqueness whenever we seek to adjust him to the ways of life and thought of any specific national community. It further means that we reject the views of those democratic educators who seek to reduce education to a bare process of inquiry and criticism, and who assert that the inclusive moral aim in a democracy is "to teach the child to think, not what to think," and that we therefore should not seek to commit the child to the life ways of our nation, but should rather let him decide for himself whether he wants to be an American citizen, and if so, what kind, and to what extent. It means finally that we reject the view of those who hold that the concept of the nation is a sheer abstraction invented to delude and manipulate people, and that the social and moral realities are the different economic groups and classes, and that education for enlightenment will seek to identify the child not with his nation, but with the interests and needs of the class of industrial workers.

In earlier discussions we have described some of the grave difficulties that we find in these theories of the meaning of liberal or democratic education. Here we shall mention only two crucial objections. These theories are grounded in a mistaken view of the meaning of individuality and of the nature of human freedom; the newborn become significant and "free" human personalities in and through their participation in the life of some historical group. The school should not try to make its program a rival or a substitute for this process of participation, it should rather strive to make the participation of the young in the life and thought ways of their country, a process of liberation, not of enslavement. All of these theories fail, in the second place, when put to the test of actual school practice. They fail because educators, including the propounders of these theories, simply cannot direct the growth of the young by exclusive reliance on a body of abstract concepts. Teachers necessarily refer in innumerable ways to the modes of life and thought of the society in which they and their pupils, live, think, and have their real beings. The children of our country will become Americans in any event, our problem as responsible educators is not to ignore this basic psychological fact, but rather to seek to make our young as adequate as we can in their rôles as citizens of our country. Nor is it probable that for many, membership in an economic class can substitute for citizenship in their country.

In the actual practice of the American schools, education for citizenship has been given a primary place, and it has taken many and various forms. We turn now to describe some of the major ways in which our schools have sought to prepare our children for their careers as citizens of the American nation.

§ 3. *Education and the Making of an American*

Judged by the emphasis of American educational practice, the people of our country are united in the conviction that a good American is one who loves the land in which he lives. Through our geographies and histories, through American novels, poems and dramas, through school pageants, through the pictures we have hung in the halls and the classrooms, as well as through the national hymns and folk-songs we have taught the young to sing in the schools, we have sought to nurture our children in affectionate regard for the motherland. The majesty of our mountains, the fertility of our prairies, the spacious grazing lands of the plains, the rich and varied mineral resources of our continental domain, the beauty of our wooded hills, lakes, rivers, and waterfalls, the grandeur of our public parks, the natural protection provided by the two great oceans; these and similar features of the homeland have been constantly celebrated in the schools. Our children have also been introduced to points of natural beauty and historical interest in their immediate surroundings, and the schools have sought to cultivate in them a sense of particular pride in their own state and region. Obviously many influences in addition to those of the schools have served to nurture a love of America in our young, but it cannot be doubted that the schools have played a primary rôle in the cultivation of this sentiment.

A good American not only loves his motherland, he also has a respect and a regard for his people, and our schools have been encouraged to nurture this regard in our young. They have emphasized that a citizen of America is a member of a distinguished human group marked by great and worthy traditions. They have taught the young that our nation is unique in that it is composed of many different groups who have left the lands and cultures of their birth in order to make their homes in America—the land of opportunity, freedom and tolerance. The schools have made a national virtue of the fact that so many of our immigrants came from the oppressed, the down-trodden, and the working classes of the Old World. The millions of immigrants who have sought a new life here have been viewed as exponents of that quality in the spirit of man which will not submit to oppression, injustice, and a brutish existence. Our ancestors have been pictured as plain men and women who nevertheless achieved real distinction because of their willingness to take great risks and to endure cruel hardship in order that they might live as free men in a free society.

Our schools have also celebrated the initiative, the courage,

and the endurance of those groups who for more than three cen-
turies continued to pioneer in the epic movement to win and
settle the American continent, and to make it the foundation for
a great new civilization characterized by decent standards of
living and a genuine equality of opportunity. The schools have
equally cherished the inventive genius, the technological competence, and the organizing ability of the American people.
They have pointed with pride to superior personal traits of
Americans—to their generous human sympathy as manifested
by their ready response to the emergency needs of people anywhere who suffer from flood, famine, earthquakes, volcanic
eruptions, plagues or other natural disaster. They have emphasized their public spirit and philanthropy as shown by their
huge and never ending gifts to schools and colleges, to hospitals
and charitable organizations, to research foundations, to libraries, museums and art galleries, and to public parks and playgrounds. In sum, the schools have conceived the patriot as the
individual who loves his land and his people, and they have had
considerable success in breeding this attitude in the lives of the
young.

But the schools have recognized that patriotism involves
more than attachment to the land and the people of our country; it also involves loyalty to a common way of life. The record
shows that the schools have faithfully served as the agencies of
the nation in the development of this respect for the basic patterns of American life. Our country was born in a revolution,
and our schools have nurtured the young in the conviction that
this revolutionary war was fought for a holy cause. The men who
resisted the soldiers of the English king at Lexington and Con-
cord, who suffered and died during the hard winter at Valley
Forge, and who ultimately won through to victory at Yorktown,
have been featured by our schools as heroic participants in the
age-long struggle of the human race for freedom and equality.
Our schools have also paid tribute to those who have continued
this struggle for human freedom within the life of our own

Republic—Washington, Jefferson, Jackson, Lincoln, Wilson, and Roosevelt are some of the public figures that our schools have held before the children of our country as examples of the ideals and the aspirations of the American people. Many of our schools bear the names of honored leaders of our democracy. In the nurture of loyalty to the American way of life our schools have made constant use of such great public documents as the Mayflower Compact, The Declaration of Independence, The Federalist Papers, The Constitution of the United States, The Bill of Rights, The Madison Memorial and Remonstrance, The Gettysburg Address, and the Charter of the United Nations.

Our schools have emphasized that, in the main, the United States has not been an aggressive, military power bent on imperialist expansion. Our military adventures in Latin America and the Far East have never enjoyed the solid support of the people, and most American educators consider the principles of the "good neighbor" policy as a more authentic expression of American interests and purposes. Indeed this policy which combines national independence and sovereignty with international good will is a true symbol of our historic world outlook. Our schools have also stressed that in our country the military authorities are subordinate to the civilian, that we have never believed in peacetime conscription, that we have persistently opposed universal military training, and that we have never fortified the long frontier between the United States and Canada. Our teachers have believed that loyalty to America was wholly compatible with loyalty to the wider interests of humanity, and we have not sought to make ardent patriots out of our children by instilling in them a fear and hatred of other peoples. Undoubtedly, the fact that we were relatively a self-sufficient, continental nation, favored by the security of our general geographical position, has made it simpler for us than for many other nations to adopt this attitude of non-aggression and general international good-will. But the American people have also sincerely believed that the ways of peaceful coöperation are superior to the ways of aggression and war, and we have tried to use our schools to nurture this moral faith in our young.

Pride in our own achievements and traits as a people has not led the American school to deny or belittle the merits and the achievements of others. On the contrary, we have sought to develop a positive appreciation of the peoples of other lands and cultures. Our bias, to be sure, has been in favor of democratic social and political systems, but we have also believed that each people has the right to determine in its own form of economy and government, and historically we have not refused to coöperate with peoples whose systems of life and government were different from ours. We have assumed that world security and peace could be attained if all nations would adopt this policy of "live and let live," and would refrain from aggressive designs on their neighbors. In brief, peace through the voluntary coöperation of independent, sovereign nations has been the major premise of American thought. It has been our conviction that the patterns of democratic civilization would in time become the patterns of all peoples and that universal peace would be a product of this growth of democracy. The American schools, however, have not been concerned with the mere cultivation of loyalty to the political state, for we have always believed that democracy is a social as well as a political concept. For the most part, American education has attempted to nurture the view that government is the servant, not the master, and that the state exists solely for the purpose of serving the needs and protecting the interests of the people. It cannot be denied that there has been some tendency in the schools toward flag-patriotism and the narrow, nationalist attitude of "my country right or wrong," but many teachers have been alert to the dangers inherent in this effort to exalt the nation and to remove its foreign deeds and policies from critical inspection. These teachers have endeavored to counteract this tendency toward an unreflective patriotism by emphasizing that democracy is a way of life as well as a form of government, and that the citizen of a democracy has the responsibility of examining on the basis of democratic values all actions of his government—foreign as well as domestic. Thus patriotism in American education has been given social as well as political meaning. Our schools have worked to strengthen the conception that the community is primary, and that all governments derive their purposes and their powers, in the last analysis, from the community that creates them.

More has been involved, therefore, in the nurture of the good American than education in political functions and responsibilities. Love of country has also meant more than love of the political state; it has involved as its deepest meaning love of American civilization. Through their studies in literature, in history, and in science, our children have learned how much American civilization owes to the cultural and the scientific discoveries of other peoples—particularly the peoples of Europe. They have learned from their studies in the fine and practical arts that much of significance in the experience of the American people cannot be subsumed under the category of the political. Patriotism as cultivated in the young in our schools has meant loyalty to our whole democratic civilization, not fanatical devotion to an all-comprehending state.

But American education has, nonetheless, been devoted to the making of an American. Our schools have been deliberately organized to nurture in our children a love for their mother country, a love for the people with whom they share a common heritage and a common destiny, an appreciation of our American system of life and government, as well as a readiness to live and, if need be, to die for it. The mind out of which the typical American citizen thinks and acts is clothed with the meanings and the values of this American national community. His interests and his allegiances undoubtedly can be broadened to include the whole human race—many Americans already cherish these more inclusive values and loyalties—but the average American is not so constituted in his psychological make-up that he could seriously entertain the ideal of becoming a citizen of the world, if world-citizenship meant that he would have to cease being an American. It is quite possible that a program of citizenship education could be developed that would nurture a person who would feel, think and respond as a world-minded American, but in any world situation that we can responsibly pre-figure at this time, it would be difficult to make a generation of American children world-minded if that involved the abandonment of the right to be American-minded. What is true of America is also true of most of the other nations of the world.

The reality of this situation defines the problem of education for citizenship at this time. We live in an interdependent world in which security from lethal means of human destruction must be global if it is to be real. But we also live in a world that is organized in the pattern of these seventy or more sovereign nations. These nations are solid political, economic, and psychological facts. They are the cultural and political forms that the evolution of the human race has produced. The sentiments and the loyalties which these different nations and cultures breed in their people are as real as the integrated and interdependent world that science and technology have built.

All plans for education, as well as all plans for political and social action, must be judged by the way in which they take account of these two basic social facts. Both political and educational plans are utopian if they assume that we can enjoy reasonable security by the mere perpetuation of the historic system of separate and absolute nation-states; they are equally utopian if they assume that we can achieve security by the immediate organization of a world-state that will supplant these more than seventy independent nations that are the product of human history. Modern man may be obsolete, as some declare, but he is not as obsolete as the political theory and the social psychology which assume that we can educate and organize human beings for a world system that ignores the actual nations in which they live, and which so profoundly mold the psychological natures which they acquire.

The great strength of the United Nations is that it is grounded in the recognition of the existence of nations—large and small—and in the recognition of the human need for collective security. It has encountered great difficulties but these difficulties are real and cannot be avoided if we want to develop a trustworthy system of world organization.

§ 4. The Experiment of the United Nations

American initiative played a primary part in the organization of the United Nations. In working out the plans for this world organization our leaders were controlled by a number of considerations. They recognized that our historic policy of "continental Americanism" is dead. "Continental Americanism" is a term used by some to denote the dual policy through which Americans voluntarily coöperated in many financial, economic, and humanitarian world-undertakings, but our government never became officially involved in any alliance or world arrangement that would impair our full right of national self-determination. In spite of this desire to concentrate on our own internal affairs, events had actually involved us in two costly world wars within the short space of twenty-five years. Our leaders perceived that the growth of America—its vast resources and expanding world interests—meant that we would almost surely become involved were further world-conflicts to develop. They therefore concluded that our own interests, and the interests of the world as a whole, would be better served if America abandoned her historic policy of absolute national independence and assumed a responsible part in the shaping of world-affairs.

Our leaders also recognized that transformations in the modes of warfare had destroyed the security from outside attack so long provided by the two great oceans. They realized that technological developments, including the invention of the atom bomb, meant that if we continued to adhere to the policy of

national self-sufficiency, it would no longer lead in actual practice to the peaceful and relatively unarmed "cultivation of our
own domestic garden." Inevitably we would seek to make America secure through a program of military preparedness. Hence
our leaders were convinced that the real choice now before us
was a choice between some form of collective security on the
one side, and a grim effort to turn America into a self-sufficient
fortress on the other. They believed that the prospect of peace
would be stronger if we entered upon a program of mutual
security rather than upon a policy of national self-sufficiency
which, under the life conditions of today, would almost surely
evolve into a program of increasing militarism at home and of
imperialist expansion abroad. Our leaders perceived that any
unilateral program to make our own country secure would gradually expand to include the whole Western hemisphere as the
area to be defended, and that the drive for strategic naval and
air bases as well as for secure access to essential raw materials and
world markets would soon involve us in the discredited practice
of power politics. They were agreed that the search for a substitute for war through the development of a general world organization was a more desirable program for the United States to
adopt.

But our leaders also realized that the American people were
not at all disposed to support a program of world organization
if that program would require us to abandon the sovereign right
of self-determination and to place the material and human resources of our country at the disposal of a world agency in which
we obviously would not have the controlling voice. Much as we
believed in security through collective means, America, as one
of the major powers of the modern world, was not prepared to
give up its right to decide in each concrete situation the purposes
for which our forces were to be used. Our leaders also knew from
their conferences with the leaders of the Soviet Union that what
was true in the case of America was equally true of Soviet Russia. It was therefore mutually decided that special representation

should be given five major powers—the Soviet Union, the United States, Great Britain, France and China—in the Security Council, the agency of the United Nations that has primary responsibility for dealing with any situation in the world where a threat to peace might develop. In order to give further protection to the sovereign rights of each of the major powers the principle of unanimity was adopted; this principle meant that the United Nations could not commit the forces of any one of these five nations to a program organized to deal with a disturbed situation without the explicit consent of that nation. Although subsequent experience has shown that the Soviet Union has made an unanticipated use of this right of veto, the fact remains that American leaders were as concerned as the Russians to have this provision incorporated into the Charter of the United Nations.

It was the faith of the American leaders that the road to world security and peace would be better provided by this functional and non-coercive approach to world organization than by reliance on a formal world organization equipped with abstract legal authority to compel all members to obey its decisions. Our leaders realized that if the major powers really wanted to coöperate for the ends of world security, and economic and cultural progress, they could do it through the agency of the United Nations, even though its Security Council was bound by this "principle of unanimity." They were equally convinced that if one of the major powers considered a given line of action to be in conflict with its vital interests, that there was no means short of war that could compel it to accept the proposed program. Their sense of the reality of the nation made them unwilling to trust an abstract legal system to dispose of all that national interest and allegiance meant in the world of today.

Our leaders were committed to another strategy—they believed that through an experience of working together for constructive ends, the various members of the United Nations could evolve through their coöperation an agency that would become a genuine world authority. As our leaders viewed it, the actual forces of history had brought these five major powers and the nations associated with them, into an effective coalition to resist the aggressions of the Axis. They hoped that this functioning coalition forged by the demands of the World War could be transmuted into a permanent agency for the maintenance of peace once the war was over. Thus the plan of the United Nations was grounded in two basic presuppositions: one, that following the defeat of the Axis powers, the victor nations would agree upon a plan of world settlement; and, two, that this world settlement would be of such a nature that all of the members of the United Nations would not only have a vital stake in maintaining it, but would be prepared on the basis of that settlement to join in a program of political, economic, cultural and humanitarian coöperation which would gradually develop a structure of policies and institutions that would supply a real alternative to the historic system of militarism and war.

It was devotion to purposes of this sort which led the American Secretary of State, Cordell Hull, to make his long and arduous trip to Moscow in the Fall of 1943, so that he could confer about postwar plans with the representatives of the Soviet Union, the United Kingdom and China. Clear commitment to these basic principles is shown in the Joint Four Nation Declaration which resulted from this Moscow Conference. In this agreement the Four Powers jointly declare:

That their united action, pledged for the prosecution of the war against their respective enemies, will be continued for the organization and maintenance of peace and security.

That they recognize the necessity of establishing at the earliest practicable date a general international organization based on the principle of the sovereign equality of all peace-loving States, and open to membership by all such States, large and small, for the maintenance of international peace and security.

That for the purpose of maintaining international peace and security pending the re-establishment of law and order and the inauguration of a system of general security, they will consult with one another and as occasion requires with other members of the United Nations with a view to joint action on behalf of the community of nations.[1]

In his report to the House of Commons, Anthony Eden, the head of the United Kingdom delegation at the Moscow Conference, expressed both the hopes and the fears of the leaders of the Western democratic countries about the projected program when he said:

> The truth must be faced that it is on the part of these powers principally that will lie the responsibility for insuring that this war will be followed by lasting peace. If they could agree together there is no point that is not capable of final solution. If they do not agree together there is no international event which could not become an international problem.[2]

In an editorial at the time the American weekly, *The New Republic,* gave its view of the significance of the Moscow agreement when it declared, "it is no exaggeration to say that, despite all the difficulties that still lie ahead, last week's actions by the Moscow Conference and by the U. S. Senate have swung open the portals to a new world." [3] Today, five years after the total defeat of the Axis powers, we are not nearly so sure that we have succeeded in opening "the portals to a new world" of security and peace. Although the organization of the United Nations has been completed, our world is still tragically divided. Indeed, it is possibly more seriously divided than at any other period in the history of mankind.

The Soviet Union and the democracies of the West have not as yet discovered the means by which they can "agree together." They have even failed in large measure to agree about the nature of the world settlement. In Europe, they have reached no common plan for the future of Germany, and in Asia they have their separate zones of postwar control. As a result of this failure to make an over-all peace settlement, the United Nations

---

[1] *Four Nation Declaration,* printed in *The New York Times,* November 2, 1943.

[2] *The New York Times,* November 8, 1943.

[3] *The New Republic,* Vol. 109, No. 20, November 15, 1943.

has had to function without the foundation that a solid agreement about the contours of the postwar world would have provided. Even those preliminary agreements that were reached during the period of the war have been nullified by the manner in which the Soviet Union has since chosen to interpret them.

Although the Soviet Union has shared in the work of the General Assembly and the Security Council of the United Nations, she has not been willing to participate in the economic, social, scientific, cultural, and educational activities of many of its most important departments. The failure of Russia to share in the work of these commissions is serious, for it was originally assumed that as a result of coöperation in these constructive programs, the different nations would grow in mutual understanding and in their ability to work together for world unity and security. In the sessions of the Security Council, the Soviet Union has made such frequent and unexpected use of her veto power that this crucial agency of the United Nations has been all but paralyzed.

Most important of all has been the failure to reach an agreement about the instruments of atomic warfare. The far-reaching American proposal for a genuine system of international control and inspection of the development and use of atomic energy has earned the hearty support of fourteen members of the United Nations Commission, but the Soviet Union, Poland and Ukraine have steadfastly voted against this plan. After discussions in 220 meetings of this United Nations Commission, extending over a period of two years, the Commission has announced that: "It has been unable to secure the agreement of the Soviet Union to even those elements of effective control considered essential from the technical point of view, let alone their acceptance of the nature and extent of participation in the world community required of all nations in this field by the first and second reports of the Atomic Energy Commission."

Similar failure has marked the effort of the United Nations Commission to get an accord about the regulation of the more conventional forms of armament. As a result of these failures to achieve understanding, the burden of military preparation has continued to grow heavier. Today, in the heart of the strategic land mass of Europe and Asia, the Soviet Union has developed one of the most powerful military machines of human history, and on its side America is making unprecedented investments to keep her defense forces at a high level of efficiency.

Since the close of the war against the Axis powers, the forces of the Soviet Union and those of the Western democracies have been engaged in a struggle for influence and control in many different theatres in Europe, the Near East, and the Far East. This struggle has become so severe that it now is popularly described as "the cold war." On her side, the Soviet Union has created a bloc of Communist nations which act as a unit in all world affairs. She has also revived the world Communist political organization under the new name of the "Cominform." In all parts of the world, the constituent national parties of this world Communist movement now operate under directives developed by the leaders of the Kremlin. The strength of these Communist parties varies enormously in different countries, but their Trojan horse practices of infiltration and exploitation of depressed and discontented groups have given them real power in every continent. Their influence is naturally greatest in those countries which suffered most from the devastation of the war, and among those colonial peoples that are struggling to throw off foreign imperialist controls. In China, the Communists have all but completed their conquest of that vast nation with a population of more than 450 millions of people. Even in such mature and technologically advanced countries as Italy and France, the Communists have penetrated deeply into labor and political movements and exert a strong influence over all public affairs.

These militant and unilateral actions on the part of the Soviet Union and its associates have brought about a great change in the attitudes of the leaders and the citizens of the Western democratic countries. The possibility of ultimate coöperation in and through the United Nations is still retained, and no responsible leader has accepted the defeatist view that another world war is inevitable, but the critical nature of the present situation is now frankly recognized. The American Secretary of State, Dean Acheson, refers to this deterioration in world affairs in a paragraph in the letter he prepared for President Truman in connection with the transmittal of the official White Paper on United States-Chinese relations. In discussing earlier American policies he states:

> This was of course the period during which joint prosecution of the war against Nazi Germany had produced a degree of coöperation between the United States and Russia. President Roosevelt was determined to do what he could to bring about a continuance in the postwar period of a partnership forged in the fire of battle. The peoples of the world, sickened and weary with the excesses, the horrors, and the degradation of the war, shared this desire. It has remained for the postwar years to demonstrate that one of the major partners in this world alliance seemingly no longer pursues this aim, if indeed it ever did.[4]

As they have observed these developments in the policies of the Soviet bloc, the Western democratic countries have tended to unite for the defense of their own interests. Under the Truman doctrine and the Marshall plan, our country has given extensive aid to the governments of Greece and Turkey, and it has assumed an unprecedented rôle in a comprehensive program for the economic rehabilitation of the nations of Western Europe. These financial and economic measures are now being broadened by the organization of what is called the North Atlantic Community. The stated purpose of this North Atlantic alliance is to unite the United States and Canada with the nations of Western and Northern Europe for the collective defense of "the freedom, common heritage and civilization of their peoples, founded on the principles of democracy, individual liberty and the rule of law." According to the Articles of this Treaty, which has already been ratified by the U. S. Senate and signed by the President of the United States:

---

[4] Printed in *The New York Times*, August 6, 1949.

The Parties, separately and jointly, by means of continuous and effective self-help and mutual aid, will maintain and develop their individual and collective capacity to resist armed attack.

The Parties will consult together whenever, in the opinion of any of them the territorial integrity, political independence or security of any of these Parties is threatened.

The Parties agree that an armed attack against one or more of them in Europe or North America shall be considered an attack against them all; and consequently they agree that, if such an armed attack occurs, each of them, in exercise of the right of individual or collective self-defense recognized by Article 51 of the Charter of the United Nations, will assist the Party or Parties so attacked by taking forthwith, individually and in concert with the other Parties, such action as it deems necessary, including the use of armed force, to restore and maintain the security of the North Atlantic area.

Any such armed attack and all measures as a result thereof shall immediately be reported to the Security Council. Such measures shall be terminated when the Security Council has taken the measures necessary to restore and maintain international peace and security.

Obviously the acceptance of this North Atlantic Treaty marks another momentous development in the foreign policies and responsibilities of our country. Although under its terms the United States retains the right to determine the nature of its specific responsibilities in any situation which may arise, there can be no doubt that we are committed by the Treaty to make common cause with the countries of Western Europe in their effort to defend themselves against any "potential aggressor." Although every effort has been made to bring the provisions of the North Atlantic Treaty within the general framework of the United Nations, it is apparent that the Treaty is a frank recognition of the fact that affairs have not at all developed in the postwar world as we had hoped they would.

In fine, the Treaty is solid evidence that our world is not united, it is divided. It is divided because the major partners of the coalition that was formed to defeat the Fascist powers have not been able to make a living thing of their pledge to continue their united action "for the organization and maintenance of peace and security." Differences in history, in systems of value and belief, and in systems of economy and government, underlie their difficulty in making an operative reality of their partnership in the United Nations. These differences, and the fears, suspicions, and rival ambitions that they breed, have divided the world into two power blocs. The Soviet Union is the dominant factor in one of these blocs, and our own country, somewhat against the will of the American people, has been thrust into a position of primary responsibility in the other. It is within the context of this divided world that education must be carried on, and that education for citizenship must re-define its essential meanings.[5]

§ 5. *Education and the Struggle for a Democratic World Civilization*

American education must take full account of these grim developments in the world situation. Our country has become one of the power centers of the modern world and is involved in a structure of international relationships that puts new demands on its citizens. The fate of democratic civilization may depend upon the use we make of our power during this critical period.

Education must define the significance of these new world relationships for the nurture of our young. We have abandoned our historic isolationism. We have ratified the Charter of the United Nations and we are committed to the effort to create a general system of collective security. But our postwar experiences have convinced us that the United Nations cannot be formed into a genuine system of collective security so long as the Soviet Union persists in its present program of aggression. We have learned that measures of appeasement will not induce the Russian leaders to renounce their present power drive. Concessions

---

[5] Since the above was written, it has been officially announced that the Soviet Union has succeeded in the production of the atom bomb. Obviously, this development makes the problem of the divided world more serious and urgent, although it is too early to say whether it will help or make more difficult the effort to find a common approach to the problem of world security.

of this kind are taken as signs of weakness, and they tend to strengthen the very tendencies that we are seeking to eradicate. We have therefore entered upon a program of firm resistance. We have refused to be forced out of Berlin. In coöperation with Britain and France we are sponsoring a separate organization of Western Germany. Under the Marshall plan we are providing substantial economic aid to the countries of Western Europe. We are pledged by the North Atlantic Pact to a program of the collective defense of the nations of the North Atlantic Community. We have given extensive help to the governments of Greece and Turkey, and we are beginning to search for means by which the advance of Communist forces can be halted in the Far East. We continue to stock-pile atom bombs. Our appropriations for the armed services are greater than at any other period of our history.

In the main, these policies of our government are national policies, supported by the members of both major parties. In spite of the burdens they put upon us, these policies are backed by the major functional groups of our country—business, labor, and agriculture. The leaders of organized labor, for example, are coöperating both at home and abroad in the formulation and the administration of these policies. Both the American Federation of Labor and the Congress of Industrial Organizations are vigilant in the effort to keep Communists out of control of their various unions, and they are uniting in the effort to develop a non-Communist world labor movement. Although most Americans realize that there are dangerous potentialities in these world policies of our country, they are convinced that they are necessary. They believe that the prospect of organizing a world in which freedom can survive is being strengthened by this demonstration in action that we are resolved to do our part to protect democratic civilization against all forms of aggression—political and cultural as well as military.

Whether the eventual outcome will be peace or a disastrous third World War, no one can predict with assurance at this time.

Much will depend upon the forces in our country that will control the further development of these policies and that will determine the way in which they will be applied in the different areas of need and tension. Much will also depend upon the reactions of the peoples of the world to these measures—will they eventually come to be viewed as expressions of a policy of American aggrandizement, or will they be welcomed as genuine efforts to maintain and create the conditions for democratic world organization and peace. Obviously, much will also depend upon the ultimate response of the members of the Soviet Bloc. As they witness the evolution of these policies will they be led to conclude that another world war is inevitable, or will they gradually show by their actual practice that they believe what Stalin has so often affirmed, namely, that it is possible for Communists and non-Communist nations to coöperate for world security and peace? The period of tension and uncertainty may be prolonged for decades. Nothing but harm will result from the assumption on our part that world affairs must rapidly take the form of total peace or total war. There is another alternative. Relations may continue strained for a prolonged period, and then gradually improve as the two Power Blocs begin to find ways of adjusting to one another.

In any case, American educators would do well not to underestimate the elements of strength in the world movement headed by Soviet Russia. Although the Soviet Union is not so technologically advanced as the countries of Western Europe, she is rapidly developing the scientific and technological competence of her people. The Soviet Union and the nations associated with her have a strategic geographical position. The great land armies of Russia are within walking distance of Western Europe and the Near East. Now that China has entered her orbit, Soviet Russia has also become a dominant factor in the Far East. Her vast domain possesses natural resources that provide an adequate material base for the development of a powerful industrial civilization. Her people have demonstrated in the ordeal of war their devotion to their country and their capacity for heroic resistance. The leaders of the Soviet Bloc are inspired by the Marxist system of philosophy which gives them the assurance that the forces of history are working on their side. Even in many non-Communist lands, the belief spreads that we are restricted today to a choice between a reactionary and repressive Fascist movement on one side, and the dynamic, liberating, and revolutionary movement of world Communism on the other. The Russian policy of equal treatment of all peoples has great appeal, particularly in those regions where colored peoples have suffered from the domination of the white race. Through the existence of seasoned and disciplined Communist movements in all parts of the world, the Soviet Union has the service of an agency that is unprecedented in the cultural and political life of mankind. By their grip on labor and other underprivileged and exploited groups, these national Communist parties have repeatedly shown their ability to exploit the civil liberties of democratic countries, to abort regular Constitutional processes, and, when conditions become favorable, to seize power by direct and violent action. The World Communist movement is directed by leaders who are well informed about world economic and political conditions, who have learned how to combine long-run purposes with flexible strategies adjusted to the peculiar conditions of different countries, and who have mastered the arts of propaganda. Those who have had most experience with these Communist leaders in world conferences, in labor and political movements, and in cultural and educational affairs have the highest regard for their abilities, even though they deplore the ends to which these personal abilities are so uniformly subordinated. The democratic forces have, to be sure, their own peculiar strengths, but American leaders would make a cardinal error if they were to assume that the Soviet Bloc does not signify a movement of great present and potential power in the modern world.

American educators would make an even more serious error were they to permit the strength and threat of the Soviet forces to lead them to unite with those who are moved by their fears to urge a program of repression and to put their trust solely in the military strength of our country. We may be sure that a mood of hysteria will not be favorable to the development of the mature American policies that are required to meet the varied demands of the present world situation. The world is divided into two great power blocs, but that does not mean that war is inevitable. The fact that an unarmed America would almost surely encourage the leaders of the Soviet Bloc to undertake bolder programs of aggression, does make it imperative that we do our part to equip the democratic forces for effective armed resistance. But the clear recognition that adequate military preparation is desirable does not mean that it is our only, or even our first, line of defense. A united and educated citizenry, informed about world affairs, including the history, the philosophy, and the economic and political practices of revolutionary Communism, trained in the disciplines and the techniques of modern science and technology, and inspired by the democratic values of American and Western civilization, still remains our first need if our concern is to organize by peaceful means a world system of collective security.

America undoubtedly must be strong if she is to be equal to her present responsibilities. But the strength of a democratic nation is a product of many factors. It derives from the unity of its people, a unity that develops when the members of the various constituent groups believe that they live under just arrangements that do not subject them to economic, political and cultural discrimination. It is rooted in the health and vigor of a people that results when all are adequately nourished, housed, and provided with essential medical and social services. It is grounded in the sense of security that is bred in a people when all have opportunity for remunerative work and realize that the productive powers of their country are not being wasted, but are rather being efficiently used to meet human needs. It is also grounded in the knowledge, the intellectual competence, and the technical skill which a people acquires through a universal and diversified program of education, equally available to all. It is fostered by a system of civil and political liberty that makes it possible for the members of different economic and social groups to share their needs and their hopes with their fellow-citizens, and to unite with them in the discussion and the formulation of programs to meet their needs. It is also nurtured by the knowledge that a people has of the values and the institutions of a free society, and by its appreciation of the struggles and sacrifices that men have undergone in order to develop this organized life of freedom and equality that we call democracy. Most basically of all it is grounded in the devotion of a people to their institutions and laws, and to their conviction that the government which is formulating the policies of their nation is led by men of their own choosing, and that these leaders are seeking the welfare of the plain people who have elected them to their offices of public trust. These are the ultimate elements of strength in our country, and without these deeper conditions of health and unity and devotion, no program of military preparation can in and of itself make America secure.

The development of an America that will have the strength to take her full part in the struggle for a democratic world civilization defines the deepest purpose of our system of education at this time. It is from the perspective of this world need and purpose that education of the American citizen should develop its concrete meanings. There is no conflict between this broadened conception of the meaning of American citizenship, and the need of humanity for a world organized for security, peace, freedom, and social progress. Today, we know of no alternative means by which these great human ends can be achieved.

INDEX

AMERICAN EDUCATION:
ITS MEN, IDEAS, AND INSTITUTIONS
An Arno Press/New York Times Collection

Series I

Culver, Raymond B. **Horace Mann and Religion in the Massachusetts Public Schools.** 1929.

Curoe, Philip R. V. **Educational Attitudes and Policies of Organized Labor in the United States.** 1926.

Dabney, Charles William. **Universal Education in the South.** 1936.

Dearborn, Ned Harland. **The Oswego Movement in American Education.** 1925.

De Lima, Agnes. **Our Enemy the Child.** 1926.

Dewey, John. **The Educational Situation.** 1902.

Dexter, Franklin B., editor. **Documentary History of Yale University.** 1916.

Eliot, Charles William. **Educational Reform: Essays and Addresses.** 1898.

Ensign, Forest Chester. **Compulsory School Attendance and Child Labor.** 1921.

Fitzpatrick, Edward Augustus. **The Educational Views and Influence of De Witt Clinton.** 1911.

Fleming, Sanford. **Children & Puritanism.** 1933.

Flexner, Abraham. **The American College: A Criticism.** 1908.

Foerster, Norman. **The Future of the Liberal College.** 1938.

Gilman, Daniel Coit. **University Problems in the United States.** 1898.

Hall, Samuel R. **Lectures on School-Keeping.** 1829.

Hall, Stanley G. **Adolescence: Its Psychology and Its Relations to Physiology, Anthropology, Sociology, Sex, Crime, Religion, and Education.** 1905. 2 vols.

Hansen, Allen Oscar. **Early Educational Leadership in the Ohio Valley.** 1923.

Harris, William T. **Psychologic Foundations of Education.** 1899.

Harris, William T. **Report of the Committee of Fifteen on the Elementary School.** 1895.

Harveson, Mae Elizabeth. **Catharine Esther Beecher: Pioneer Educator.** 1932.

Jackson, George Leroy. **The Development of School Support in Colonial Massachusetts.** 1909.

Kandel, I. L., editor. **Twenty-five Years of American Education.** 1924.

Kemp, William Webb. **The Support of Schools in Colonial New York by the Society for the Propagation of the Gospel in Foreign Parts.** 1913.

Kilpatrick, William Heard. **The Dutch Schools of New Netherland and Colonial New York.** 1912.

Kilpatrick, William Heard. **The Educational Frontier.** 1933.

Knight, Edgar Wallace. **The Influence of Reconstruction on Education in the South.** 1913.

Le Duc, Thomas. **Piety and Intellect at Amherst College, 1865-1912.** 1946.

Maclean, John. **History of the College of New Jersey from Its Origin in 1746 to the Commencement of 1854.** 1877.

Maddox, William Arthur. **The Free School Idea in Virginia before the Civil War.** 1918.

Mann, Horace. **Lectures on Education.** 1855.

McCadden, Joseph J. **Education in Pennsylvania, 1801-1835, and Its Debt to Roberts Vaux.** 1855.

McCallum, James Dow. **Eleazar Wheelock.** 1939.

McCuskey, Dorothy. **Bronson Alcott, Teacher.** 1940.

Meiklejohn, Alexander. **The Liberal College.** 1920.

Miller, Edward Alanson. **The History of Educational Legislation in Ohio from 1803 to 1850.** 1918.

Miller, George Frederick. **The Academy System of the State of New York.** 1922.

Monroe, Will S. **History of the Pestalozzian Movement in the United States.** 1907.

Mosely Education Commission. **Reports of the Mosely Education Commission to the United States of America October-December, 1903.** 1904.

Mowry, William A. **Recollections of a New England Educator.** 1908.

Mulhern, James. **A History of Secondary Education in Pennsylvania.** 1933.

National Herbart Society. **National Herbart Society Yearbooks 1-5, 1895-1899.** 1895-1899.

Nearing, Scott. **The New Education: A Review of Progressive Educational Movements of the Day.** 1915.

Neef, Joseph. **Sketches of a Plan and Method of Education.** 1808.

Nock, Albert Jay. **The Theory of Education in the United States.** 1932.

Norton, A. O., editor. **The First State Normal School in America: The Journals of Cyrus Pierce and Mary Swift.** 1926.

Oviatt, Edwin. **The Beginnings of Yale, 1701-1726.** 1916.

Packard, Frederic Adolphus. **The Daily Public School in the United States.** 1866.

Page, David P. **Theory and Practice of Teaching.** 1848.

Parker, Francis W. **Talks on Pedagogics: An Outline of the Theory of Concentration.** 1894.

Peabody, Elizabeth Palmer. **Record of a School.** 1835.

Porter, Noah. **The American Colleges and the American Public.** 1870.

Reigart, John Franklin. **The Lancasterian System of Instruction in the Schools of New York City.** 1916.

Reilly, Daniel F. **The School Controversy (1891-1893).** 1943.

Rice, Dr. J. M. **The Public-School System of the United States.** 1893.

Rice, Dr. J. M. **Scientific Management in Education.** 1912.

Ross, Early D. **Democracy's College: The Land-Grant Movement in the Formative Stage.** 1942.

Rugg, Harold, et al. **Curriculum-Making: Past and Present.** 1926.

Rugg, Harold, et' al. **The Foundations of Curriculum-Making.** 1926.

Rugg, Harold and Shumaker, Ann. **The Child-Centered School.** 1928.

Seybolt, Robert Francis. **Apprenticeship and Apprenticeship Education in Colonial New England and New York.** 1917.

Seybolt, Robert Francis. **The Private Schools of Colonial Boston.** 1935.

Seybolt, Robert Francis. **The Public Schools of Colonial Boston.** 1935.

Sheldon, Henry D. **Student Life and Customs.** 1901.

Sherrill, Lewis Joseph. **Presbyterian Parochial Schools, 1846-1870.** 1932 .

Siljestrom, P. A. **Educational Institutions of the United States.** 1853.

Small, Walter Herbert. **Early New England Schools.** 1914.

Soltes, Mordecai. **The Yiddish Press: An Americanizing Agency.** 1925.

Stewart, George, Jr. **A History of Religious Education in Connecticut to the Middle of the Nineteenth Century.** 1924.

Storr, Richard J. **The Beginnings of Graduate Education in America.** 1953.

Stout, John Elbert. **The Development of High-School Curricula in the North Central States from 1860 to 1918.** 1921.

Suzzallo, Henry. **The Rise of Local School Supervision in Massachusetts.** 1906.

Swett, John. **Public Education in California.** 1911.

Tappan, Henry P. **University Education.** 1851.

Taylor, Howard Cromwell. **The Educational Significance of the Early Federal Land Ordinances.** 1921.

Taylor, J. Orville. **The District School.** 1834.

Tewksbury, Donald G. **The Founding of American Colleges and Universities before the Civil War.** 1932.

Thorndike, Edward L. **Educational Psychology.** 1913-1914.

True, Alfred Charles. **A History of Agricultural Education in the United States, 1785-1925.** 1929.

True, Alfred Charles. **A History of Agricultural Extension Work in the United States, 1785-1923.** 1928.

Updegraff, Harlan. **The Origin of the Moving School in Massachusetts.** 1908.

Wayland, Francis. **Thoughts on the Present Collegiate System in the United States.** 1842.

Weber, Samuel Edwin. **The Charity School Movement in Colonial Pennsylvania.** 1905.

Wells, Guy Fred. **Parish Education in Colonial Virginia.** 1923.

Wickersham, J. P. **The History of Education in Pennsylvania.** 1885.

Woodward, Calvin M. **The Manual Training School.** 1887.

Woody, Thomas. **Early Quaker Education in Pennsylvania.** 1920.

Woody, Thomas. **Quaker Education in the Colony and State of New Jersey.** 1923.

Wroth, Lawrence C. **An American Bookshelf, 1755.** 1934.

Series II

Adams, Evelyn C. **American Indian Education.** 1946.

Bailey, Joseph Cannon. **Seaman A. Knapp: Schoolmaster of American Agriculture.** 1945.

Beecher, Catharine and Harriet Beecher Stowe. **The American Woman's Home.** 1869.

Benezet, Louis T. **General Education in the Progressive College.** 1943.

Boas, Louise Schutz. **Woman's Education Begins.** 1935.

Bobbitt, Franklin. **The Curriculum.** 1918.

Bode, Boyd H. **Progressive Education at the Crossroads.** 1938.

Bourne, William Oland. **History of the Public School Society of the City of New York.** 1870.

Bronson, Walter C. **The History of Brown University, 1764-1914.** 1914.

Burstall, Sara A. **The Education of Girls in the United States.** 1894.

Butts, R. Freeman. **The College Charts Its Course.** 1939.

Caldwell, Otis W. and Stuart A. Courtis. **Then & Now in Education, 1845-1923.** 1923.

Calverton, V. F. & Samuel D. Schmalhausen, editors. **The New Generation: The Intimate Problems of Modern Parents and Children.** 1930.

Charters, W. W. **Curriculum Construction.** 1923.

Childs, John L. **Education and Morals.** 1950.

Childs, John L. Education and the Philosophy of Experimentalism. 1931.
Clapp, Elsie Ripley. Community Schools in Action. 1939.
Counts, George S. The American Road to Culture: A Social Interpretation of Education in the United States. 1930.
Counts, George S. School and Society in Chicago. 1928.
Finegan, Thomas E. Free Schools. 1921.
Fletcher, Robert Samuel. A History of Oberlin College. 1943.
Grattan, C. Hartley. In Quest of Knowledge: A Historical Perspective on Adult Education. 1955.
Hartman, Gertrude & Ann Shumaker, editors. Creative Expression. 1932.
Kandel, I. L. The Cult of Uncertainty. 1943.
Kandel, I. L. Examinations and Their Substitutes in the United States. 1936.
Kilpatrick, William Heard. Education for a Changing Civilization. 1926.
Kilpatrick, William Heard. Foundations of Method. 1925.
Kilpatrick, William Heard. The Montessori System Examined. 1914.
Lang, Ossian H., editor. Educational Creeds of the Nineteenth Century. 1898.
Learned, William S. The Quality of the Educational Process in the United States and in Europe. 1927.
Meiklejohn, Alexander. The Experimental College. 1932.
Middlekauff, Robert. Ancients and Axioms: Secondary Education in Eighteenth-Century New England. 1963.
Norwood, William Frederick. Medical Education in the United States Before the Civil War. 1944.
Parsons, Elsie W. Clews. Educational Legislation and Administration of the Colonial Governments. 1899.
Perry, Charles M. Henry Philip Tappan: Philosopher and University President. 1933.
Pierce, Bessie Louise. Civic Attitudes in American School Textbooks. 1930.
Rice, Edwin Wilbur. The Sunday-School Movement (1780-1917) and the American Sunday-School Union (1817-1917). 1917.
Robinson, James Harvey. The Humanizing of Knowledge. 1924.
Ryan, W. Carson. Studies in Early Graduate Education. 1939.
Seybolt, Robert Francis. The Evening School in Colonial America. 1925.
Seybolt, Robert Francis. Source Studies in American Colonial Education. 1925.
Todd, Lewis Paul. Wartime Relations of the Federal Government and the Public Schools, 1917-1918. 1945.
Vandewalker, Nina C. The Kindergarten in American Education. 1908.
Ward, Florence Elizabeth. The Montessori Method and the American School. 1913.
West, Andrew Fleming. Short Papers on American Liberal Education. 1907.
Wright, Marion M. Thompson. The Education of Negroes in New Jersey. 1941.

Supplement

The Social Frontier (Frontiers of Democracy). Vols. 1-10, 1934-1943.